A Warning for Fair Women

*Early Modern
Cultural Studies*

SERIES EDITORS
Carole Levin
Marguerite A. Tassi

A Warning for Fair Women

ADULTERY AND MURDER
IN SHAKESPEARE'S THEATER

Edited by Ann C. Christensen

UNIVERSITY OF NEBRASKA PRESS

Lincoln

Publication of this volume was assisted by the
University of Houston English Department's
Houstoun Fund.

Library of Congress Cataloging-in-Publication Data
Names: Christensen, Ann C., 1962–, editor.
Title: A warning for fair women: adultery and
murder in Shakespeare's theater / edited by
Ann C. Christensen.
Description: Lincoln: University of Nebraska Press,
[2021] | Series: Early modern cultural studies |
Includes bibliographical references and index. |
Summary: "A critical edition of A Warning for Fair
Women introduces new audiences to an important
but neglected work of Elizabethan drama"—
Provided by publisher.
Identifiers: LCCN 2020041093
ISBN 9781496208361 (hardback)
ISBN 9781496225528 (paperback)
ISBN 9781496226242 (epub)
ISBN 9781496226259 (mobi)
ISBN 9781496226266 (pdf)
Subjects: LCSH: Sanders, George, –1573—Drama. |
Murder—England—London—Drama.
Classification: LCC PR2411 .W17 2021 |
DDC 822/.3—dc23
LC record available at
https://lccn.loc.gov/2020041093

Set in Adobe Caslon by Mikala R. Kolander.

Contents

Illustrations

Preface

The first London audiences for *A Warning for Fair Women* already knew the sensational story of the murder of George Saunders (Sanders, in the play) by his wife's lover; this news had circulated in popular ballads, at least one pamphlet, and other print texts. Some viewers might have known the parties involved or witnessed the executions some twenty years earlier in 1573. Similarly, most of us know, for example, about the Los Angeles police chasing O. J. Simpson's white Chevy Bronco, yet this knowledge of events from June 1994 doesn't keep us from watching a new TV series about the case. Just as people today pay to see remakes of old movies or stage or film adaptations of novels, so sixteenth-century audiences did not expect a brand-new story at the theater either. Therefore, a spoiler alert here can only be half-hearted. *A Warning* (printed in 1599 and performed earlier) is based on events that occurred in and around London in 1573: the murder of a prominent and well-connected merchant by Irish-born Captain George Browne, who had a sexual relationship with Anne Sanders, the merchant's wife. Browne was tried, convicted, and executed for murder, and Mistress Sanders, her neighbor, Nan Drurie, and Drurie's servant, Roger Clement (nicknamed "Trusty Roger") were also tried, convicted, and executed as accessories to the crime.

The writer of *A Warning* likely used more than one source for the characters and contours of the plot, but the main source is a thirty-two-page pamphlet, *A briefe discourse of the late Murther of master George Sanders* (signed A. G. in 1573, reprinted with attribution to Arthur Golding in 1577) that gives an account of the case and instructs the readers on moral behavior (see appendix). Another text, "The wofull lamentacon [*sic*] of mrs. Anne Saunders, which she wrote with her own hand, being prisoner in newgate, Justly condemned to death" is the only known extant ballad, a manuscript contemporary with the murder (and with Golding's tract). This twenty-eight stanza verse lamentation takes the form of a confession to "O high and mighty God" on the eve of the speaker's execution; she also speaks in apostrophes directed at Satan, her coconspirators, and different groups of women, warning "tender mothers," "honest wives," and "finest London dames" to hear her. The speaker also names Drurie and Roger and herself, but neither Browne nor another suitor, a minister Mell, appears in her account (see appendix). In her study of early modern accounts of husband murder, Emma Whipday shows that the "murderous wives" in lamentations like this one appear not as sinners but as tragic heroines who have narrative control, even though they lack agency.[1] In any case, this was the kind of news story that would have garnered other ballads, and at least one more seems to have been in circulation in 1596 since Thomas Lodge's "Wit's Misery" published that year quips about a ballad—"the story of Mistress Sanders"—pasted above the mantel of an unsavory brothel keeper named "Cozenage," which means trickery or deception.[2]

Arthur Golding was already well known for his English translations of major classical texts, such as Ovid's *Metamorphoses* (1565), and religious works including Protestant reformer John Calvin's *Sermons* (1577). In fact *A briefe discourse* is only one of perhaps three of Golding's original works; that is, not translated from ancient or foreign sources. This pamphlet, published as it was so soon after the trials and by a writer of "exceptional cultural authority,"[3] became the source for other records, including two chronicle histories that the playwright may also have consulted, John Stow's *Annales of England* (1592) and Raphael Holinshed's *Chronicles of England, Scotland, and Ireland* (1577, 1587), both of which reprint entire passages from *A briefe discourse* with few additions of their own. (Since they are nearly identical, I excerpt only one, Stow, in the appendix.) About half of Golding's pages concern what we might call the "facts" (who, what, where, and when), while the rest grapple with more general question of why. Golding instructs his readers on good spiritual practice, namely, neither committing similar sins themselves nor judging the accused. Golding's pamphlet closes with two pages that claim to transcribe Anne Sanders's "confession" and a prayer that she purportedly recited, along with "a note of a certain saying" of Master Sanders found "in his study."[4]

Another contemporary reference to the case that suggests its wide reach was Anthony Munday's 1580 collection of strange and wonderful news items, whose title lists trending atrocities, with Sanders's murder at the top: "A View of Sundry Examples. Reporting many strange murders, sundry persons perjured, signs and tokens of God's anger towards us. What strange and monstrous children of late been born; And all memorable murders *since the murder of Master Sanders by George Browne*, to this recent and bloody murder of Abell Bourne Hosyer, who dwelled in Newgate Market" (italics added). Munday uses this "example" to illustrate how "the world [is] bent on all kind of wickedness" by asking a series of seemingly rhetorical questions about fear of God and duty to country that he then answers with scripture.[5]

Though ostensibly telling the "same" story, the different versions of the murder stress different dimensions and facets because their creators had distinct audiences and purposes in mind. For example, the chroniclers, Stow and Holinshed, add some new information to Golding's account, specifically that Browne "flung himself" off the scaffold and that "Anthony Browne, brother to the forenamed George Browne, was for notable felonies conveyed from Newgate to York, and there hanged" (see appendix). Munday assumes his readers already know the story, using it to point to wickedness. As Randall Martin points out, Calvinist Golding similarly moralizes about the events, but selectively downplays or redacts information that he finds unworthy of repeating. Because Golding wanted a sinner's dramatic repentance to reform his readers, Martin asserts, Golding makes Anne Sanders out to be worse than merely "an alleged accessory after the fact."[6] I discuss sources further in the introduction, but for now, I note that the playwright transformed the source material's outline of events into a grisly—if also often homey—drama that initially follows Anne and George Sanders's movements through an ordinary day: from a neighborhood meal to George's business meetings on the Exchange, where merchants and others gathered; from an unsought flirtation and a burnt supper to petty resentments. Of course, the day does not remain ordinary or we would have no drama and certainly no tragedy!

A Warning is an entertaining story not only of the extraordinary events of adultery, conspiracy, and murder, but also of more everyday practices of friendship, motherhood, and spirituality. Arrests, prison cells, and legal proceedings combine with memorable characters (such as the widow who is willing to commit serious crimes to build up her daughter's dowry) and imaginative theatrical devices, including a "bloody banquet," a tree springing up, and a dying person's wounds suddenly spouting blood. First performed by the Lord Chamberlain's Men, which was the theater company where Shakespeare worked, *A Warning* had never been revived on stage and remained known only to scholars until now. A 2018 production based on this edition constitutes what I believe to be the world revival, discussed below in "The Play in Performance."

Few if any modern critics think *A Warning* is very good. The scholar who compiled materials in the 1870s for the indispensable compendium, *The School of Shakspere* [*sic*], for example, faulted the dramatist's "(generally) servile" rendering of news.[7] Peter Berek's complaint more than a century later that it is "a clunky, highly moralized retelling of a celebrated 1573 murder" is fairly typical.[8] For theater historian Andrew Gurr, *A Warning* features a "banal narrative and moralistic sentiments," though Gurr also acknowledges that the play's London setting and espousal of a "citizen-minded orthodoxy . . . argue that the company's repertory values were not exclusively Shakespearean."[9] In other words, Gurr observes that other kinds of plays were regularly produced and performed by the company that we now associate almost "exclusively" with Shakespeare's style. So *A Warning*'s audiences might not have expected to witness political intrigue as in *Julius Caesar*, also published in 1599; or admire love plots resolved by act 5, whether star-crossed (*Romeo and Juliet*) or cross-dressed (*As You Like It*); or hear interiorized tragic speeches like Hamlet's (*Hamlet* pub. 1601). Viewers may have also enjoyed the features of *A Warning* that we never see in Shakespeare, such as long final courtroom scenes (a finale that Ben Jonson perfected in his city comedies, such as *Volpone*) and neighbor women who corrupt young wives (familiar in domestic tragedies such as *King Edward IV* and *Women Beware Women* by Thomas Heywood and Thomas Middleton, respectively). In fact *A Warning*'s importance arguably stems from the fact that Shakespeare never wrote a domestic tragedy (*Othello*, however, is sometimes considered in this genre), relied on silent or "dumb" shows to advance his plots, or set a play in contemporary London (his English history plays are, by definition, not contemporary and the Windsor of *Merry Wives* is a contemporary, middle-class setting, but not at all urban).

Jeremy Lopez, a scholar committed to (re)publishing plays by other playwrights (including Anonymous), discusses the limited scope of what he calls "a 'Shakespearean' aesthetic"—that is, a "predilection for an essentially 'Shakespearean' dramatic style, one that foregrounds poetic richness, individuated characters, and a high degree of structural unity."[10] Lopez shows that what used to be called the "non-Shakespearean" canon is a mere sliver of the output (about twenty-five plays of many hundreds) that conform more or less to this "aesthetic," characterized by five-act structures and so-called three-dimensional characters. Given this mission of Lopez and other early modernists, we ought not to fault *A Warning*'s failure to comply with a Shakespeare-based "norm." Instead we can pursue the more intellectually satisfying routes that consider, inter alia, which other plays were produced by the company and how *A Warning*'s differences may expand our sense of popular entertainment in the period in order to get at the kind of cultural work this play seems to perform. We can also ask how *A Warning* could be staged today. Additionally, with Lopez, we can interrogate why certain elements of early modern dramatic form are omitted from anthologies of Elizabethan and Jacobean drama today. How did early modern viewers appreciate what, for us, seem like lacks—"uneven" structures, "underdeveloped" characters, and "unpolished" lines? How does the current canon limit our access to other works?

Having spent many years working closely with the text and, more vitally, seeing it performed by the Resurgens Theatre Company in Atlanta (November 2018), participating in a spirited read-aloud with the Shakespeare Institute (June 2020), hearing it read aloud by University of Houston students and faculty at various times, and seeing it performed ("readers' theater" style) at the Attending to Women in Early Modern Europe conference in June 2018, I can attest to its many merits for students of Shakespeare as well as directors and dramaturgs. I witnessed unexpected moments of high hilarity and also expressions of poignancy and pathos in each different reading and performance. I hope you will have similar experiences as you read this book.

A Note about the Text and Previous Editions

The printing derived from authorial papers bearing some theatrical notations. The title was entered in the Stationers' Register on November 17, 1599; the Stationers' Company of London was the office that regulated the English publishing industry, including printers, bookbinders, booksellers, and anyone with a request to publish something. *A Warning*'s title page includes a long version of the title with plot summary embedded (a common spoiler): "A WARNING for Faire Women. Containing, The most tragicall and lamentable murther of Master George Sanders of London Marchant, nigh Shooters hill. Consented unto By his owne wife, acted by M. Browne, Mistris Drewry and Trusty Roger agents therin: with their severall ends." The title page also includes a performance statement: "As it hath beene lately diverse times acted by the right Honorable, the Lord Chamberlaine his Seruantes"; an imprint: "Printed at London by Valentine Sims for William Aspley 1599"; the company: "Lord Chamberlain's (Hunsdon's) Men"; and date: "1599." The text is a seventy-six-page quarto with no scene or act divisions. Copyright as we know it did not operate in the period, and no copyright was ever transferred for this play. There were no subsequent editions for about three hundred years.

Richard Simpson reprinted *A Warning* in his two-volume anthology of plays in *The School of Shakspere* (1878), dividing it into two acts (his act 2, for example, begins with the first dumb show, when Tragedy enters "with a bowl of blood in her hand"). In 1893 another editor, A. F. Hopkinson, issued a reprint with five act divisions and scenes and scene locations inserted; in 1904 Hopkinson reissued a slightly corrected and enlarged reprint. J. S. Farmer published a photo-facsimile text in 1912 as part of the "Tudor Facsimile Text" series. Not until 1975 did a modern scholarly edition appear, and this was Charles Dale Cannon's PhD thesis publication with a ninety-one-page introduction and appendixes (including transcriptions of the published accounts of George Sanders's murder written by Arthur Golding, John Stow, and Raphael Holinshed—all notably sources for many of Shakespeare's work as well). Cannon restored the play to running lines (from 1 to 2734), marginally inserting twenty-one scene numbers. In 2011 Gemma Leggott modernized the text, wrote a new introduction, and updated the bibliography on the play for her master's thesis.[1] I am indebted to all of these editors, Cannon above all.[2] My edition follows his choices closely and is based on the 1599 quarto—"the only substantive text," which Cannon prepared by collating seven of the eight known copies of the 1599 quarto, named for the libraries and collections where they are held: Bodleian (Oxford), Dyce (Aberdeen), Folger (Washington DC), Harvard (Cambridge, Massachusetts), Huntington (Pasadena, California), Pforzheimer Library (Austin, Texas, at the Harry Ransom Center), and Yale (New Haven, Connecticut). Readers seeking more information concerning textual variants, or other textual issues, should consult Cannon's excellent volume.

Following Cannon, I believe that the initial printing came from the author's own copy, in contrast to other sorts of manuscript copies that might have been available to printers, such as a version of a performance script, usually marked up in the course of preparing to produce the play. As Cannon observes, the quarto text of *A Warning* is "relatively free from tangles, false starts, and blotting characteristic of foul papers."[3] Cannon supports this contention by enumerating different types of evidence, such as the fairly consistent speech tags (i.e., the way a character is tagged or named before their lines appear) and the fact that certain types of stage directions that describe props and movements are "permissive or indefinite" or "full or literary" as opposed to directions that merely mark entrances and exits or that prescribe a number or actors, such as "enter two lords."[4] (A permissive stage direction might say "enter several lords," permitting various numbers of actors playing lords.) Among many of the full directions, one example is "Beane left wounded and for dead, stirres and creepes (8.219)."[5] Such level of detail, in Cannon's reconstruction, represents an "authorial hallmark," which means that, rather than being an acting script, the printer had a copy that at least started with the writer's words.[6]

Textual Notes

I have modernized the punctuation and spelling, except in cases where the unique early modern spelling is interesting (such as "handkercher") and the meaning is clear, and/or the meter demands it. For example, I do not change "conducteth" to "conducts," but I change "my self" to "myself." For each new scene, I propose a location to clarify where an event is supposed to take place in the story. I use italics for all stage directions; brackets set off my own suggestions, added to help the reader imagine the moment on stage. I place stage directions as "opposite" the line where they are called for, rather than making a separate line in effort to follow the quarto lineation as closely as possible. I regularize spellings of proper names in the text and in the speech tags or headings and print the full names, which are often abbreviated in the quarto; for instance, Anne Sanders is usually tagged with her full name, but occasionally as "A. San." or "Anne." "1 Lo." becomes First Lord; "M. James," short for "Master James," which I change to "James." Short defining notes and longer explanatory notes are included in the notes section that follows the appendix.

Acknowledgments

I am deeply grateful for the professional and personal friendships that I enjoyed while I ate, drank, and slept *A Warning for Fair Women*. Folks read, responded to, and helped improve drafts of some parts of this book at some point in the process, or they answered my questions, helped me function, and in many instances also generously shared their own work with me. Any errors or weaknesses are, of course, my own.

A Warning for Fair Women by Anonymous was performed at the Shakespeare Tavern Playhouse, Atlanta, Georgia, November 19–21, 2018. All images are reproduced with kind permission from the Resurgens Theatre Company. The production was directed and text-edited by Brent Griffin (based on an earlier draft of this critical edition), stage-managed by Julia Pettigrew, and choreographed by Sims Lamason. Costumes were created by Catherine Thomas, fight choreography was staged by Tamil Periasamy, and music was composed by Matthew Trautwein. Performers included Catie Osborn (Tragedy, Lord Justice), Matthew Trautwein (History, Roger, Keeper), Ash Anderson (Comedy, Anne Drurie), Robert Bryan Davis (George Sanders), Sims Lamason (Anne Sanders), Tamil Periasamy (George Browne), Trey Harrison (Barnes), Bob Lanoue (Beane), Richard Herren (Old John), Catherine Thomas (Joan), Teagan Williams (Girl), Emily Nedvidek (Fury, Lord 1), and Lauren Brooke Tatum (Fury, Lord 2). Music was performed by Ash Anderson (vocals), Sims Lamason (vocals), Catie Osborn (drum), Catherine Thomas (harp), and Matthew Trautwein (lute, violin, vocals).

I appreciate advice and support from Emma Atwood, Ariane Balizet, Cheryl Birdseye, Patricia Cahill, Kate Christensen, Stephen Deng, Alan Dessen, S. P. Cerasano, Brent Griffin, Erin Kelly, Jeremy Lopez, Carol Neely, Sarah O'Malley, Cathy Patterson, Ana Rodrigues, Todd Romero, Barbara Sebek, Iman Sheeha, Leslie Thomson, Amy Tigner,

Laura Turchi, Maggie White, Martin Wiggins, and Miranda Wilson. Tamara Fish, Michael Osborne, Elizabeth Stavoski, Wayne Thomas, and Claude Willan helped prepare the manuscript and illustrations. The Shakespeare Institute of Birmingham University invited me to read the play with them (via Zoom) as part of their King's Men Repertory Marathon, which was both entertaining and instructive, thanks to Martin Wiggins and company. I appreciate the University of Houston students who studied the play with me, especially my Spring 2018 Shakespeare class, who kindly (but with no choice, really) permitted me to sneak *A Warning* onto the syllabus, as well as the plucky volunteer readers from the UH SHX Club and Improv Club, who did wonderful table readings organized and led by Vinh Hoang and Aubrey Cowley, in which Wendy Wood and Jeffrey Villines shined particularly bright. My colleagues at the Attending to Women in Early Modern Europe conference (Milwaukee, June 2018) performed a rollicking condensed version of the play. DeeDee Guzman hosted a cast party for Resurgens. I also appreciate the feedback from auditors, readers, respondents, and fellow panelists at meetings where I have discussed aspects of this work: the Resurgens Theatre "Death and Domesticity" conference (Atlanta, September 2018), the Shakespeare Association of America seminar, "The King's / Lord Chamberlain's Men" (April 2019); and the Durham Early Modern conference (July 2019). My UH colleagues, too numerous to name, helped me shoulder other burdens as I worked on this book. Thanks, y'all. I am grateful to Carole Levin, the University of Nebraska Press editorial team, and the anonymous reviewers for their commitment to the project, creative ideas, and humanity.

I dedicate this book to my three sons, Wilson, Sam, and Elliot Miller, and the memory of their father, my beloved yokefellow, Reagan Miller.

Introduction

Genre: True Crime and Domestic Tragedy

A Warning for Fair Women is one of a small handful of plays performed on the early modern London stage that modern scholars classify as "domestic tragedy" for their common treatment of family and/or marriage in crises that end in tragic ways (usually including adultery and death, often by murder).[1] An early, influential critic to consider how this genre appealed to London playgoers was Louis B. Wright, whose *Middle-Class Culture in Elizabethan England* (1935) emphasized the bourgeois or "middling sort" aspects of character, setting, and plot. Another scholar who attended to the genre was H. H. Adams, whose *English Domestic or Homiletic Tragedy: 1575–1642* (1943) argued that such plays were basically versified sermons for husbands and wives. Indeed, this admonitory and didactic mode was common in ballad titles from the period as well: "A warning to wanton wives" (1564), "A warning to all maids that brews their own bane," and "A warning for widows that aged be" (1565), to name a few.[2] Along with middle-class values and an instructional tone, the use of realistic details also typifies domestic tragedy, as when the Sanders boy and his school chum, Harry, toss a coin on the stoop (sc. 17), and when Beane fantasizes about bringing home the delicacy of calf's head from London (sc. 6). Other domestic tragedies give elaborate stage directions about such homey activities as meals—specifying the use of candles, napkins, and even crumbs.[3] Another important generic distinction is the self-conscious reduction in tragic scale, offering likewise, as one critic suggests, "some significant reflection on [the theatrical tradition]."[4] Holbrook supports this claim by noting the frequency with which these tragedies openly admit their distinction from the usual tragic fare—the fall of the great: "'look for no glorious state,' declares the prologue to *A Woman Killed with Kindness*, 'our Muse is bent / Upon a barren subject, a bare scene'" (86). *Arden's* epilogue presents a similar metatheatrical disclaimer, calling the preceding performance a "naked tragedy" conveying "simple truth" that "needs no other points of glozing stuff," statements that draw attention to the artlessness of the piece, relative to "high" tragedy (ep. 14, 17–18). The epilogue to *A Warning* in a similar vein proclaims itself a "true and home-borne Tragedy" (Ep.17).

A Warning, like *Arden of Faversham*, uses a prologue and epilogue to proclaim its middling-sort concerns and familiar city sites, while Elizabethan tragedies more commonly focused on historical kings and queens and ancient or distant empires, as in Shakespeare's Roman *Titus Andronicus* and Christopher Marlowe's *Tamburlaine the Great* and *Edward II*.[5] No royalty appear in *A Warning*, though members of Queen Elizabeth's Privy Council take part in the investigative and judiciary phases, aided by local magistrates and jailers. Showing the distinction between this play and other tragedies, the character of Tragedy tells viewers to "look for no glorious state" (epilogue). After Tragedy successfully eliminates the competition from Comedy and History in the opening induction, she turns to the spectators to announce: "My scene is London, native and your own, / I sigh to think, my subject too well known" (Pro. 7–8). This statement does two things: it places the setting for the action in the immediate location of the theater itself—in England's capital, a city that was home to an expanding population and a thriving commercial theater industry—and it acknowledges that the story to be performed was already familiar to this audience.[6] Tragedy argues that her kind of play is new, mocking the usual suspects of revenge tragedies—choruses, ghost, and tyrants. Gurr explains this "new form" as "a drama documentary," noting, for instance, that Melpomene avers the story is "not 'fained' [or invented] but 'true.'"[7]

Taken together these elements—nonaristocratic, bourgeois characters, small-scale domestic (or private) settings, and contemporary, "realistic" touches—are generally agreed to constitute domestic tragedy, and readers will note these elements at work in *A Warning*. Although modern playgoers tend to think of plays within distinct genres or categories, and although the hybrid category "tragicomedy" did not come into practice until arguably 1606 with George Wilkins's and Shakespeare's *Pericles*, it is important to remember that no play was purely tragedy or comedy. Elizabethan playwrights blended styles, tones, and moods, as evidenced in a title like Marlowe's history play published the same year as *A Warning: The Troublesome Reign and Lamentable Death of Edward the Second, King of England, with the Tragical Fall of Proud Mortimer*. This wording suggests the audience can feel sorry for the death of even a "troublesome" king and that a "proud" man's fall can still be tragic. *A Warning* for its part mingles moods when it juxtaposes an everyday, realistic setting, such as a woman sitting on her doorstep, with the elevated, romantic rhetoric of the captain who courts her there, or when a highly stylized and ritualistic "bloody banquet" immediately precedes a jovial farewell after a normal meal.[8]

Beginning in the 1980s English domestic tragedy and the history of domesticity in general have received extensive critical attention, most notably from feminist scholars who usefully complicate both the ideas of domesticity and of genre, acknowledging, for example, the limited scope for middling-sort women in public life on the one hand, yet their relatively greater authority in their households, on the other, and also expanding what counts as tragic. Paramount in this discussion and evident in the genre is that Englishwomen's legal status—in *potestate maritorum*—placed them under the absolute power of their husbands, yet their actual lived experience placed them in charge of the personnel and materiel of their households.[9] Additionally, the presence of servants and other social groups crucially shape this class of play, as Lena Cowen Orlin and others observe, reminding us that households, not individuals or even families, were the units that were taxed in this period. Orlin explores the way that "private matters," including love and marriage, in fact helped constitute "public culture."[10] Frances Dolan and, following her, Randall Martin, asked new kinds of questions about domestic crime, such as husband-murder, which was notably classified as petty treason in this period, a crime against divinely ordered hierarchies.[11] Catherine Richardson's and Marissa Greenberg's work on domestic tragedy looks in different ways at the plays' representations of and engagements with spaces and objects in the home, and the intersections among the home, the street, the city, and other locales.[12] Ariane Balizet contributes to this growing feminist scholarship by exploring the ways that domesticity and the body were understood in the period through the staging of "blood and home[s]," and my own previous work shows the important connection between men's absence for business and the tragic consequences at home.[13] Women's status in their communities as gossips or wise women, for example, and the problematic nature of their legal testimony—these are current focal points in scholarship on the play pursued by Iman Sheeha, Cheryl Birdseye, and Emma Atwood.[14]

In her book *The Subject of Tragedy*, Catherine Belsey emended the definitions of "man" as the tragic hero and liberal humanist subject as she considered the genre of tragedy, concerned as it is with agency, law, ethics, the state, and the human subject. Her observation that "woman [*sic*] was produced in contradistinction to man, and in terms of the relations of power in the family" was a central tenet of the feminist literary criticism of this era, when gender and class were newly foregrounded categories of analysis, and the household and marriage were seen less as "natural" than as historically specific sites of potential struggle and even violence.[15]

In sum, when we follow the paths of this historicist feminist scholarship to recognize that people's experiences of social structures like neighborhood, friendship, work, and professional life that are central in our own lives nonetheless have distinct and distant histories, we see the play's engagements with the society and culture of its time on a deeper level. So, for example, a theme of "marriage" seems familiar yet must be historicized. When we consider the social and institutional contexts for the play's depiction of marriage, family, religion, and the law, as well as tragedy as a genre, we can better appreciate both *A Warning*'s novelty and its participation in aesthetic and cultural traditions. The laws, customs, and experiences that organized early modern life were also the topics of sermons, conduct books, and political debates.[16] Finally, because *A Warning* stages uneven power and affective relations within a household space that is permeable, while also dramatizing, for example, facets of the legal system and the commercial economy, it offers insights into older forms of everyday life that still concern us today.

Dating, Theater Company, and Authorship

The composition of *A Warning for Fair Women*, like many period plays, is difficult to date with perfect accuracy; the obvious latest date for the writing of the play is 1599, when it was printed, and the earliest is 1573, when George Sanders and John Beane died. Still, some narrowing can be done: its performance run was likely completed in the 1597–98 playing season, or possibly into the 1599 season, when it was released to the printer in London.[17] Modern scholars agree that the writing and first (and only) performances took place some years before the publication date (and some believe later than 1590, the date first suggested by Hopkinson). Dating is based on various kinds of evidence—internal (from inside the play itself, such as real-life people and events that can be fact-checked) and external (such as records of a performance, actors' dates, and so on). While the play mentions real people, such as the minister and martyr, John Bradford, whose *Works* (i.e., *Godly Meditations on the Lord's Prayer*, published in 1562) Anne Sanders owns, and a medical cure known as Dr. Stephens's (or Stevens's) water, the book and the medical cure had reputations far beyond their creators' life spans, so their dates are not limited enough to firmly date the play.[18] The reference to a tobacco pipe (induction) might be more useful for helping to date the play because, though the leaf was imported to London as early as 1565, smoking gained widespread use only after the mid-1580s.[19] Scholars also use evidence from theatrical practices that emerged, developed, and fell out of fashion over a period to help date a play. The dumb show is one such practice whose popularity climaxed in the first two decades of the sixteenth century and declined from 1571 to 1580.[20] This information, combined with other evidence, places the performance most likely after 1580. Andrew Gurr groups *A Warning* among the plays acquired by the Lord Chamberlain's Men between 1594 and 1597.[21] The editors of the catalogue of *British Drama 1533–1642*, Martin Wiggins and Catherine Richardson, give 1597 as their "best guess" for performance.[22]

A Warning, in any case, is an Elizabethan text that extends the canon of non-Shakespearean drama for the Lord Chamberlain's Men and enlarges our sense of this playing company that housed Shakespeare's plays and for which Ben Jonson, Thomas Dekker, Francis Beaumont and John Fletcher, and John Webster also wrote.[23] *A Warning for Fair Women* played in the repertory of the Lord Chamberlain's Men, Shakespeare's Company, at the Curtain or the Theatre (not, as some earlier critics believed, at the Globe Theatre, which was newly rebuilt and renamed only in 1599). What we can say for sure is that the playwright of *A Warning* had to be an active contributor to the repertory of the Lord Chamberlain's Men in the years before 1599 since, as noted, the title page identifies this company and that date. The immediate known repertory context for *A Warning* is William Shakespeare's *1 and 2 Henry IV* and *The Merry Wives of Windsor* and a two-part play, *The Seven Deadly Sins*, which is no longer extant.

The theater company is important for at least two reasons: one, the play is unattributed, or, anonymous, although a number of potential authors has been suggested as I summarize below; and two, audiences in this period went to plays based more on the theater and the players than on an individual playwright's name recognition. The practice of including authors' names or their initials on the title pages for printed plays developed only gradually, and, even then, the identification usually appeared below the title and other verbiage.[24] While a printed play without an author's name was not unusual in this period, title pages did identify the theater company and playhouse (the King's Men and the Curtain, for example), a habit that later faded away as plays began to be considered "works" of literary merit rather than theatrical ephemera.[25] Title pages often included an image, bookshop information, and dedications to patrons or readers, and might also advertise the play the way that *A Warning* does: "lately diverse times, acted." This printed information is a trove for scholars interested in the print trade, issues of authority and performance, and other facets of book and theater history.[26]

With no official identification of an author, scholars and editors have advanced and/or refuted theories of authorship; these theories and refutations necessarily shape their views of *A Warning*. For example, if an editor believes that an unattributed play was written by a playwright whose other works rely on, say, one kind of resolution or reflect a certain religious viewpoint, the editor's subsequent work might highlight these aspects of the play in question. Candidates for *A Warning*'s authorship have been proposed based on *A Warning*'s formal and thematic similarities to other contemporary drama, dating (from internal references), and information about publication and the theater company's practices and personnel (such as a resident clown). In brief, popular playwrights Thomas Lodge, Anthony Munday, Thomas Kyd, Thomas Heywood, and Shakespeare have been put forth, along with Robert Yarington, whose work includes a domestic tragedy based in part on a true murder story, *Two Lamentable Tragedies* (1601).[27] John Lyly, who wrote for the elite indoor playhouses (not the Curtain), has also been suggested. Before relatively recent computer-assisted analytics that use tools like plagiarism software to trace patterns, for example, nineteenth- and early twentieth-century editors pointed less systematically to patterns in words and turns of phrase and/or structural, dramatic, and thematic techniques, and other devices shared by both *A Warning* and one or more plays by a known playwright. More recently scholars show that some of these correspondences are far too common to be attributed to just one playwright (for example, the use of an induction). Some late nineteenth- and early twentieth-century attribution studies admit to or are accused of deriving their claims through the process of elimination, "guesswork," or "conjectur[e]" rather than well-supported positive claims.[28] All this having been said, one can only admire this older scholarship for its learning and painstaking textual analysis.

Two of the more influential authorship claims were made by A. F. Hopkinson (1904) and Joseph Quincy Adams (a descendant of the presidential Adams family and the first director of the Folger Shakespeare Library in Washington DC). Hopkinson was convinced that Thomas Kyd wrote the play, showing many parallels with *The Spanish Tragedy* among Kyd's other plays, such as the use of court/judgment scenes, allegorical figures, dumb shows and choruses, and a propensity for "murder, bloodshed and lust."[29] Hopkinson's additional evidence is that Kyd's plays were initially published anonymously, like *A Warning*, and that another play of Kyd's used the "murder will out" theme found in *A Warning*. Cannon dismisses this attribution on "linguistic, ideational, and technical grounds."[30]

In 1913 Adams put forth Thomas Heywood as the author, since Heywood wrote other plays with domestic-tragedy themes (among Adams's other rationales), a claim refuted by Otelia Cromwell in her 1928 book, *Thomas Heywood: A Study in the Elizabethan Drama of Everyday Life*.[31] Cannon also entertains and dismisses Adams's evidence.[32] Despite this well-substantiated refutation, Leggott finds the Heywood argument "convincing" based on both Adams's review of "characterization, staging and language" and her own comparisons to the Heywood canon.[33] Most current scholars concede to a yet unidentified author, into which ranks I place myself. Recently, however, Martin Wiggins attributed *A Warning* to Thomas Dekker. Wiggins first placed *A Warning for Fair Women* squarely in the Dekker oeuvre when he sponsored the Shakespeare Institute's annual read-aloud on Dekker in 2016 at Stratford-on-Avon (see Shakespeare blog post).[34] We await further news on this front.

Structure

Originally printed with no formal act or scene breaks, *A Warning* comprises twenty-one distinct scenes and three separate dumb shows (i.e., the stage is cleared twenty-four times in all). Although the induction claims the play for Tragedy, and though it seems to split into two uneven parts—before George Sanders's murder (scenes 1–7) and after (scenes 8–21)—it might make more sense to view it in three parts that in some ways correspond to the three generic allegorical figures competing in the induction: Comedy, Tragedy, and History.[35] In other words, as in the Shakespearean tragedies, *A Warning*'s tones, moods, and dramatic sequences structure the play beyond monochromatic tragic. The induction, prologue, scenes 1–7, and the first two dumb shows make up the first part. This covers the preliminary fight for dominance of the stage in the induction and the main plot's conspiracy against Sanders, the merchant; Drurie's seduction of Mistress Sanders; and the first two murder attempts. This section also includes the scenes in Woolwich and on the road, where John Beane meets up with the rustic characters, Old John and Joan. This initial part of the play feels like dark comedy, suggested in the recitation of dreams foretelling Beane's death, on the one hand, and Browne's anguished response to his failure to stab Sanders, on the other: "Night, I could stab thee; I could stab myself!" (5.80). The settings in part 1 vary, but cluster mainly around dwellings (Drurie's, Sanders's and Barnes's), London's streets, and the River Thames.

The second part—and the shift to a full-on tragic mode—is suggested not only by the induction's revelation that "the stage is hung with black," but also by Tragedy's predictive line in the first dumb show: "in these sable curtains shut we up / The comic entrance of our play" (9), preparing for the murder that does not occur until scene 8. The murder, following Golding's account, transpires along the road near Shooter's Hill, an area to the southeast of London proper (now part of the city); successive scenes shift rapidly from the road to court, and then back to London. The imagery of "sable curtains" and the violent attack that ends in death (of Sanders and, later, Beane) suits a tragedy similar to *Macbeth*. As another example, "sable Night, mother of dread and fear" is the setting for Shakespeare's narrative poem *The Rape of Lucrece*.[36] In addition, like other tragedies, *A Warning* dramatizes the immediate and chaotic aftermath of a horrible crime; in this case extending from Browne's bloodying and puncturing his handkerchief, his alibi-seeking flight to Greenwich Court, and his swooning at the sight of Young Sanders in London, to Anne's attempted violence on herself and the fallout among the conspirators (scenes 8–11). The second dumb show represents the murder of George Sanders as a tree chopped by an axe-wielding Browne and shows Anne Sanders following Lust to Browne.

From here, *A Warning*'s final segment (comprising nearly half the play, i.e., scenes 12–21 and the final dumb show) follows the source plot fairly closely to trace the legal and spiritual resolutions of the murders. Critics have rightly observed the play's lopsidedness because of the early climax—the death of the cuckolded husband (leaving thirteen scenes and one dumb show to be performed). Ariane Balizet helpfully summarizes the subsequent action—from "tedious [legal] procedure" to "*actual* gallows humor and serious spiritual reflection" (original italics):

> *A Warning for Fair Women*'s performance of justice spans seven scenes and roughly one-third of the play's lines; the action after the murder includes Browne's apprehension and arrest by the mayor of Rochester; testimony from the surviving witness, John Beane; Browne's trial and condemnation; the joint trial and condemnation of Anne Sanders, Roger, and Drury; Browne's scaffold speech and execution; last-minute repentance on the part of the two women; and a scene in which two carpenters discuss building a gallows big enough for three conspirators.[37]

In this way *A Warning* seems like the new kind of history play that Tragedy introduces and that Gurr calls "documentary drama."[38] Taking place mostly in public or nondomestic settings (courtrooms, prison, scaffold), these last scenes introduce an entirely new set of characters—civil magistrates, officers, prison workers, and clergy—whose collective role is to gather evidence, extract confessions, and determine and execute punishments. Yet even the seemingly "factual" courtroom drama mode is peppered with moments of shock, suspense, and pathos, as when Beane's wounds suddenly bleed, when Anne Sanders's white flower darkens and when she kisses her children goodbye en route to her execution.

Staging

A Warning uses distinct yet complementary theatrical modes and devices to advance the action and themes—namely, the metatheatrical induction, prologue, and epilogue; the realistic drama of the Sanders plot; and the emblematic pantomime of dumb shows. Inductions are explanatory or framing scenes that prepare the audience for, but remain separate from, the play proper. Students may be familiar with this device from Shakespeare's *The Taming of the Shrew*, in which a drunken tinker,

Christopher Sly, is tricked by a lord to believe that he himself is also a lord; these framing scenes set up (or offset) the main plot of Petruchio's tricks to transform Katherina into a good wife (the induction is often cut from performances today).[39] In *A Warning*'s induction the debate among the figures of Tragedy, Comedy, and History frames the play to come, commenting on theatrical practices of the day and trying to define what is proper to tragedy. The tone feels generally comical. Tragedy also later plays the role of a chorus, commenting on the silent "dumb show" action and breaking up the play into units that Dieter Mehl likens to "acts" and Frances Dolan calls "movements."[40] "The Custom House" that prefaces Nathaniel Hawthorne's *The Scarlet Letter* and the deflating postscript to Margaret Atwood's *The Handmaid's Tale*—these operate like inductions and epilogues, respectively. Prologues work similarly to introduce a play and are usually spoken by one character or a chorus directly to the spectators, like the famous sonnet prologue to *Romeo and Juliet* that begins "Two households both alike in dignity" (1.1.1). Tragedy's prologue to "all you spectators" informs us that the play she presents is local, familiar, and true: "My scene is London, native and your own, / I sigh to think, my subject too well known, / I am not feigned" (Ind.).

Epilogues likewise break the fourth wall as Rosalind does in *As You Like It*: "good plays prove the better by the help of good epilogues" (ep. 6–7). The epilogist is either an actor stepping out from the play but remaining in character or a choral figure whose speech defends the play just performed and sometimes also asks for applause in the way that Prospero does in *The Tempest*: "But release me from my bands / With the help of your good hands" (ep. 9–10). In *A Warning*, it is Tragedy who offers this closing speech, again reminding the spectators that her play was not invented, but a "true and home-born tragedy" as she also promises a comedy or history play tomorrow (ep.). In this way, the epilogue returns us to the induction's debate over genre.

Along with these metatheatrical elements *A Warning* uses the public stage's full slate of technical facilities, demonstrating the dramatist's knowledge of popular and useful elements of stagecraft, if not necessarily innovative ones. One such technique mentioned previously is

the "dumb show"—symbolic or allegorical action performed silently and, in this play, orchestrated by Tragedy who appears at three points in the play proper to narrate and comment on the silent movements that the audience watches. These performances are called "dumb shows" not in the sense of being stupid, of course, but because they are mutely acted out "scenelets" that arguably advance the plot of the main play and, as some critics suggest, limn such actions as sexual behavior in a symbolic rather than literal way for reasons of propriety. Whatever else their function, dumb shows certainly give the audience another dimension or "alternative logic" to the main plot.[41] Diane Purkiss, in her study of staged banquets, ranks *A Warning*'s "bloody banquet" (the first dumb show) as a "noticeably metaphorical representation . . . [that illustrates] the ominous aspects of feasting onstage."[42] Cannon points out dumb shows' more prosaic uses—to present information more economically than speech through silent gestures and also to "preserve decorum" by treating the lovers' consummation only symbolically.[43] Most critics agree on the ritualized manner of the scenes with allegorical figures as Lust and Mercy; M. C. Bradbrook emphasizes that these scenes take place "outside time or space," show events about to happen in the play proper, and, in the particular case of *A Warning*'s "bloody banquet," might have inspired *Macbeth*'s cauldron scene.[44] Alan Dessen and Leslie Thomson's *Dictionary of Stage Directions* provides a number of illustrative period examples along with a succinct explanation of the stage direction "dumb show":

> *dumb show* This term refers to mimed performances of various lengths in about forty-five plays (in more than fifty other plays with a *dumb show* the terms are not used in [stage] directions); 1) many *dumb shows* are simply or primarily an expedient means of summarizing events not presented due to time and/or staging constraints; 2) others are more complex, often revealing information to the audience in order to create dramatic irony; 3) still others are overtly allegorical, requiring explication; [4 some] *dumb shows* represent usually well-known stories or events, [such as a wedding].[45]

A Warning's three dumb shows combine these different facets using a "mixed" form in which "dumb" allegorical figures interact at times with human characters from the play; this happens, for example, when the Furies usher in Anne Sanders, Drurie, and the two men involved in the murder plot. For Mehl, the effect of this mixing is to hit a pause button, relieving the verse from conveying complicated "mental processes and moral decisions," such as the rationale Anne Sanders uses to submit to Browne.[46] Mehl and Dolan separately also analyze the dumb show in relation to classical and medieval drama. Dolan insightfully concludes that the playwright's reliance on both modes of representation (i.e., realistic and symbolic) "expos[es] the inadequacies of each to explain the crime. The allegorical motive, 'Lust,' does not connect with the grim journalistic detail of the re-enacted crime, nor with any of the previous representation of Anne's motives for allying with Browne."[47] That these pantomimes are also spectacularly elaborated through staging and props lends a grander dimension to the facts of the case, extending, in Mehl's words, a "moral application" beyond "a personal tragedy."[48] (My own summaries of scenes and dumb shows are found within the text proper.) Finally, the three dumb shows are also visually and aurally compelling, with such props as skull-goblets, black candles, and an axe; musical accompaniment and dance; and—in the second show—the shocking image of a tree suddenly popping up only to be chopped down in effigy of George Sanders.[49]

Beyond the dumb shows, *A Warning* is remarkable for other spectacular stage moments. Most notable is the gallows or gibbet, rarely seen in Elizabethan theater, but here the focus of the final scenes. In scene 18 Browne is walked to a scaffold where he gives a long confession about his bad life; eventually the actor "leaps off" to hang himself, surely a shock to the audience.[50] A second gallows is built on stage and discussed at some length in scene 20 when two London workingmen meet by chance on the morning of the execution of the murder accomplices. One of them, Tom Peart, a carpenter, reports that he has been before dawn "setting up" gallows where the criminals will "swing"; the wooden structure remains on stage, provoking Anne Sanders's panic over her impending execution. Other unusual stage moments

include Beane's spontaneous revival and bleeding afresh days after his attack, explained as his wounds reacting at the sight of his attacker; the presence of young children in more than one scene, including their own mother's walk to her execution; the dramatic darkening of Anne Sanders's white corsage to prove, as one lord proclaims, her guilt; and the handkerchief steeped in Sanders's blood and punctured with the same dagger used to slay him.[51] That these striking properties and stage spectacles have little or no basis in Golding's account suggests an experienced dramatist at work.[52]

Domesticity and Business as Interrelated Themes

Clashes and connections between the cultures of business and domesticity structure this play, where merchants do their business away from home (Sanders on the Exchange and Lombard Street; Barnes and Sanders at St. Mary Cray, a nearby town) and women and servants work to manage and sustain the home. With the master away so often, the Sanderses' home seems to lack what we call in the twenty-first century a work-life balance. Although *A Warning*'s plot, characters, and themes are shaped by domesticity and business, still these are physical and ideational spaces that we should take care not to reduce to women's and men's "spheres," respectively. Domestic life in this period was not based primarily in the private affective dyads between husband and wife, or parents and children, as people sometimes think of family life today (whether heterosexual or same-sex couples). Whereas critics have understandably concentrated on the marriage that shapes the main plot of *A Warning* and other domestic tragedies, marriage and "the nuclear family" were neither as stable nor as normal as we might have expected. With high mortality rates, widowhood was common, and so many households were headed by single women; the average age for a first marriage for women and men was about twenty-four and twenty-six, respectively, only slightly younger than current figures in the United States.[53] Romeo and Juliet were not the norm. Rather, domestic life encompassed a broad range of affective, sexual, familial, and even communal and professional relationships that also changed over time. Historians remind us that in early modern London—and

indeed throughout Europe—a household might include extended family, servants, neighbors, apprentices and other workers, and sometimes guests. People whom we call "relatives" today were sometimes called "friends" in early modern England, and readers may be familiar with Shakespeare's use of the word "cousin" (or "coz") to mean a close friend who may or may not be part of one's extended family. "Family" or kinship was a more fluid concept than it may seem today.

In *A Warning*, for example, households are made up of nonrelated people: consider the woman-headed home of the widowed Nan Drurie, her daughter (though not among the cast of characters), and her male servant, Roger; the country folk, Old John and his servant Joan; and the Queen's Greenwich household staffed on stage by men, the yeoman of the buttery, and Master James (though of course, female servants and ladies-in-waiting were plentiful in the actual royal household). Domestic relationships extend to various merchant-gentlemen, who appear with their peers, servants, or apprentices, and who refer to offstage wives; the immigrant Brownes are brothers, but clearly have not seen each other in years, and so on. Along with these varied domestic/occupational formations, *A Warning* associates "family" with bloodline, a meaning implied when Browne is disturbed to see the fatherless child at play on the stoop where he had previously accosted Mistress Sanders (sc. 11). A sweeter glimpse into the meaning of family occurs earlier at that very same stoop in scene 2: waiting for Master Sanders to return from business, the son pesters his mother for treats and new clothes; she calls him "prattling boy" and also mentions his sister. It seems notable that, as a couple, Anne and George Sanders share the stage alone only once, and then very briefly—when he finally arrives home from the Exchange at the end of scene 2. Meanwhile, the playwright is more interested in the complex and shifting relationships that circle around them—those among masters, mistresses, children, and servants and among merchants, neighbors, and friends. The neighbor exerts a powerful influence: Mistress Drurie is responsible for both leading her friend astray and leading her to repent and confess. The women share a number of long scenes together, most notably the palm-reading session in scene 4 and their change-of-heart talk in Newgate Prison (sc. 21). George Sanders's primary relationships consist of business associates; he is seen with other merchants and his man and is less often at home than he is expected to return home from the Exchange or from travels.

Furthermore, the home is a permeable economic unit: Mistress Sanders hosts the linendraper and milliner in order to make her dry-goods selections; the servant "man" crosses in and out of household space, clearly demonstrating his intimacy with both domestic and commercial matters at once. Mistress Drurie seems a fixture at her neighbors' house; for example, George and Anne Sanders each invite her to "sup" on separate occasions, and they are all together in the opening scene, George offering to escort the widow home (1.33). This brief review of the household makeup in this play illustrates scholars' expanding definition of early modern domestic life—from the sense of "natural" heterosexual married pairs and male-headed households to a model that more accurately reflects the changing dynamics among the householder and housewife and their business associates, guests, the domestic and occupational workers (such as apprentices) who might live with them at any given time, along with same-sex and queer friendships and neighborhood networks.

When we account for these broader definitions of domesticity at work in both *A Warning* and in the experience of audiences, we appreciate the public dimensions of the apparently "private" home.[54] Recognizing that boundaries were permeable rather than fixed—between home and street, household and community, and inside and outside work—challenges assumptions about rigid divisions between, say, personal and economic life, and women and men. Domesticity was inseparable from economy; the original meaning of "economic" was in fact closer to "home economics" than to Wall Street: *oikos* in Greek means the family, the family's property, and the house, and thus "œconomic" originally referred to the management of the home and estate. As Craig Muldrew explains in his important book *The Economy of Obligation*, from about the middle of the sixteenth century "the culture of credit" helped a coin-poor population to combat uncertainties in their ability to repay loans and wealthier households to defray suspicions of

overspending. In a word, domestic culture and business culture were interdependent:

> The culture of credit was generated through a process whereby the nature of the community was redefined as a conglomeration of competing but interdependent households which had to trust one another. Credit was an attribute of the household and individuals within it, but each individual unit of creditworthiness was serially linked with others and as a result the idea of the community was interpreted as something problematic, which could only be maintained through trust in the credit of others in the face of increased competition and disputes.[55]

Women contributed to their domestic economies through work that organized the household, filled the larder, fed and clothed the family, and disciplined the children and servants, the latter of whom also performed housework. Less tangibly than but as crucially as selling eggs at market or brewing her own beer, as many urban and rural women did, a married woman's good name, modest behavior, and thrifty habits supported her household because her husband's standing in the community depended on these qualities. A wife's skills in cookery, medicine (called "physic"), and household management, along with her demeanor, speech, and other behaviors, worked together with the husband's skill in crafts or trade, trustworthiness, and so on to advance a family's reputation and hence ensure their credit. In addition, women worked in many industries at various points in their lives, although generations of history books misunderstood or overlooked these roles and evidence about women's economic lives generally.[56] Even though most trades and guilds officially prohibited women's training and membership, female family members performed nearly the same work as men in the trade, often including skilled tasks, and widows commonly took over their deceased husbands' trades. Women's medical work is a notable example of this "hidden-from-history" problem. Feminist scholars have upturned earlier assumptions about the negligible role women played in the healing arts in early modern Europe. As Debo-

rah E. Harkness asserts, "Women were at the very heart of London's medical world. They were not marginal, they were not laughable, and they were not expendable. Perhaps that is why so many male practitioners found them so very threatening."[57]

Setting to one side women's essential contributions to their domestic economies and their participation in the broader economy through often informal wage work, men dominated most large-scale commerce, and *A Warning* reflects this with the ever-absent Master Sanders and his busy associates. As I have argued elsewhere, men and business occupy significant discursive space but little actual stage time in domestic tragedy.[58] We hear of but rarely see places where husbands do business, such as shops, docks, and markets (in contrast to citizen comedies, for example, that highlight such locales). Such settings are often represented offstage, such as the Exchange and the other reported stops in George Sanders's daily itinerary in *A Warning*. One such stop is Lombard Street, where Sanders dines in scene 5; a social more than a work space, it was "the open-air meeting place for international trade prior to the building of the Exchange, [and] got its name from the foreign merchants who once gathered there."[59] Playwrights use domestic thresholds (stoops and windows) and interiors to suggest the master's presence elsewhere, while dramatizing fully the impact of his absence on the home. *A Warning* enacts the merchant-characters' comings and goings and bodies forth the streets and ferries that convey them, but not so much what these men do when they arrive. Instead of properties associated with commerce (e.g., shop stalls and merchandise), which are common in city comedies, domestic tragedy keeps the focus on domestic life and husbands' travel that disrupts it. This genre of play uses props, staging, and characterization to represent domesticity and travel, calling for home interiors and exteriors (such as stoops, doors, or windows) and roads and ferrymen, among other signs of domestic life, liminality, and transit.[60]

Scene Study

In this section I offer a close reading of one scene (4) to illustrate the themes I have been discussing.[61] The tensions between domesticity

and business in Sanders's urban, commercial household culminate in the so-called "breach of credit" scene when the mistress of servants, objects, and activities cannot pay her bills. Anne Sanders—practicing what we might call the housewife's trade—controls the household goods, including their purchase, storage, and consumption; but on this occasion, her merchant-husband (and his male servant) control and restrict her access to the communal purse strings. She has arranged for tradespeople to deliver certain wares to her house (linens, purse, and gloves), but is unable to complete the transaction. Beginning in medias res (or, in the middle of things), the scene presents a dialogue between George Sanders and his man concerning "bills of debt," payments, "bond[s]," "credit," and "quittance" as George sets out from the house for his workday (4.1–17). The merchant acknowledges that he is expected "on the Exchange tonight" and "upon the Burse" (7, 16) even as he learns that his wife is inside expecting to conduct her own business "here" at home (24). The servant reports that she has "appointed [linen and 'other things'] should be brought her home," and that she "bade [him, the servant] tell out thirty pounds even now" to pay for those purchases (26, 19–20). The problem is that the master needs the "whole sum" (1,500 pounds) that same day to complete his own business deals, trumping the mistress's prior claim on a tiny portion, though a still-large amount for linens (30 pounds), evidence of the Sanderses' financial success. The situation is immediately apparent to the servant: "What shall I say unto my mistress, sir?" This problem gives Sanders no pause: "She must defer her market till tomorrow, / I know no other shift: my great affairs / Must not be hindered by such trifling wares" (4.18–23).

Parsing this statement lays bare a central problem in *A Warning* and indeed in other period discourses about business culture and domestic culture: men's "great affairs," activities, and business relationships outside the home are troped as vocational "ventures," while, at the same time, the reduced category of "trifling wares" typifies the realm of women and domesticity. Further, in particular, as the word "wares" connotes in George's statement, that realm is a place of consumption rather than production. The stereotypes of female vanity and of women wasting money on luxuries—these ideas persist today (as in

the bumper sticker, "Shop 'Til You Drop"). In *A Warning* the perceived hierarchy between the merchant's important commercial obligations and his wife's minor home business had some validity; for example, his term, "hindered," conveys his sense that housewifery ought to support or be subordinated to his business, not hinder it—a belief that Anne Sanders herself shares and behind which is the recognition of the absolute necessity of a housewife's skill in establishing and maintaining a home, as scholarship, including my own previous work, has shown.[62] That a household's survival depended on a good housewife was acknowledged as fact, famously illustrated in the common advice to bachelors: "to thrive one must wive." But, with the wave of a hand that dismisses his wife's claim to household money, George Sanders devalues his spouse's housewifery as mere shopping, rather than acknowledging her as the "director of a small factory," as one scholar characterizes premodern housewifery.[63]

The next beat of the scene opens in medias res as well. "Enter Anne Sanders, Mistress Drurie, a Draper, and a Milliner" (osd 34). Anne confidently surveys the goods with the Milliner's and Draper's men, while Nan Drurie looks on:

Come near, I pray you, I do like your linen,
and you shall have your price. But you my friend, the
gloves you showed me and the Italian purse are both
well made, and I do like the fashion. But trust me,
the perfume, I am afraid, will not continue. Yet upon
your word, I'll have them too. (4.36–41)

This mere six-line speech to the vendors is what we could call "an isolated incident" in the play; yet this brief and bounded moment is often rendered monumental evidence of a city wife's social ambition and excessive desire for consumer goods. To this list that damns Anne, critics add the French "hood, and gown of silk," coach, and livery that Mistress Drurie holds out to her later in the scene (lines 151–56). Blaming Anne for hoods and goods that she in fact rejects, and for gloves and purses that she cannot buy seems to me both reductive and ahis-

torical.[64] Reductive, because such a reading stresses the luxury goods while overlooking Anne's routine management of household stores and children and her responsibility for the feeding, outfitting, discipline, supervision, and entertainment of her household (seen elsewhere in the play, especially scene 2). Such judgment is also ahistorical, because these activities constituted housewifery and *required* purchasing power.[65] Indeed, Anne's matter-of-fact assessment of the thwarted exchange suggests her regular and unquestioned access to funds: "I have brought these men / To have their money for such necessaries, / As I have bought" (4.73–75). I propose that we read the character's interaction with the merchants' men not as some uniquely feminine shopping spree, but simply as the parallel to her husband's opening line in the scene: "Sirrah, what bills of debt are due to me?" (4.1). Both wife and husband are economic agents in keeping with the interdependencies between domestic culture and business culture as discussed above. The image of Anne Sanders as a confident and industrious housewife off-sets the consuming woman/city-wife stereotype. Though critics often readily point out how little demonstrable desire Anne seems to have for Browne, they too quickly infer her desire for fine fashions.[66]

Crime and Punishment (and Performance)

Is Anne Sanders guilty? And, if so, what is she guilty of—adultery, conspiracy, murder, none or all of the above? This question is primary for most readers of the play (as it was for the actors and audience at the Attending to Women conference.) The text leaves this point ambiguous. Historically, as in the play, she, Mistress Drurie, and Roger were tried, convicted, and executed for murder as accessories before and after the fact.[67] They each confessed sooner or later to knowing about the plan to kill George Sanders, but *A Warning* handles Anne Sanders's guilt with much less conviction (in only one sense of the word); it is less clear what she knew and when.[68] Golding takes "editorial jabs" throughout his pamphlet on the matters of Mistress Sanders's adultery, perjury, and conspiracy in murder until eventually he is able to commend her good death.[69] However, on stage, the character enjoys an apparently earned reputation as a good wife: "respective of her good name" (1.71) and protective of her marriage, though later committing adultery and lying in court. The same person who handily rebuffs Browne in scene 2 vociferously refutes Roger's accusation about her plate pawning, even falsely accusing him under oath (17.159–60).[70] Her words often contradict her actions as she transitions from loyal wife to remarrying widow. In scene 7, just when Browne is poised to stab her husband, she worries in an aside that Browne has "been moved / By some ill motion to endanger [her spouse]" (98–99). Is this a voice of regret by someone who has already signed on to the murder plot or the true hope of someone left out of the loop? Or is her aside the performance of an insincere prayer? As Mihoko Suzuki argues, "In *Warning*, it is not entirely clear whether Anne Sanders is even aware of the plan to kill her husband, though the title page unequivocally states that it concerns 'the most tragicall and lamentable murther of Master George Sanders . . . *consented unto by his owne wife*'" (italics added).[71] At no point do the plotters mention murder to her.

Anne Sanders's culpability comes exclusively through the dumb show performances: in the first, Tragedy dips only Anne Sanders's finger in the bowl of blood that signifies the murder pact, while smearing the other plotters' hands more thoroughly:

To Browne

Thy hands shall both be touched for they alone
Are the foul actors of this impious deed!

To Drurie and Roger

And thine and thine, for thou didst lay the plot,
And thou didst work this damnéd witch devise,
Your hands are both as deep in blood as his.

To Anne

Only thou dips a finger in the same. (lines 81–90)

In the next dumb show, she is handed an axe to chop down her husband/a tree, which she refuses, but Browne takes it up (lines 28–31).

As for confessing, Anne Sanders holds out until the eve of her execution, when she tells the Doctor that she earned God's wrath "Not
only by consenting to the death / Of my great husband, but by wicked
lust, / And willful sin, denying of the fault" (21.71–73). Aside from this
eleventh-hour admission, evidence against her extends to the letter that Browne reads at Shooter's Hill (sc. 8) and the pawned plate
to help fund his escape. Still, no aspect of these activities is enacted
(such as writing a letter or gathering up her silver). There is also the
strange case of her hue-changing corsage that the Lord sees (reason-
ably enough) as proof of her guilt:

ANNE Ah, good my Lords, be good unto Anne Sanders,
   Or else you cast away an innocent.
   [*The rose changes color—to black or red.*]
2 LORD It should not seem so by the rose you wear!
   His color is now of another hue.
ANNE So you will have it. But my soul is still
   As free from murder as it was at first. (lines 17.210–18)

These props and her confession appear—if you'll excuse the expression—
after the fact. This is not to corroborate her claim to be spotless as that
white flower she wears to her hearing, only to note that the play refrains
from dramatizing her performance of either adultery or conspiracy.[72]
   What *is* fully dramatized, in contrast, is what they do on the gallows.
The final scenes of *A Warning* participate in a cultural form known as
the "scaffold speech"—the phenomenon of the convicted person's last
dying speech made in public and often printed and circulated later.
Both Browne and Anne Sanders deliver versions of these speeches, with
Anne instructing her children and others in general not to follow her
bad example, and Browne cursing the "vile world" and confessing to
everything from indulging in extravagant fashion and prostitution to
heresy and blasphemy (18.74–92). Public confessions played important
social functions in this period, the impact of which scholars continue
to debate: did speakers of these last words toe the official church line
as a deterrent to crime, or did they rather flout the norms of the society

that witnessed the execution in a play to literally "get the last word," or, as I believe, did these speeches resonate in different ways for different hearers (and later readers, including us today)?

Browne's flamboyant center-stage farewell illustrates the powerful allure of such a moment in the theater, especially since it culminates in his shocking "leap" from the scaffold; in fact, "scaffold," the word for the raised platform or stand for proclamations and theatrical performances, came to refer to the site for public executions only in the mid-sixteenth century. In any case, Browne's "confession" that in the end is meant as a warning to "all careless men . . . by my fall your wicked lives amend," indulges in scandalous assertions that he has blasphemed scripture, the sacraments, the Sabbath, and so on (18.95–96).[73] When an audience heard the convict's claim to be the "the worst that live" and "the most accursed," they may have felt a mingled sense of admiration and fear for this bravado, along with disdain for how low Browne had stooped. But how truthful are his boasts? Why confess all those outlandish crimes before dying? One answer lies in a theatrical tradition of over-the-top gallows speeches. Another play performed by the Lord Chamberlain's Men in the 1590s was the revenge drama, *Titus Andronicus*, considered Shakespeare's first tragedy. In this play the villain Aaron the Moor is captured and about to be executed when he confesses to having engineered some horrifically cruel events that the audience has witnessed over the course of previous acts. But Aaron adds another twenty lines inventorying crimes that have not been part of the play, only to conclude with perverse regret what one critic calls his "extended anti-repentance speech": "And nothing grieves me heartily indeed / But that I cannot do ten thousand more" (*Titus Andronicus* 5.1.143–44).[74] The shock value of scaffold speeches like Aaron's and Browne's would entertain audiences if also making them squirm.

Another explanation for this phenomenon within the performance and print scaffold speeches is that church and state authorities engineered them to prove the value of true repentance as a route to salvation and to justify their own roles in this process. Golding's pamphlet demonstrates this in its insistence that Mistress Sanders was "utterly unprepared to die at that time."[75] The idea here is that the more terrible the sins committed, the more dramatic and hence instructive the repentance and subsequent forgiveness by God. The clergy took active roles in leading convicted prisoners to craft these speeches. For example, as Martin has shown, Protestant prison chaplains played "forensic and spiritual" roles for their charges, and these clergymen became a common "narrative focus of murder news in the first half of the seventeenth century."[76] Although not part of the denouement of *A Warning*, Browne's edification by a chaplain is important in Golding's *A briefe discourse*:

> During the time of his imprisonment, [Browne] coming to a better mind than he had been in time past, confessed that he had not heretofore frequented sermons, nor received the holy sacrament, nor used any calling upon God, private or public, nor give[n] himself to reading of holy Scripture, or any books of godliness. . . . Nevertheless, God was so good unto him, and schooled him so well in that short time of imprisonment, as he closed up his life with a marvelous appearance of hearty repentance, constant trust in God's mercy . . . and willingness to forsake this miserable world.[77]

Perhaps the playwright had the last two words quoted above in mind when his Browne bids farewell to the "vile world." In the play Browne undergoes a kind of self-catechism when he weighs the pros and cons of revealing his lover's guilt in scene 18, delivers a semiconfession (deciding not to reveal her guilt), and assists his own execution.

In contrast, *A Warning*'s Anne Sanders is instructed mostly offstage by prison chaplains, specifically an unnamed minister who is later punished for trying to protect her in order to marry her (the Mell of the prose pamphlet) and a "Doctor," whom she says has counseled her to confess and repent. Ultimately, however, Sanders's change of heart comes about through the unlikely ministrations of her one-time confidante, Anne Drurie. These onstage and offstage counsels, along with Sanders's frightened response to the carpenters' overheard chatter about gallows—these events partly depend on the way that the character is gendered as a criminal: as a woman, she is susceptible, even malleable to reform, just as earlier she had been easily duped by Drurie's "prognostications." Sanders's demise illustrates a good soul moved toward God, but Browne stays firm in defending her and dies in a lie.

Anne Sanders's gender is "performed" in her scaffold speech as well.[78] Englishwomen's speech, writing, and movements were restricted by law and custom. As Kate Aughterson shows in her sourcebook of primary documents about women from the period:

Strictures against public speaking by women sounded forth from pulpit conduct manuals and household instruction; nevertheless, some women did speak out in public, through preaching, petitioning, or publication of their translations, mother's advice, household or medical advice or poems; or in private through letters, unpublished autobiography and in the unmeasurable education of their children at home.[79]

Furthermore, as Aughterson also notes, spirituality was one arena where women might be encouraged to speak.[80]

What would a woman like Anne Sanders say at the fraught hour of her public execution? Explaining the different subjectivities of male and female scaffold speakers, Dolan notes the relative rarity of staging executions in the theater at all, adding, "while women are killed in Renaissance drama with alarming frequency, they are rarely executed on stage." Dolan further argues that accounts of women's executions stress less the spectacle than "the moral self-assertion it occasioned" and emphasize not their bodies, but their speech or, in the case of the hanging of Mistresses Drurie and Sanders, "the huge and eager audiences that gathered for a last sight of these women, who conspired in the murder of Sanders's husband."[81] As Golding's *A briefe discourse* records:

For almost the whole field, and all the way from Newgate, was as full of folk as could well stand one by another: and besides that, great companies were placed both in the chambers near abouts (whose windows & walls were in many places beaten down to look out at) and also upon the gutters, sides, and tops of the houses, and upon the battlements and steeple of S. Bartholomew's.[82]

Anne's dying words demonstrate another early modern English discursive phenomenon—the mother's blessing—a genre of advice books by women (some published later in the period) called mothers' manuals, the most popular of which were Dorothy Leigh's *The Mothers Blessing* (1616) excerpted in the appendix, and Elizabeth Jocelin's *The Mothers Legacie to her unborne Childe* (1624). In these texts "the authors/mothers provide their children with domestic, worldly, and spiritual counsel."[83] As Iman Sheeha discusses, "Whether the mother is actually on her deathbed, painfully aware of her pressing mortality, or a young pregnant mother experiencing anxieties that she will not survive the childbirth, the figure of the dying mother occupying a liminal, thus powerful, space between life and death is crucial to the genre."[84] In the final scene of *A Warning*, Anne performs a number of exemplary "last acts": she confesses and repents her crimes, accepts her punishment ("I am . . . resolved to go to death"), blesses her children, and says her good-byes. Dolan connects the unique moment of a woman speaking in the public spectacle of her own hanging to the intimate form of mother's blessing: "Like the mothers who, anticipating their deaths in childbirth and addressing texts to their unborn children, first erase and then assert themselves as authoritative agents, condemned women achieve public voice through the effacement of their bodies."[85] In fact, Anne Sanders's final moments on stage actually combine both genres since she answers her children's request for her "blessing" and counsels onstage audiences (21.117, 140–47, 165). Like the later printed advice books that Poole and Sheeha discuss, Anne Sanders presents herself as an advisor to her audience, in this case, neutralizing her position as a negative exemplar.

Scaffold speeches suggest a kind of "afterlife" for these stories that, as stated earlier, could be "spun" or understood in different ways over time. In Browne's case, his body undergoes an immediate afterlife. Peter Lake and Michael Questier observe the important postmortem phase of punishing criminal bodies like Browne's: "by dismembering, defiling and displaying the body of the criminal, the state sought to use the resulting physical remains as almost literal embodiments of the majesty of monarchy, ghastly bill-boards."[86] The Lords who handle Browne's arraignment vaguely promise to abide by his request to be buried, not "hanged in chains": "Let not that trouble thee" (17.77), and after he dies, promptly order just that (18.102). For her part, Anne Sanders's legacy extends to the book of meditations that she gives to her children, and her instruction that they take care of their spiritual lives. In fact, Iman Sheeha shows that "this scene on the scaffold [is] clearly link[ed] with other mothers' legacies[:] the play stages a mother who is about to leave her legacy with her children literally as a dying woman."[87]

The Play in Performance

The world revival of *A Warning for Fair Women* was mounted in late November 2018 by the Resurgens Theatre Company at Atlanta's Shakespeare Tavern, a specially constructed, Globe-inspired Elizabethan playhouse. With a script based on my edition, this revival was overseen by artistic director Brent Griffin, with whom I consulted during the text-wrangling process. I attended two of the three performances and interviewed some of the actors, along with Griffin, on casting and the use of stage space, breaking the fourth wall, finding the humor, making cuts, and so on. The company used modified "original practices" techniques, based in what they describe as "judicious editing, minimalist staging, organic music, original pronunciation, period costuming . . . [no] intermission, universal lighting, and a very strong emphasis on verse-speaking."[88] These performances—the culmination of the company's season of "Death and Domesticity," which also included *Arden of Faversham* and *A Woman Killed with Kindness*—introduced invaluable dramaturgical and thematic insights into the genre of domestic tragedy. They also proved that *A Warning*—apparently never staged past its first run—is more than stageworthy; it is hugely entertaining and even moving.

For the two-hour performance of *A Warning*, characters and some of the minor plot lines and settings were streamlined, cut, or combined and each change made logical and/or aesthetic sense. For example, whereas the full script stresses various community dimensions of the story—the neighborhood, including working-class London characters like the ferryman and carpenters; wider commercial and civic contexts; Queen Elizabeth's court at Greenwich; Newgate Prison with keepers and chaplains, and so on—this show spared torch-bearing servants, officious mayors, and nosy courtiers. Cutting the Rochester scenes, where Browne is apprehended, omits the butcher Browne figure; one actor seamlessly collapsed the butcher's plot functions and other roles: the merchant who entertains George Sanders on Lombard Street, Master James, and the yeoman of the buttery; the last two are introduced in the Greenwich Palace scenes, which were also cut. In the absence of the text's palace (though the Queen herself never does appear), the Privy Council is not appointed, and the idea of order trickling down through a female monarch is arguably lost. These alterations mean that regular Londoners, rather than courtiers, investigate the crime. Furthermore, the restoration of order in the performance *did* fall to women, since women actors play the Justice and Lords (as Ladies) in the final scenes, arbitrating aloft from the balcony. The protracted denouement was wisely trimmed (after all, George Sanders is killed in scene 8 of a 21-scene text).[89] Clearly the cuts in this production put the focus less on marital crisis and more intently on other relationships—especially those between and among the neighbors, Mistresses Drurie and Sanders; the male servant Roger; and Captain Browne—showing how the murder impacted the little child, the wife, the lover, and the plotters.

The performance began with Griffin's address to the audience, explaining the "candlelight wash" over the house, the threat of audience participation, and the lack of intermission. Subsequently, two dancers (Lauren Brooke Tatum and Emily Nedvidek) as the Furies entered with Tragedy (Catie Osborn), and the three continued to propel the prologue/induction and the three dumb shows to follow; these actors also doubled as the Justice and the "Lords" in the final court scene. Mocking Tragedy behind her back for the over-the-top paean to herself (i.e., the superior genre of tragedy), History (Matthew Trautwein) and Comedy (Ash Anderson) rolled their eyes, gagged, and performed other behind-your-back gestures, some quite obscene, reminiscent of the *Weekend Update* Chevy-Chase character on the American TV show, *Saturday Night Live*. Although my edition suggested this stage direction, their realization was perfect, deriding Tragedy's declamation that she "must have passions that move the soul." She cracked her whip (literally) to stop the action in order to transform History and Comedy into the main human villains, Trusty Roger and his mistress, Drurie, respectively. The Furies valeted them into minor costume changes (masks and some costume pieces removed; apron adjusted).

Significantly, this transformation implied that Tragedy controls the action, an interpretation advanced by her stomping a foot or clapping her hands to freeze and redirect the action, as when Anne Sanders is led in a dance to embrace Lust over Chastity. This integration of allegorical and human worlds left one wondering about the scope of human agency and autonomy: in particular, where do Comedy's antics end and Drurie's machinations begin? When Griffin first proposed this interpretation to me, I worried that the human passions and conflicts would fall from the story, but the cast played the roles as fully human and even sympathetic, as in the scene when sweet, simple Beane sheepishly ducks under Joan's wide-brimmed hat to bestow a kiss, and in the obvious affection that Anne Sanders shows for her child in scene 2. Although Tragedy was a forceful stage manager, it was in many ways Captain George Browne's (Tamil Periasamy's) show, in part because of how he worked the crowd with his pathos-filled soliloquies, in turns desiring a married woman and her husband's life, and his subsequent expression of total regret. His entrances came almost always from the floor-level (rather than from the stage doors or steps), and he often spoke directly to the viewers. Particularly charming (I thought) was his awkward courtship at Anne's stoop; no smooth operator, his vain attempts to play it cool included nearly sliding down the post he leaned against and scrambling for reasons to prolong his stay: "I would be loath to prejudice your pleasure" (sc. 2). This wooer was, in the words of one reviewer, more "a feckless yet charismatic Romeo-type" than a killer, though my students found even his Romeo tack unappealing.[90]

After the murder, Browne's guilt makes him manic, as Periasamy titters, sputters, and zig-zags around the stage in the alibi scene (sc. 9), where he accepts a mug of ale from Barnes, guzzling it so fast that it left a frothy mustache, and racing off the stage after delivering an excuse for his bloody hose. When Barnes sighed that the man is "an honest proper gentleman as lives," the audience guffawed. It's like calling Heathcliff a "capital fellow." That Periasamy delivered his final "scaffold speech" from half-below the trap door, looking like a bedraggled "mad" Malvolio meant that this Browne did not shockingly "leap off" the scaffold as the script dictates. But shock returned when the discovery space later revealed a tableau of all three dead men—Sanders and Beane draped around Browne, with a noose around his neck—a vision that sent Anne into her final faint. Periasamy's height and fit physique suited his role as a romantic rival, while his dark skin, unique in the cast, emphasized his outsider status as an Irishman in London.

The versatile Sims Lamason, who played Anne and choreographed the show, brought musical theater talents to her role, with a voice to match the character's emotional pivots from kind and loyal wife/mother to brassy desperado to soulful penitent. Throughout the company's season of domestic drama, Lamason played each "fallen" wife in the entire Scarlet Letter A-team: Alice Arden and the Annes (Frankford and Sanders).[91] Meg Pearson celebrated the actor's lively rendition of the role that on paper many critics find one-dimensional, compared, for example, to the more vibrant Alice Arden. Another reviewer observed the "sympathetic texture" of *A Warning*'s Anne:

> When we first meet her, Anne is sewing upstage, embodying dutiful boredom and feeling the neglect of her absent husband. This domestic confinement contrasts with her balletic seduction during the dumbshow. As she moves from confinement into dance, drinking from a skull and wrapping herself in red cloth, Anne's dangerous foray into adultery is also an embodied freedom. Employing a resonant vocal range, Lamason made it difficult to see Anne as a villain and painted the question of Anne's guilt in contemporary shades of gray: we hear coy coquetry with her lover,

confident defiance in the courtroom—her "not guilty" plea was shockingly raw—and heartfelt penitence in her jail cell, singing softly from the 16th century ballad "The Woeful Lamentation of Mistress Anne Sanders."[92]

Soon after this song, the women reconcile at that threshold; Anne Sanders is "strangely changed," and both women accept their fates. As an unpassionate adulteress this Anne Sanders rises in stature, in part because Lamason is physically imposing (in Griffin's words, she "plays taller than she is; she projects a big stature"), but also because her "Lamentation" was the emotional turning point in the show.

The Resurgens production can boast the modern world premiere of a newly scored ballad, "The wofull lamentacon of Mrs. Anne Saunders, which she wrote with her own hand, being prisoner in Newgate, justly condemned to death," elaborated from a ballad that was contemporary with the murder that the play stages.[93] It was transcribed from manuscript by Hyder Rollins in 1920 and is not much discussed in current criticism; I include the full text in the appendix. In the performance this ballad constituted the musical motif and was sung twice: first, accompanied by Tragedy's hand-drum beats, a delightful as-if spontaneous duet by Drurie and Roger to clinch their pact (punctuated by a hilarious secret handshake); then reprised by Lamason at the grate of Mistress Sanders's prison door to Trautwein's (now as the prison keeper) lute accompaniment. As Emma Atwood observes in her review, "This combination of Renaissance instrumentation (lute and drum) with layered vocal duets . . . harness[ed] the immediacy of live performance in a way that never felt jarringly modern."[94] Many play ballads were sung to the tune of "Fortune my Foe," which was "the standard tune for first-person [ballad and lamentation] accounts of husband murder," stressing, as Emma Whipday has argued, the speaker not as sinner but as tragic heroine.[95] In all, the musical score shadowed the human world of the play with its tonal shifts.

Theatrical space itself fostered crucial interpretative possibilities. Atlanta's Shakespeare Tavern, according to Griffin, necessitates audience interaction: the stage is not as deep as an early modern stage, so the "thrust" becomes the aisle between two groupings of tables, "constructed so that actors want to spill out into the audience." Additionally, dance, song, and props carried the shifting tones, as when period instruments opened the show; when the dancers/Furies took on the text's roles of Lust, Chastity, Diligence, and so on—pushing and pulling the human figures like marionettes captured in the figures' gossamer scarves; and when Browne is accidentally hit by a door opened by his beloved and thwarting the second murder attempt.

The material parameters and the fact that *A Warning* is a highly metatheatrical play justified the breaking of the fourth wall, evidenced in the organic way that the (black) humor in this production came off, as when Periasamy "played straight" the moment of waving a bloody handkerchief to proclaim his intent to send it "as a token to my love," forcing Roger to turn away in disgust (sc. 8). Some other memorably funny moments occurred in the final scene, when the Lord Justice monotonously delivered the arraignments' legalistic language (sc. 18); at Beane's "deathbed," when Barnes and the Justice exchanged strange tales of murder will out; and earlier, when Anne Sanders appears genuinely surprised that her palm-reading neighbor should "know so much" about her recent encounter with Browne (sc. 4). The audience knows that it was Drurie who had engineered Browne's interview with Anne Sanders to begin with.

The threatened if minimal "audience participation" occurred when actors gestured to the audience to suggest an offstage person. Members of the audience were also unwittingly conscripted into the nominal roles of the text's "milliner and draper" from whom Anne Sanders has ordered merchandise in the "breech of credit" scene. At the Shakespeare Tavern, she and Drurie entered as if shopping at the dining tables, admiring the "cloth" for sale (a paper napkin or a program), while Drurie boldly nibbled from someone's bag of pretzels. (All the world's a food court?) The center space was deployed to stage Beane's attack; left for dead in the aisle, he later crawled back up the center steps to the main stage as Browne ducked behind tables/bushes. Much of the audience eye contact was encouraged by Trautwein and Anderson, who had previously paired up as the low- and high-energy (respectively) servants in the 2017 Resurgens touring show of Jonson's city comedy, *Volpone*. For instance, when first changed from allegorical into human figures, they frantically eyed each other and the audience as if for help in catching up with the plot; Drurie mouthed to her partner for our benefit, "Who am I again?" They ad-libbed (Anderson even told a few jokes one night to kill time) and, in character, promoted each other in efforts to garner tips from Browne and applause from the audience.

A Warning illustrated the company's commitment to early modern versification practices. For Griffin "the language makes the character, rather than Stanislavskian notions of the opposite. . . . There is no entity beyond the words on the page."[96] Griffin also suits the script to his actors (working early modern dramatists did). So, for instance, the energetic Anderson used facial and bodily gymnastics to great comic effect, while Catherine Thomas commanded attention in a quieter way as Joan. The play calls for a young boy, the Sanderses' son, but the company found a girl, who performed "child" ably. An unexpectedly chilling scene was when Browne symbolically chopped down the tree/ Sanders in the dumb show: George Sanders held up the small girl with her doll on his shoulder, and when he fell, she and her doll tumbled down as well. This moment—when only imagined by reading the dumb-show stage directions—hardly feels real, let alone poignant, but the theatrical enactment showed how the murder that the conspirators are plotting has deep and long consequences. This contemporary theater company—with its evocative range from high hilarity to horror, from the quotidian to the transcendent—made the play at once early modern and new.

For Further Exploration

I have taught *A Warning* in a graduate seminar on "'Misgoverned Kings,'" which focused on corrupt, abdicating, or absent rulers (including "domestic kings") and in undergraduate sections of Renaissance Drama and Shakespeare (included in the latter because the play was part of Shakespeare's company repertory, if not *his* play). My Shakespeare students, and, on a separate occasion, a group of students and faculty sponsored by the UH Improv and Shakespeare Clubs, did read-alouds in 2017, and participants at the Attending to Women in Early Modern Europe conference in June 2018 performed a shortened script in a readers' theater format—standing, scripts in hand, with some props, most memorably a box of donut holes for the child's after school snack. As discussed above, the Shakespeare Institute sponsored a Zoom reading (June 2020) and the Resurgens Theatre Atlanta mounted a full-scale production in November 2018 at the Shakespeare Tavern. From these classroom and performance experiences, I have observed a number of themes and organizing ideas that I outline here, offered as topics for discussion, research, and writing assignments. Under each topic heading, I recommend some additional resources, the references for which can be found in the bibliography.

Place, space/setting. How are different spaces represented, occupied, and valued, including those that are not depicted on stage, such as the Brownes' Ireland, the Royal Exchange, and the village of St. Mary Cray? Inventory interior spaces, such as homes, the butcher shop, Newgate Prison, and courtrooms, along with exterior or public/outdoor spaces: the Thames, city streets, country roads, the scaffold. Another aspect of setting is temporality: consider daytime and darkness and the fact that the murder occurs during the Easter season. Marissa Greenberg's chapter on the play is especially fascinating for this topic. Also see the essays in Lena Orlin's collection, *Material London*. The chapter "Writing about Setting" in Edgar Roberts's *Writing about Literature* outlines a clear step-by-step process for drafting essays on setting. On stage props as part of setting, see Teague's *Shakespeare's Speaking Properties* and Harris and Korda's *Staged Properties in Modern English Drama*.

Economic exchanges/economic language. How do economic concerns impact the way that characters conduct professional and personal relationships? For example, George Sanders's financial solvency constitutes a large part of his reputation; he instructs his man to "take heed unto my credit: / I do not use (thou knowest) to break my word, / Much less my bond" (sc. 4). Meanwhile the husband's resolve results in his wife's own "breach of credit"; his "great affairs" impact hers. Look for instances in which payments, tips, gifts, and bribes are transacted or promised, and notice "econolingua"—words that connote money and transaction: "trust," "credit," "debt," "dowry," and "requite" (the last of which means to pay back). What counts as currency in the play? In addition to coins, for instance, note how jewelry and even clothing act as tokens of exchange and payment. As another example, Browne seems to "get by on his good looks" as we might say today; Londoners trust him in part because he is a "fair" or handsome man. His appearance, thus, seems a kind of currency. Sandra Fischer's book *Econolingua* is a glossary of money-related terms from the period; her introduction contextualizes the words within the society and culture of the time. See also Deng on money, the Mint, and coins; Gillen on economic metaphors for women and sexuality; and two important studies of cloth and clothing in the period: Jones and Stallybrass, and Hentschell.

Roles of the church and the state. Today it would be unusual for a judge in the United States to lecture a defendant on their immortal soul, but in Elizabethan England, the church was not separate from the state; the Queen was also the head of the Anglican Church. Protestant Christianity was the air people breathed. How are such concepts as divine Providence, repentance, sin, and salvation discussed and represented in *A Warning*? How do these concerns overlap with more strictly legalistic ones? The last part of the play is especially interesting for this topic since it is peopled with clerical figures (the Doctor, Mell) and public officials, including two mayors, Justices, and jailers. How do these figures and the institutions they represent shape the "warning" of the play? Inventory the props and stagecraft that convey church and state, such as the gallows and the book of meditations or prayers that Anne Sanders gives to her orphaned children.[97] A classic work that addresses both this topic and the following is Keith Thomas's *Religion and the Decline of Magic*. On the law, especially relating to women and marriage, see Dolan (*Dangerous Familiars* and *Marriage and Violence*), Dowd, Giese, Ingram, and Gowing, Martin, and Mukherji.

The supernatural and the occult. How does the play represent belief in dreams, signs, and omens (such as Beane's sense that his stumbling foretells danger in scene 6, and Anne Sanders's interpretation that the spots on her hands bode trouble in scene 4)? While Old John pronounces that dreams "are but fancies" (6.79–80). Beane and Joan seem fully invested in them. *A Warning* participates in the "murder-will-out" tradition, seen after Beane's death, when Barnes and James compare stories of murderers' spontaneous confessions brought on by actors' performance or some eerie coincidence. Another way that the occult functions in the play is through palmistry. A common folk belief in the period, palm reading and other forms of "fortune-telling" grew increasingly suspect. For reformed theologians, Luther and Calvin in particular, palmistry was demonic. Given this complex context for chiromancy, then, the moment when Drurie reads her friend's palm might be familiar to some theatergoers, but also dangerously strange. While Anne Sanders believes that Providence (or God's plan) was disclosed through Drurie's "skill," she (and audiences) might also know that the church condemned such practices. Compare examples of the supernatural from Shakespeare to this play, noting which characters "believe" in or practice occult arts, and which do not. For example, Macbeth's alternating trust in and distrust of the weird sisters' prophesy might be an interesting contrast to this earlier case of the two neighbor women's beliefs; compare Cicero's skepticism of "omens" in *Julius Caesar* with that of another old man, John in *A Warning*. On the occult, see Floyd-Wilson, Poole, and Thomas.

Work and professional identity. What constitutes work in the play? Who performs work on stage? We see a London ferryman, carpenters, merchants, apprentices, and housewives; rural agricultural workers; servants in the royal household; magistrates and civil servants; and a provincial tradesman (the butcher). For example, the two carpenters talk about the shape of their workday—when they rise, what they do, and when they'll kick back for a drink afterward (6.36–40). George Sanders's commercial business is also often talked about, yet his place of work, the Exchange, never appears on stage. The medical profession is associated exclusively with women in *A Warning*: both Mistresses Drurie and Sanders are skilled in "physic" or the healing arts; they share recipes and cures—skills routinely outlined in housewifery manuals in the period. Before formal medical schools were in place, women's work as herbalists and healers was visible and valued in their communities.[98] Beyond this—and more unusually—Drurie is reported a surgeon, and Roger tells Browne that she is also "studying the law" (1.162). She herself claims income from her palmistry. Compare men's and women's work and the rural, agrarian economy embodied by Old John and Joan to the urban, commercial one. See the collection of articles on various kinds of work in Michelle Dowd and Natasha Korda's *Working Subjects* and also *The Recipes Project*, an excellent online research collective for information about "Food, Magic, Art, Science, and Medicine" in the period.

Masters and servants. Master/servant relationships are significant indices of the extremely hierarchical Elizabethan world. Most English people spent some portion of their lives in service—as apprentices or domestic or agricultural servants. For example, when Roger explains that he has "served [Drurie] (man and boy) this seven years" (1.40), "man and boy" refers to aging out of the typical term of service as an apprentice; likely Roger came to the Drurie household in his early teens, and now he may be in his early twenties and legitimately able to leave. Roger may also intend this detail on his résumé to signal his availability to serve Browne. Meanwhile, Drurie speaks of her dependency on her "trusty" servant: "I use his [Roger's] counsel in as deep affairs" (1.154) in the same way that the Sanderses' servant is both essential to his master's trade and intimate with the domestic affairs, including their finances, as demonstrated in scene 4 when he shudders to explain to his mistress, "my master gave me charge I should deliver none [money]," only to promise "twice the sum" at a later time. When the chagrined mistress takes out her frustration on him, we see the different hierarchies of age, gender, class operating:

How's that, sir knave?
Your master charged you should deliver none?
Go to, dispatch and fetch me thirty pound,
Or I will send my fingers to your lips. (4.49)

See the groundbreaking book *Masters and Servants in English Renaissance Drama and Culture: Authority and Obedience* by Mark Thornton Burnett, Fumerton's study of the precarity of servants and others in the period, and "The Apprentice's Cap" episode of the BBC Radio podcast *Shakespeare's Restless World* (see MacGregor).

Public and private. Domestic tragedies such as *A Warning* and *Arden of Faversham* challenge on many levels the idea that public and private life are separate "spheres." First, in these stories, the private or secret dealing of adultery is exposed, becoming matters of public knowledge, record, and performance. Second, these accounts of private citizens (rather than public figures, like kings) were chronicled in popular ballads and drama and also made their way into more formal documents such as John Stow's *Annales of England*. Third, imagined divisions between public and private fall away, given the vital role of reputation in public life fueled by the networks of gossip and surveillance. Explore the private forms of affection and spirituality in the play, on the one hand, and their externalized forms of marriage and prayer (as in the public confessions), on the other. See the fine article on the topic by Longfellow; Helgerson, *Forms of Nationhood* on the intersections of public and private in chronicles, drama, and other genres of writing in the period; and Orlin's *Private Matters and Public Culture in Post-Reformation England*. Bernard Capp's work on neighborhoods and gossip is indispensable, as is Richardson's scholarship on domestic life. See also *Middling Culture: The Cultural Lives of the Middling Sort, Writing and Material Culture 1550–1650*.

Source material. Comparing and contrasting specific points in the play and the pamphlet can lead to productive insights about how and why the playwright used the various materials he inherited. What does the playwright choose to emphasize, cut, add, and so on? What seems to be gained, lost, or significantly altered by certain choices? Do any patterns emerge? Most critical studies of *A Warning* engage to some extent with the sources, and students' readings should also make use of source material. See especially Dolan and Martin.

Beauty and virtue. In early modernity people often saw outward beauty as a sign of inward virtue or goodness, while external "deformity" might show an inward defect. (The bad treatment of Quasimodo, the "Hunchback of Notre Dame," illustrates this assumption persisting for centuries.) While we are unfortunately used to cultural representations of women's physical attractiveness as a measure of their worth, in this play, it is a man, Browne, who is universally hailed as attractive. Although he praises Anne Sanders as an exceptional beauty (3.75–76, 108–9), he himself is notably handsome—"goodly a creature," "so fair a gallant," and "a proper man who hath good store of coin" (1.180, 195; 3.31). The fact that "fair" was a term that meant beautiful, virtuous, and also light-complected (white) shows how whiteness was interpolated with positive traits, and the opposite bias linked dark skin and features with ugliness and vice. In a reference to the Sanders's murder story (that preceded the play), Anthony Munday cites a version of the aphorism, "pretty is as pretty does" in relation to Browne: "Not long since, one George Browne, a man of *stature goodly and excellent*, if life and deeds thereto had been equivalent; but as the ancient adage is, goodly is he that goodly doth, and *comely* is he that behaveth himself comely"[99] (italics added). Focus on gendered and raced ideas of beauty in the play and the period. On early modern European notions of beauty, see Snook and Karim-Cooper; on antiblackness, see Burton and Loomba, Burton and Hall, and Thompson and note 252 in this volume.

Cast of Characters

Allegorical and Silent Figures (Appear in the Induction and Dumb Shows)

INDUCTION

Tragedy, also called Melpomene:[1] the goddess or Muse of tragedy, and one of the nine Mousai (Muses) or goddesses of music, song, and dance. Melpomene was portrayed holding a tragic mask or sword and sometimes wearing a wreath of ivy and buskin boots. She opens the play and later acts as a chorus, commenting on the action in the dumb shows, which are silent enactments of an often-symbolic event. She also speaks the prologue and epilogue.

History: another female figure; she represents and defends the genre of the history play, which dramatized stories of royal families, courtly intrigue, and wars, as in Shakespeare's *Richard III*.

Comedy: a third female figure; she represents and defends comic plays that usually concern nonaristocratic characters end in marriage, as *The Taming of the Shrew*.

DUMB SHOWS

The Furies:[2] These female characters from Greco-Roman mythology are the goddesses of vengeance, also called the Destinies.

Lust: a male figure

Chastity: a female figure, dressed in white

Justice: male

Mercy: female

OFFICERS

Diligence: a servant of Justice

Households and Families (in the Main Play)

SANDERS, LONDON MERCHANT FAMILY

George Sanders: a merchant, husband, and father who lives and trades in London

Anne Sanders: wife of George Sanders, mother, and friend of Mistress Drurie; courted by Browne

Man: a servant in the Sanders household and assistant to George

Young Sanders: school-aged son of George and Anne Sanders

Daughter of George and Anne Sanders (appears and speaks only at the end of the play)

Other children (appear and speak only at the end)

Harry: a young boy, friend of Young Sanders (does not live in the household)

MISTRESS DRURIE'S HOUSEHOLD, LONDON

Anne Drurie: a widow, palm reader, and surgeon, neighbor to the Sanders family

Roger Clement, also called *"Trusty Roger"* and *"Hodge"*: a manservant to Anne Drurie

Drurie's daughter (mentioned, but does not appear on stage)

BARNES HOUSEHOLD, WOOLWICH (The town in East London was a dockyard and naval station from the early 1500s, and from 1808 through World War II, housed the Royal Arsenal; now Woolwich is the home of the Arsenal Football Club. It is eight miles east of London Bridge along the Thames.)

    Master Barnes: a merchant, business associate of George Sanders

    John Beane: a servant of Master Barnes, friend of Old John and Joan. He delivers messages and accompanies George Sanders on the road.

BROWNE BROTHERS, IRISH BORN, LIVING IN LONDON

    George Browne: a captain who seems to be living in London for some period of time before the play begins

    Anthony Browne: a convicted murderer (appears in the final scene)

LONDON MERCHANTS

Draper (or linendraper): a manufacturer or dealer in cloth and other textiles. In this play, he is a representative or agent for the tradesman he works for.

Milliner: a dealer in such personal accessories and dry goods as hats and gloves, sometimes imported; a Milliner was originally someone from Milan. Like the draper, this man is a "rep" or agent who answers to someone else.

Gentleman 1: a merchant friend of George Sanders, whom he visits in London's Lombard Street, where foreign merchants settled, some from the Lombardy region of Italy.

Prentice: an apprentice to merchant/Gentleman 1

Gentleman 2: another merchant/business associate of George Sanders

LABORERS

Waterman: pilot of the ferry across the River Thames from London proper to Greenwich, where the Tudors held court

Old John: a farmer or cattle drover, John Beane's friend

Joan: Old John's maid, who seems to be in love with Beane

Butcher Brown of Rochester: proprietor of a butcher shop and home where George Browne tries to hide, acting as though this Browne is his kinsman. Rochester in this period was a provincial town.

Will Crow: a London carpenter

Tom Peart: a London carpenter

GREENWICH PALACE OFFICIALS

Yeoman of the Buttery: a servant or attendant in a royal or noble household, usually high ranking; in this case, the sort of steward of the Queen's stores at Greenwich Palace; a buttery is like a pantry where provisions were stored. This is the room where visitors might enter.[3]

Master James: a kind of court functionary at Greenwich, who is appointed to the Privy Council that investigates the murder case

Four Lords

Two Messengers

CIVIC OFFICIALS

Lord Mayor of London

Lord Justice of London

Clerk of London: officer who reads formal arraignments

Sheriff of London

Mayor of Rochester

OFFICERS

Halberdiers: officers or guards who carry halberds, a long-handled, sharp spear/battle-axe (nonspeaking role)

Pursuivant: A royal or state messenger, especially one with the power to execute warrants; a warrant officer (nonspeaking role)

Page (nonspeaking role)

Master Humphries (nonspeaking role)

NEWGATE PRISON FUNCTIONARIES (Newgate was a London prison used in part as a holding tank for the accused to await their trials).

Minister: anonymous spiritual advisor to prisoners, including Anne Sanders. In the source material, he is named Mell.

Keeper of Newgate Prison: he is like Anne's personal cell keeper, who assists her

Doctor: Not a medical doctor but a doctor of divinity or theology, a minister; he counsels Anne and Drurie in prison

Jailor of Newgate Prison: the head of the prison

A Warning for Fair Women

Induction

Three female allegorical figures who represent the three main dramatic subgenres—Tragedy, History, and Comedy—engage in a vicious insult exchange as they fight over who will control the stage that day. Tragedy comes storming in, first yelling at History to quit playing the drum, a sound effect that signaled historical plays (with their military themes) and then complaining of the "filthy sound" of Comedy's "fiddle strings." The ensuing argument threatens to become violent (Tragedy wields a whip) and also reveals interesting things about stage practices of the time. For example, the figures make fun of the different styles of acting: while Tragedy demands "passions that must move the soul," Comedy mocks the tragic tropes of tyrants and political intrigue, poison, and revenge. Later, when History points out that because "the stage is hung with black," the "auditors" would be prepared for a tragedy, she and Comedy retreat, and Comedy admits, "These ornaments [the black cloth] beseem not thee and me."

Enter at one door, History with drum and ensign,[1] *Tragedy at*
another, in her one hand a whip, in the other hand a knife.[2]

TRAGEDY Wither away so fast? Peace with that drum:
   Down with that ensign which disturbs our stage.
5   Out with this luggage, with this foppery.[3]
   This bawling sheepskin[4] is intolerable.
HISTORY Indeed no marvel, though we should give place
   Unto a common executioner.
   Room, room, for God's sake, let us stand away!
10   O, we shall have some doughty stuff[5] today.

Enter Comedy at the other end [of the stage].[6]

TRAGEDY What, yet more cats' guts? O, this filthy[7] sound
15   Stifles mine ears!
   More cartwheels creaking yet?[8]
   A plague upon't, I'll cut your fiddle strings,
   If you stand scraping thus to anger me.
COMEDY Gup[9] mistress buskins with a whirligig; are you so touchy?
20   Madam Melpomene,[10] whose mare is dead
   That you are going to take off her skin?
TRAGEDY A plague upon these filthy fiddling tricks,
   Able to poison any noble wit!
   Avoid the stage or I'll whip you hence.
25 COMEDY Indeed thou mayest, for thou art Murder's Beadle,[11]
   The common hangman unto Tyranny.

   [She suddenly notices that History is also present; does a cartoonish
   double-take.]

30   But, History—what all three met at once?
   What wonder's toward that we are got together?[12]
HISTORY My meaning was to have been here today,   [*to Comedy*]
   But meeting with my Lady Tragedy,

She scolds me off.

And, Comedy, except[13] thou canst prevail,   35

I think she means to banish us the stage.

COMEDY Tut, tut, she cannot: she may for a day

Or two perhaps be had in some request,

But once a week if we do not appear,

She shall find few that will attend her here.[14]   40

TRAGEDY I must confess you have some sparks of wit.

Some odd ends of old jests scraped up together,[15]

To tickle shallow injudicial ears,

Perhaps some puling[16] passion of a lover, but slight and childish,

What is this to me?   45

[Comedy and History stand behind her and mock Tragedy's elevated rhetoric, perhaps making funny faces.]

I must have passions that must move the soul,

Make the heart heavy, and throb within the bosom,   50

Extorting tears out of the strictest[17] eyes,

To rack a thought and strain it to his form,

Until I rap the senses from their course.[18]

This is my office.

COMEDY How some damned tyrant, to obtain a crown,[19]   55

Stabs, hangs, empoisons, smothers, cutteth throats,

And then a Chorus, too, comes howling in,

And tells us of the worrying of a cat,

Then of a filthy whining ghost,

Lapped in some fowl sheet, or a leather pelch,[20]   60

Comes screaming like a pig half sticked,

And cries, "*Vindicta*, revenge, revenge!"[21]

With that a little rosen flasheth forth,[22]

Like smoke out of a tobacco pipe, or a boy's squib.[23]

Then comes in two or three like to drovers,   65

With tailors' bodkins, stabbing one another.[24]

Is not this trim? Is not here goodly things?[25]

That you should be so much accounted of,
I would not else.

70 HISTORY Now, before God, thou'lt make her mad anon.[26]
Thy jests are like a wisp unto a scold.[27]

COMEDY Why, say I could—what care I, History?
Then shall we have a tragedy indeed:
Pure purple buskin, blood and murder right.[28]

75 TRAGEDY Thus with your loose and idle similes,[29]
You have abused me, but I'll whip you hence.   *She whips them.*
I'll scourge and lash you both from off the stage!
'Tis you have kept the theaters so long,
Painted in playbills, upon every post,[30]
80 That I am scorned of the multitude,
My name profaned; but now I'll reign as Queen
In great Apollo's name and all the Muses,
By virtue of whose Godhead, I am sent.[31]
I charge you to be gone and leave this place.

85 HISTORY Look, Comedy, I marked it not till now: [*pointing to the
upper stage*]
The stage is hung with black and I perceive
The auditors prepared for Tragedy.[32]

COMEDY Nay then, I see she shall be entertained;[33]
These ornaments beseem[34] not thee and me.
90 Then, Tragedy, kill them today with sorrow,
We'll make them laugh with mirthful jests tomorrow.

HISTORY And, Tragedy, although today thou reign,[35]
Tomorrow here I'll domineer again.   *Exeunt*[36]

Prologue

Left alone, Tragedy addresses the audience directly, drawing attention to their location in the public theater (the "fair circuit" and "this round"), as she sets the scene: "My scene is London, native and your own." With this locale and the "subject" of the play that is "too well known," Tragedy tells the audience that this drama is a new kind of play, since few plays were set in contemporary London, and she also hints that "many" of the viewers present may once have cried about the events in the performance that had actually transpired in their lifetimes.

Turning to the people

TRAGEDY Are you both gone so soon? Why then I see
　　All this fair circuit here is left to me.[37]　　[*gesturing widely around
　　　　the theater*]
5　　All you spectators, turn your cheerful eye,
　　Give entertainment unto Tragedy.
　　My scene is London, native and your own;
　　I sigh to think my subject too well known.
　　I am not fained: many now in this round,[38]
10　　Once to behold in sad tears were drowned,
　　Yet what I am, I will not let you know,
　　Until my next ensuing scene shall show. [*Exit*]

Scene 1. A street in London

We meet all the main characters as they separate after having supper together. Mr. Sanders and Captain Browne chat briefly about Ireland, where Browne was born, and which in the 1590s was occupied by English settlers or "planters," who were given land and expected to "reduce" or bring the "wild Irish" under English rule. The Sanderses begin the walk home with their neighbor, Mistress Drurie, when Browne calls Roger back because he wants to talk to Drurie. In the play's first soliloquy, Browne reveals his desire for Anne Sanders, adding a graver tone to the scene, with his vow to "lose my life" if he fails to "win" her; he thinks that Drurie can help him. When Roger returns with her, Browne wants to speak alone with Drurie, who insists that her man is trustworthy (his nickname, after all, is Trusty Roger). Because Browne is not totally direct about the actual nature of his "surfeit," she has to decode; commonly the term refers to a stomachache brought on from overindulgence. Having just left the meal, Drurie assumes that Browne simply ate too much and needs medical attention—perhaps a purgative ("physic") that she or Anne Sanders can supply. Drurie and Roger both comment a number of times on Browne's handsomeness (he is "fair"), and they see that they can profit from doing him service. They attest to the excellent reputations that the Sanders couple enjoys in London. After weighing the pros and cons of betraying their friends, eventually they strike a deal for Browne to gain "access" to Anne for a fee. Drurie eyes Browne's jewelry, and he takes the hint and gives her at least two pieces (a turquoise broach or earring and a ring; he also promises a necklace or "chain"); he tips Roger, who asks for Browne's hand-me-downs ("cast" off suit).

Enter [George] Sanders, Anne Sanders, [Mistress Nan] Drurie,
[Captain] Browne, Roger, and Master Sanders's servant.

SANDERS Gentleman, here must we take our leave,
    Thanking you for your courteous[39] company,
5   And for your good discourse of Ireland,
    Whereas it seems you have been resident,
    By your well noting the particulars.
BROWNE True sir, I have been there familiar,
    And am no better known in London here
10   Than I am there unto the better sort,
    Chiefly in Dublin, where ye heard me say
    Are as great feasts as this we had today.[40]
SANDERS So have I heard, the land gives good increase,
    Of every blessing for the use of man,[41]
15   And 'tis great pity the inhabitants
    Will not be civil, nor live under law.[42]
BROWNE As civil in the English pale as here,
    And laws obeyed, and orders duly kept,
    And all the rest may one day be reduced.[43]
20 SANDERS God grant it so: I pray you what's your name?
BROWNE My name's George Browne.
SANDERS God be with ye, good Master Browne.[44]
BROWNE Many farewells, Master Sanders to yourself,
    and to these Gentlewomen. Ladies, God be with you.
25 ANNE God be with ye, sir.
DRURIE Thanks for your company.
    I like your talk of Ireland so well
    That I could wish time had not cut it off.
    I pray ye, sir, if ye come near my house,
30   Call, and you shall be welcome, Master Browne.
BROWNE, I thank ye, Mistress Drurie: is't not so?
DRURIE My name is Anne Drurie.
SANDERS Widow, come, will ye go?
DRURIE I'll wait upon you sir.

Exeunt Sanders. Anne Sanders makes a curtsy and departs, and all   35
the rest [exit] saving[45] *Roger, whom Browne calls.*

BROWNE Hark ye, my friend,
 Are not you servant unto Mistress Drurie?
ROGER Yes indeed, forsooth,[46] for fault of a better,
 I have served her (man and boy) this seven years.[47]   40
BROWNE I pray thee do me a piece of favor then,
 And I'll requite it.[48]
ROGER Anything I can.
BROWNE Entreat thy mistress when she takes her leave
 Of Master Sanders and his wife, to make retire   45
 Hither[49] again, for I will speak with her.
 Wilt thou do it for me?
ROGER Yea, sir, that I will.
 Where shall she find ye?
BROWNE I'll not stir from hence.   50
 Say I entreat her but a word or two;
 She shall not stay longer than likes herself.
ROGER Nay, sir, for that as you two can agree;
 I'll warrant you I'll bring her to ye straight.   *Exit Roger.*
BROWNE Straight or crooked,[50] I must needs speak with her,   55
 For, by this light,[51] my heart is not my own,
 But taken prisoner at this frolic[52] feast,
 Entangled in a net of golden wire,
 Which love had slyly laid in her fair looks.[53]
 O, Master Sanders, th'art[54] a happy man,   60
 To have so sweet a creature to thy wife,
 Whom I must win or I must lose my life.
 But if she be as modest[55] as she seems,
 Thy heart may break, George Browne, ere thou obtain.
 This Mistress Drurie must be made the mean,   65
 What ere it cost to compass[56] my desire,
 And I hope well. She doth so soon retire.

Enter Roger and Drurie.

70 Good Mistress Drurie, pardon this bold part
That I have played upon so small acquaintance
To send for you; let your good nature hide
The blame of my bad nurture for this once.[57]
DRURIE I take it for a favor, Master Browne,
75 And no offence. A man of your fair parts[58]
Will send for me to stead him anyway.
ROGER Sir, ye shall find my mistress as courteous a gentle-
woman, as any is in London, if ye have occasion to use her.
BROWNE [*to Roger*] So I presume, friend. Mistress, by your
leave, *Takes her aside [and whispers to her]*
80 I would not that your man should hear our speech,
For it concerns me much it be concealed.
DRURIE I hope it is no treason[59] you will speak.
BROWNE No, by my faith, nor felony.[60]
DRURIE Nay then, though my man Roger hear it, never care.
85 If it be love, or secrets due to that,
Roger is trusty, I dare pawn my life,
As any fellow within London walls.[61]
But if you have some secret malady
That craves my help, to use my surgery,[62]
90 Which though I say 'tis pretty, he shall hence.
If not, be bold to speak; there's no offence.
BROWNE I have no sore, but a new inward grief, [*Roger stands off to*
one side of the stage.]
Which, by your physic,[63] may find some relief.
95 DRURIE What, is't a surfeit?[64]
BROWNE Aye, at this late feast.
DRURIE Why, *Aqua coelestis*, or the water of balm,
Or *Rosa solis*, or that of Doctor Stevens
Will help a surfeit.[65] Now I remember me,
100 Mistress Sanders hath a sovereign[66] thing,
To help a sudden surfeit presently.

BROWNE I think she have; how shall I compass it?

DRURIE I'll send my man for some on't.

BROWNE Pray ye stay.

    She'll never send that which will do me good.   105

DRURIE O say not so, for then ye know her not.

BROWNE I would I did so well as I could wish.   *Aside*

DRURIE She's even as courteous a gentlewoman sir

    As kind a pet[67] as London can afford:

    Not send it, quotha[68]? Yes and bring't herself,   110

    If need require. A poor woman t'other day,

    Her water-bearer's[69] wife, had surfeited

    With eating beans (ye know 'tis windy[70] meat)

    And the poor creature's subject to the stone.[71]

    She went herself and gave her but a dram.[72]   115

    It helped her straight; in less than half an hour

    She fell unto her business till she sweat,

    And was as well as I am now.

BROWNE But that which helps a woman helps not me.

    A woman's help will rather do me good.   120

DRURIE I'faith I have found you, are ye such one?[73]

    Well, Master Browne, I warrant, let you alone.

BROWNE But, Mistress Drurie, leave me not yet alone,

    For if ye do, I never shall alone

    Obtain the company that my soul desires.   125

    Faith tell me one thing—can ye not do much

    With Mistress Sanders; are you not inward with her?[74]

DRURIE I dare presume to do as much with her

    As any woman in this city can.

BROWNE What's your opinion of her honesty?   130

DRURIE O, very honest, very chaste i'faith,

    I will not wrong her for a thousand pound.[75]

BROWNE Then all your physic cannot cure my wound.

DRURIE Your wound is love; is that your surfeit, sir?

BROWNE Yea, and 'tis cureless without help of her.   135

DRURIE I am very sorry that I cannot ease ye.

BROWNE Well, if ye can, i'faith I will well please ye.

DRURIE You wear a pretty turquoise there me thinks,[76]
    I would I had the fellow on't.

140 BROWNE Take ye this,[77]   [*Browne removes a piece of jewelry, the*
    earring or broach, and hands it to her.]
    Upon condition to affect my bliss.[78]

DRURIE Pardon me that, sir, no condition.
    For that grief I am no physician.
    How sayest thou, Roger, am I?

145 ROGER Yea, forsooth mistress. What? What did ye ask?   [*Starting*
    suddenly, acting as though he has not been listening]

DRURIE This gentleman's in love
    With Mistress Sanders and would have me speak
    On his behalf. How sayest thou; dare I do't?
    And she so honest, wise and virtuous?

150 BROWNE What mean ye, Mistress Drurie, to bewray[79]
    Unto your man, what I in secret spoke?

DRURIE Tush, fear not you, 'tis Trusty Roger, this.
    I use his counsel in as deep affairs.
    How sayest thou, Hodge?

155 ROGER Mistress, this say I: though Mistress Sanders be
    very honest, as in my conscience she is, and her husband
    wise and subtle,[80] and in all Billingsgate-ward[81] not a kinder
    couple; yet if you would wrong her husband, your dear
    friend, me thinks ye have such a sweet tongue, as will

160   supple a stone, and for my life, if ye list to labor,
    you'll win her. [*Turning to Browne*] Sir, stick close to my mistress;
    she is
    studying the law, and if ye not be strait-laced—ye
    know my mind—she'll do it for ye and I'll play my part.[82]

BROWNE Here Mistress Drurie this same ring is yours   *Give[s] her*
    a ring

165   Wear't for my sake, and if ye do me good,
    Command this chain, this hand, this heart blood.[83]   [*pointing in*
    turns to his neck, hand, and chest]

What say ye to me? Speak a cheerful word.

ROGER Faith, Mistress, do; he's a fine gentleman.

Pity he should languish for a little love.

DRURIE Yea, but thou knowest they are both my friends. 170

He's very wise, she very circumspect,

Very respective of her honest name.[84]

ROGER If ye list,[85] you can cover as great a blame.

DRURIE If I should break it, and she take it ill.

ROGER Tut, you have cunning, pray ye use your skill. 175

To her, Master Browne.[86]   [*Roger whispers in Browne's ear and
pushes him forward.*]

BROWNE What say ye to me, lady?

DRURIE This I say.   [*She pauses, increasing the tension.*]

I cannot make a man.[87] To cast away

So goodly a creature as yourself were sin. 180

Second my onset, for I will begin

To break the ice that you may pass the ford.[88]

Do your good will; you shall have my good word.[89]

BROWNE But how shall I have opportunity?

DRURIE That must be watched, but very secretly. 185

BROWNE How? At her house?

DRURIE There ye may not enter.

BROWNE How then?

DRURIE By some other fine adventure.

Watch when her husband goes to the Exchange.[90] 190

She'll sit at door; to her, though she be strange.[91]

Spare not to speak; ye can but be denied.

Women love most by whom they are most tried.[92]

My man shall watch, and I will watch my turn.

I cannot see so fair a gallant mourn. 195

BROWNE Ye bless my soul by showing me the way,

O, Mistress Drurie, if I do obtain,

Do but imagine how I'll quit your pain.[93]

But where's her house?

DRURIE Against Saint Dunstan's church.[94] 200

205   **BROWNE** Saint Dunstan's in Fleet Street?

      DRURIE No, near Billingsgate,

          Saint Dunstan's in the East; that's in the West.

          Be bold to speak for I will do my best.

      BROWNE Thanks, Mistress Drurie. Roger, drink you that,   [*handing*

          him some loose coins or a small pouch]

210   And, as I speed, expect your recompense.[95]

      ROGER I thank ye sir, nay I'll gauge[96] my hand.

          Few women can my mistress's voice withstand.

      DRURIE Sir, this is all ye have to say?

      BROWNE For this time, Mistress Drurie, we will part.

215   Win Mistress Sanders, and ye win my heart.

      DRURIE Hope you the best. She shall have much ado,

          To hold her own when I begin to woo.[97] Come, Hodge.   *Exit*

      ROGER I trust, sir, when my mistress has obtained your suit,

          You'll suit me in a cast suit of your apparel.[98]

      BROWNE Cast and uncast shall Trusty Roger have,

220   If thou be secret, and an honest knave.   *Exeunt omnes.*

Scene 2. Sanders's house, outside on the doorstep

Anne Sanders and her son sit waiting for George to come home from the Royal Exchange, a place where merchants did business in the city; they talk familiarly about suppertime, afterschool snacks, and the child's Easter outfit. When the boy goes inside, Browne enters. His soliloquy changes the tone from prosaic family chatter to elevated, poetic, and tragic blank verse; he then begins to chat up Mistress Sanders, who handily repulses his advances. For example, when Browne grandly offers to put in a good word for her spouse at court, she assures him that no such intervention is necessary, and, once Browne leaves, she comments on the "errand-making gallants" who can't let a woman sit alone in peace. At this point George Sanders returns—late—for supper. Husband and wife agree to invite Drurie for the meal: "she'll make us merry."

Enter Anne Sanders with her little son, and sit at her door.

BOY Pray ye, mother, when shall we go to supper?[99]

ANNE Why, when your father comes from the Exchange;[100]

5   Ye are not hungry since ye came from school.

BOY Not hungry, mother, but I would fain[101] eat.

ANNE Forbear a while until your father come.

    I sit here to expect his quick return.

BOY Mother, shall not I have new bow and shafts,

10   Against[102] our school go a feasting?

ANNE Yes, if ye learn,

    And, against Easter, new apparel too.

BOY You'll lend me all your scarves, and all your rings,

    And buy me a white feather for my velvet cap;

15   Will ye, mother? Yea say, pray ye, say so.

ANNE Go, prattling boy,[103] go bid your sister see

    My closet locked when she takes out the fruit.

BOY I will, forsooth, and take some for my pains.   *Exit Boy.*

ANNE Well, sir sauce, does your master teach ye that?

20   I pray God bless thee; th'art a very wag.[104]   *Enter Browne.*

BROWNE Yonder she sits to light this obscure street[105]   [*Alone*]

    Like a bright diamond worn in some dark place,

    Or like the moon in a black winter's night,

    To comfort wand'ring travelers in their way.

25   But so demure, so modest are her looks,

    So chaste her eyes, so virtuous her aspect,[106]

    As do repulse love's false artillery.[107]

    Yet must I speak, though checked with scornful nay.

    Desire draws on, but Reason bids me stay.[108]

30   My Tutoress[109] Drurie gave me charge to speak,

    And speak I must, or else my heart will break.

    God save ye, Mistress Sanders, all alone?   [*To Anne*]

    Sit ye to take the view of passengers?[110]

ANNE No, in good sooth sir, I give small regard

35   Who comes or goes. My husband I attend,

Whose coming will be speedy from th'Exchange.

BROWNE A good exchange made he for single life[111]
   That joined in marriage with so sweet a wife.

ANNE Come ye to speak with Master Sanders, sir?

BROWNE Why ask ye that?   40

ANNE Because ye make a stay,
   Here at his door.

BROWNE I stay in courtesy,
   To give you thanks for your last company.
   I hope my kind salute doth not offend?[112]   45

ANNE No sir, and yet such unexpected kindness,
   Is like Herb John in broth.[113]

BROWNE I pray ye how's that?

ANNE 'T may even as well be laid aside as used.
   If ye have business with my husband, sir,   50
   Y'are welcome; otherwise, I'll take my leave.   [She stands up and
      turns to go inside.]

BROWNE Nay, gentle Mistress, let not my access
   Be means to drive you from your door so soon.
   I would be loath to prejudice your pleasure.
   For my good liking at the feast conceiv'd,[114]   55
   If Master Sanders shall have cause to use
   The favor of some noble personage,
   Let him employ no other but George Browne
   T'effect his suit without a recompense.[115]
   I speak I know not what! My tongue and heart   Aside   60
   Are so divided through the force of Love.

ANNE I thank ye, sir, but if he have such cause,
   I hope he's not so void of friends in Court,
   But he may speed and never trouble you.[116]
   Yet I will do your errand if ye please.   65

BROWNE Even as't please you![117] I doubt I trouble ye.

ANNE Resolve your doubt, and trouble me no more.

BROWNE 'Twill never be. I thought as much before.   [Aside]
   God be with you, Mistress.

70 ANNE Fare ye well, good sir.

BROWNE I'll to Nan Drurie yet and talk with her. *Exit*

ANNE These errand-making gallants are good men

That cannot pass and let a woman sit

Of any sort, alone at any door,

75 But they will find a 'scuse to stand and prate.

Fools that they are to bite at every bait.[118] *Enter Sanders.*

Here he comes now whom I have looked for long.

SANDERS How now, sweet Nan, sit'st thou here all alone?

ANNE Better alone than in bad company.[119]

80 SANDERS I trust there's none but good resorts to thee.

ANNE There shall not, sir, if I know what they be.

Ye have stayed late, sir, at th'Exchange tonight.

SANDERS Upon occasion, Nan, is supper ready?

ANNE An hour ago.

85 SANDERS And what good company?

None to sup with us? Send one for Nan Drurie;

She'll play the wag,[120] tell tales, and make us merry.

ANNE I think sh'as supped, but one shall run and look.

If your meat be marred, blame yourself, not the cook.

90 SANDERS How ere it be, we'll take it in good part

For once and use it not. Come, lets in, sweetheart. *Exeunt*

Scene 3. Drurie's house

This scene formalizes the contract among Drurie, Roger, and Browne that they broached in scene 1. It opens with Drurie and Roger comparing notes about Browne's case, and they "marvel" that they have not heard from him lately. Roger is up-front about his mistress's role as go-between to drive or "pilot" the illicit sexual relationship for pay, and she reacts by pretending to be ignorant of this implication, denying her role (as if to say, "Who, me?") and then claiming that Browne is in fact courting her daughter. The conversation must be performative—as in putting on an "act"—since the two have already agreed to the job when Browne approached them earlier. Roger, on both occasions, acknowledges Drurie's history as a bawd. In any case, they confirm for the audience their intimate cooperation: Drurie compliments his quick wit, and Roger admires her accomplishments in tempting women. Their private conversation ends with plans to exploit Browne and possibly Anne Sanders, too, in order to extract as much "treasure" as possible. When Browne enters to update them on his "breaking the ice" with Anne, there is some pretense about whether Roger should be present and, as in scene 1, much talk of "secret[s]" and money. Roger makes a show of encouraging an apparently reluctant Drurie to accept Browne's offer and seduce Anne Sanders. The scene ends with a series of rhymed statements that seem to cement the plan.

Enter Anne Drurie, and Trusty Roger her man. To them Browne[121]

DRURIE Roger, come hither; was there no messenger
    This day from Master Browne to speak with me?
5 ROGER Mistress, not any, and that I marvel at.
    But I can tell you, he must come and send,
    And be no niggard[122] of his purse beside,
    Or else I know how it will go with him.
    He must not think to anchor where he hopes,
10   Unless you be his pilot.[123]
DRURIE Where is that?
    The fellow talks and prates he knows not what.   [*As if in an*
      aside]
    I be his pilot? Wither? Canst thou tell?
    The cause he doth frequent my house, thou seest,
15   Is for the love he bears unto my daughter.
ROGER A very good cloak, Mistress, for the rain,
    And therein I must needs[124] commend your wit:
    Close dealing is the safest; by that means
    The world will be the less suspicious.
20   For whilst 'tis thought he doth affect[125] your daughter,
    Who can suspect his love to Mistress Sanders?
DRURIE Why, now thou are as I would have thee be—
    Conceited and of quick capacity.[126]
    Some heavy drawlatch would have been this month,
25   (Though hourly I had instructed him),
    Before he could have found my policy.[127]
    But, Hodge, thou art my heart's interpreter,
    And be thou secret still, as thou hast been,
    And doubt not but we'll all gain by the match:
30   George Browne, as thou knowest, is well reckoned of.
    A proper man who hath good store of coin,
    And Mistress Sanders—she is young and fair,
    And may be tempered easily like wax,[128]
    Especially by one that is familiar with her.

ROGER True, Mistress, nor is this the first by many   35
    That you have won to stoop unto the lure.[129]
    It is your trade, your living; what needs more?
    Drive you the bargain; I will keep the door.[130]
DRURIE Trusty Roger, thou well deserve thy name.
ROGER But, Mistress, shall I tell you what I think?   40
DRURIE Yes, Hodge, what is't?
ROGER If you'll be ruled by me,[131]
    Let them pay well for what you undertake.
    Be not a spokeswoman,[132] mistress, for none of them,
    But be the better for it: times will change,   45
    And there's no trusting to uncertainties.
DRURIE Dost think I will? Then beg me for a fool,
    The money I will finger twixt them twain[133]
    Shall make my daughter such a dowry,
    As I will match her better than with Browne—   50
    To some rich attorney or gentleman.
    Let me alone. If they enjoy their pleasure,
    My sweet[134] shall be to feed upon their treasure.
ROGER Hold you there, mistress. Here comes Master Browne.
BROWNE Good morrow, Mistress Drurie.   *Enter Browne.*   55
DRURIE What, Master Browne,
    Now by my faith you are the very last man
    We talked of; y'are welcome sir, how do you?
    And how speed you concerning that you wot[135] of?
ROGER Mistress, I'll void[136] the place, if you please.   60
    And give you leave in private to confer.   [*pretends to leave the
    room; a false exit*]
BROWNE Whither goes Roger? Call him back again.
DRURIE Come hither, sirrah, Mr. Browne will have you stay.[137]
BROWNE Why how now, Roger? Will you shrink from me?
    Because I saw you not, do you suppose   65
    I make no reckoning of your company?
    What man? Thy trust is it I build upon.
ROGER I thank you sir: nay, pray you be not offended.

I would be loath to seem unmannerly.

70 BROWNE Tut, a fig's end:[138] thy counsel will do well,
And we must use thee; therefore, tarry here.
I have no other secret to reveal,
But only this—that I have broke the ice,
And made an entrance to my love's pursuit.
75 Sweet Mistress Sanders, that choice argument
Of all perfection, sitting at her door
Even now I did salute.[139] Some words there passed,
But nothing to the purpose, neither time,
Nor place consorted to my mind. Beside,
80 Recourse of servants and of passengers
Might have been jealous of our conference
And, therefore, I refrained all large discourse.[140]
Only thus much I gathered by her speech—
That she is affable, not coy, nor scornful,
85 And may be won, would you but be entreated [*speaks to Drurie,*
who may turn her back, frown, or gesture in some way that
suggests her reluctance to agree]
To be a mediator for me and persuade her.[141]
ROGER I pray you do so, Mistress. You do know
That Master Browne's an honest gentleman
And I dare swear will recompense you well.
90 BROWNE If she[142] do mistrust me, there's my purse, [*speaks to*
Roger]
And in the same ten angels[143] of good gold,
And when I can but have access to her,[144]
And am in any possibility
To win her favor, challenge of me more—
95 A hundred pound in marriage with your daughter.
DRURIE Alas, how dare I, Master Browne? Her husband
Is one that I am much beholding to,
A man both loving, bountiful, and just,
And to his wife, in all this city, none
100 More kind, more loyal hearted, or more firm.

What sin were it to do him then that wrong?   [*Drurie looking*   105
    worried, again pretending reluctance to accept Browne's offer.]
BROWNE O, speak not of his worth, but of her praise.[145]
    If he be firm, she's fair; if he bountiful,
    She's beautiful; if he loyal, she's lovely;
    If he, in all the City for a man
    Be the most absolute, she, in all the world   110
    Is for a woman the most excellent.
    O, earth hath seldom such a creature seen,
    Nor subject been possessed with such a love.
ROGER Mistress, can you hear this, and not be moved?[146]
    I would it lay in me to help you, sir,   [*to Browne, perhaps in an*   115
      aside]
    I'faith you should not need for many words.
BROWNE I know that, thou hast always been my friend,
    And, though I never see Anne Sanders more,
    Yet for my sake drink[147] this, and Mistress Drurie,   [*Browne*
      handing him coins]
    England I must be forced to bid farewell,   120
    Or shortly look to hear that I am dead,
    Unless I may prevail to get her love.
ROGER Good mistress, leave your dumps[148] and speak to him,
    You need not study so; 'tis no such labor.[149]
    Alas, will you see a gentleman cast away?   125
    All is but George; I pray you let be done.[150]
DRURIE Well, Master Browne, not for your money's sake
    So much, as I regard I love you well,
    Am I content to be your orator.
    Mistress Sanders shall be certified[151]   130
    How fervently you love her, and withal.
    Some other words I'll use [o]n your behalf,
    As you shall have access to her at last.
BROWNE I ask no more. When will you undertake it?
DRURIE This day; it shall no longer be deferred,   135
    And, in the evening, you shall know an answer.

BROWNE Here at your house?

DRURIE Yea, here if so you please.

BROWNE No better place. I rest upon your promise.
140   So farewell, Mistress Drurie, till that hour,
    What sweet can earth afford will not seem sour.   [*Exit*
      Browne.][152]

DRURIE He's sped, i'faith. Come, Roger, let us go.
    Ill is the wind doth no man profit blow.[153]

145   ROGER I shall not be the worse for it; that I know.   *Exeunt*

Scene 4. Sanders's house

Sanders and the unnamed male servant prepare for the day; they discuss current business dealings and deadlines for payment. When it appears that all available funds are tied up, the servant mentions that his mistress has asked for money for household purchases that day (a tiny fraction of what Sanders is paying out), and Sanders explains that his "great affairs" outweigh his wife's "trifling wares" or purchases. After Sanders exits, the worried servant stays on stage and the scene moves inside: the women enter with two merchants whose wares Anne Sanders examines and discusses with them. After asking the servant for the requisite thirty pounds, and hearing that her husband refuses to relinquish the amount, the angry and embarrassed mistress sends the merchants away, refusing their offer to pay on credit (i.e., the "bills of debt" that the men use on the Exchange). This upset gives Drurie the chance to stoke her friend's anger ("Your husband was to blame, to say the truth"), and then she reads Anne Sanders's palm to predict the death of George Sanders and Anne's remarriage to another, "better" George (Browne). Anne Sanders does not seem interested in this idea at all, but eventually agrees to what she has come to believe is God's will. By the end of the scene, Drurie soliloquizes about how to murder Sanders, followed by the first dumb show that changes the tone to dark and tragic.

*Enter Master Sanders and his man. [They stand on the stoop outside
the house.]*

SANDERS Sirrah, what bills of debt[154] are due to me?
MAN All that were due, sir, as this day are paid.
5 SANDERS You have enough then to discharge the bond
   Of Master Ashmore's fifteen-hundred pound
   That must be tendered[155] on the Exchange tonight?
MAN With that which Master Bishop owes, we have.
SANDERS When is his time to pay?
10 MAN This afternoon.
SANDERS He's a sure[156] man, thou needst not doubt of him.
   In any case, take heed unto my credit:
   I do not use (thou knowest) to break my word,
   Much less my bond. I pray thee look unto it,
15 And when as Master Bishop sends his money,
   Paying the whole sum, I'll be upon the Burse,[157]
   Or if I be not, thou canst take a quittance.[158]
MAN What shall I say unto my mistress, sir?
   She bade me tell out thirty pounds even now,
20 She meant to have bestowed in linen cloth.[159]
SANDERS She must defer her market till tomorrow,
   I know no other shift:[160] my great affairs
   Must not be hindered by such trifling wares.
MAN She told me, sir, the draper would be here,
25 And George, the milliner, with other things,
   Which she appointed should be brought her home.[161]
SANDERS All's one for that; another time shall serve.
   Nor is there any such necessity,
   But she may very well forbear a while.
30 MAN She will not so be answered at my hand.
SANDERS Tell her I did command it should be so.   *Exit*
MAN Your pleasure shall be done sir, though thereby
   'Tis I am like to bear the blame away.   [*remains on stage*]

Enter Anne Sanders, Mistress Drurie, a Draper, and a Milliner.[162]
[a room inside the house]

ANNE Come near, I pray you, I do like your linen,
    and you shall have your price. But you, my friend, the
    gloves you showed me and the Italian purse are both
    well made, and I do like the fashion. But trust me,
    the perfume, I am afraid, will not continue. Yet upon   40
    your word, I'll have them too. Sirrah, where is your   *[to the*
      servant]
    Master?
MAN Forsooth, he's gone to th'Exchange even now.
ANNE Have you the money ready which I called for?
MAN No, if it please you, my master gave me charge I should deliver   45
    none.
ANNE How's that, sir knave?
    Your master charged you should deliver none?
    Go to, dispatch and fetch me thirty pound,
    Or I will send my fingers to your lips.[163]
DRURIE Good fortune! Thus incensed against her husband,   50
    I shall the better break with her for Browne.   *Aside*
MAN I pray you, Mistress, pacify yourself,   *[to Anne Sanders]*
    I dare not do it.[164]
ANNE You dare not, and why so?
MAN Because there's money to be paid to night,   55
    Upon an obligation.
ANNE What of that?
    Therefore, I may not have to serve my turn?[165]
MAN Indeed. Forsooth, there is not in the house,
    As yet sufficient to discharge that debt.   60
ANNE 'Tis well that I must stand at your reversion,[166]
    Entreat my prentice, curtsy to my man.
    And he must be purse-bearer, when I need.
    This was not wont to be your master's order.

65 DRURIE No, I'll be sworn of that. I never knew,
　　 But that you had at all times, Mistress Sanders,
　　 A greater sum than that at a command.
　　 Mary,[167] perhaps the world may now be changed.
　 MAN Feed not my mistress's anger, Mistress Drurie;
70　 You do not well. Tomorrow, if she list,[168]
　　 It is not twice so much but she may have it.
　 ANNE So that my breach of credit[169] in the while
　　 Is not regarded. I have brought these men
　　 To have their money for such necessaries,
75　 As I have bought, and they have honestly
　　 Delivered to my hands; and now—forsooth—
　　 I must be thought so bare and beggarly,
　　 As they must be put off until tomorrow!
　 LINENDRAPER Good Mistress Sanders, trouble not yourself.
80　 If that be all, your word shall be sufficient,
　　 Were it for thrice the value of my ware.
　 MILLINER And trust me, Mistress, you shall do me wrong,
　　 If otherwise you do conceit of me.
　　 Be it for a week, a fortnight, or a month,
85　 Or when you will, I never would desire
　　 Better security for all I am worth.[170]
　 ANNE I thank you for your gentleness, my friends,
　　 But I have never used to go on credit.
　　 There is two crowns betwixt you for your pains.[171] *[gives each*
　　　　 man a coin]
90　 Sirrah, deliver them their stuff again,　 *[to servant]*
　　 And make them drink a cup of wine. Farewell.
　 LINENDRAPER Good Mistress Sanders, let me leave the cloth.
　　 I shall be chidden[172] when I do come home.
　 MILLINER And I. Therefore, I pray you be persuaded.
95 ANNE No, no, I will excuse you to your masters.
　　 So, if you love me use no more entreaty.[173]　 *Exeunt [merchants*
　　　　 and servant].
　　 I am a woman, and in that respect,

Am well content my husband shall control me,
But that my man should over-awe me too,
And in the sight of strangers, Mistress Drurie: 100
I tell you true, does grieve me to the heart.
DRURIE Your husband was to blame, to say the truth,
That gave his servant such authority.
What signifies it, but he doth repose
More trust in a vile boy, than in his wife?[174]   105
ANNE Nay, give me leave to think the best of him.
It was my destiny and not his malice.
Sure I did know as well when I did rise
This morning, that I should be chafed ere noon,
As where I stand.   110
DRURIE By what, good Mistress Sanders?[175]
ANNE Why, by these yellow spots upon my fingers.   [*Anne shows
her hands.*]
They never come to me, but I am sure
To hear of anger ere I go to bed.
DRURIE 'Tis like enough, I pray you let me see,   [*Drurie takes up*   115
Anne's hands and turns them over, begins to "read" her palm.]
Good sooth they are as manifest as day,
And let me tell you too, I see deciphered
Within this palm of yours, to 'quite that evil,[176]
Fair signs of better fortune to ensue.
Cheer up your heart; you shortly shall be free   120
From all your troubles. See you this character
Directly fixed to the line of life?[177]
It signifies a dissolution,
You must be, Mistress Anne, a widow shortly.
ANNE No! God forbid, I hope you do but jest.   [*pulls her hand*   125
away]
DRURIE It is most certain: you must bury George.
ANNE Have you such knowledge then in palmistry?
DRURIE More than in surgery. Though I do make
That my profession, this is my best living,

130 And where I cure one sickness or disease,
I tell a hundred fortunes in a year.
What makes my house so haunted as it is
With merchants' wives, bachelors, and young maids,
But for my matchless skill in palmistry?[178]

135 Lend me your hand again, I'll tell you more.   [picks up Anne's
hand again]
A widow, said I? Yea, and make a change,
Not for the worse, but for the better far:
A gentleman (my girl) must be the next,
A gallant fellow, one that is beloved

140 Of great estates. 'Tis plainly figured here,
And this is called the Ladder of Promotion.   [points to Anne's
palm]

ANNE I do not wish to be promoted so.   [shakes her hand free]
My George is gentle and beloved beside,
And I have even as good a husband of him

145 As any wench in London hath beside.

DRURIE True, he is good, but not too good for God.[179]
He's kind, but his love dispense with death;
He's wealthy, and an handsome man beside,
But will his grave be satisfied with that?

150 He keeps you well; who says the contrary?
Yet better's better. Now you are arrayed
After a civil manner, but the next
Shall keep you in your hood[180] and gown of silk,
And when you stir abroad, ride in your coach,

155 And have your dozen men all in a livery
To wait upon you! This is somewhat like!

ANNE Yet had I rather be as now I am,
If God were pleased that it should be so.

DRURIE Aye, marry, now you speak like a good Christian,[181]

160 "If God were pleased." Aye, but he hath decreed
It shall be otherwise, and to repine[182]
Against his Providence, you know, 'tis sin.

ANNE Your words do make me think I know not what
   And burden me with fear as well as doubt.
DRURIE Tut, I could tell ye for a need his name[183]   165
   That is ordained to be your next husband,
   But for a testimony of my former speeches.
   Let it suffice I find it in your hand   [*Drurie picks up Anne
      Sanders's hand again.*]
   That you already are acquainted with him.
   And let me see, this crooked line derived   170
   From your ring finger shows me, not long since[184]
   You had some speech with him in the street,
   Or near about your door, I am sure it was.
ANNE I know of no more than that gentleman
   That supped with us. They call him Captain Browne,   175
   And he—I must confess, against my will—
   Came to my house as I was sitting there,
   And used some idle chat might a' been spared.
   And more iwis[185] than I had pleasure in.
DRURIE I cannot tell. If Captain Browne it were,   180
   Then Captain Browne is he must marry you.
   His name is George, I take it. Yea, 'tis so.   [*as if deciphering this
      "information" in Anne's palm*]
   My rules of palmistry declare no less.
ANNE 'Tis very strange how ye should know so much.
DRURIE Nay, I can make rehearsal of the words,[186]   185
   Did pass betwixt you if I were disposed,
   Yet I protest I never saw the man
   Since nor before the night he supped with us.
   Briefly, it is your fortune, Mistress Sanders,
   And there's no remedy but you must have him.   190
   I counsel you to no immodesty.
   'Tis lawful, one deceased, to take another.
   In the mean space[187] I would not have you coy,
   But if he come unto your house, or so,
   To use him courteously, as one for whom   195

You were created in your birth a wife.

ANNE If it be so, I must submit myself

To that which God and destiny sets down.

But yet I can assure you, Mistress Drurie,

200   I do not find me any way inclined

To change or new affection, nor—God willing—

Will I be false to Sanders whilst I live.

By this time he's returned from th'Exchange,

Come, you shall sup with us.   *Exit*

205 DRURIE I'll follow you.

Why, this is well. I never could have found[188]   [*alone*]

A fitter way to compass Browne's desire,

Nor in her woman's breast kindled love's fire.

For this will hammer so within her head,

210   As for the new, she'll wish the old were dead,

When in the nick of this I will devise[189]

Some stratagem to close up Sanders's eyes.

[Dumb show 1]

The "bloody banquet" seems to replace whatever Mistress Sanders had in mind when she invited Nan Drurie to dine: "Come, you shall sup with us" (sc. 4). Though Anne Sanders expects her husband to arrive home to eat with them, he fails to appear, and instead of servants carrying dishes and candles as one might expect in a domestic-themed play, the stage directions dictate: "Enter Tragedy with a bowl of blood in her hand," followed by Furies who "cover" or set the table. There is "some strange solemn music like bells" and a kind of dance, with Lust and Chastity escorting human characters and participating in the action of the scene; the humans and Furies and Lust toast each other and embrace in various combinations before Tragedy puts them to sleep. Tragedy observes these symbolic movements, and, as in the prologue, "turn[s] to the people" to offer her interpretation of the scene. This, like the other dumb shows, is highly symbolic, ritualistic action.

Enter Tragedy with a bowl of blood in her hand.[190]

TRAGEDY Till now you have but sitten[191] to behold
 The fatal entrance to our bloody scene,
5 And by gradations seen how we have grown
 Into the main stream of our tragedy.
 All we have done hath only been in words,
 But now we come unto the dismal act,
 And in these sable curtains shut we up
10 The comic entrance to our direful play.[192]
 This deadly banquet is prepared at hand,
 Where ebon tapers[193] are brought up from hell
 To leave black murder to this damned deed.
 The ugly screech owl and the night raven,
15 With flaggy wings and hideous croaking noise,
 Do beat the casements[194] of this fatal house,
 Whilst I do bring my dreadful Furies forth

They [the Furies] come to cover [that is, set the table].

20

 To spread the table to this bloody feast,

The while they cover [the table].

25 Come forth and cover, for the time draws on.
 Dispatch, I say, for now I must employ ye
 To be the ushers to this damnéd train.[195]
 Bring forth the banquet and that lustful wine,
 Which in pale mazors[196] made of dead men's skulls,
30 They shall carouse to their destruction.
 By this they're entered to this fatal door.
 Hark now the ghastly fearful chimes of night
 Do ring them in, and with a doleful peal.

35 *Here some strange solemn music like bells is heard within.*[197]

Do fill the roof with sounds of tragedy.
Dispatch, I say, and be their ushers in.

[This is the direction for the silent performance that Tragedy subsequently narrates.]

40

The Furies go to the door and meet them:[198] first the Furies enter before leading them, dancing a soft dance to the solemn music. Next comes Lust [walking] before Browne, leading Mistress Sanders covered with a black veil. Chastity all in white pull[s] her back softly by the arm. Then Drurie thrust[s] away Chastity, Roger following. They march about and then sit to the table. The Furies fill [the skulls with] wine; Lust drinks to Browne, he to Mistress Sanders; she pledges him.[199] Lust embraces her; she [Anne] thrusts Chastity from her.[200] Chastity wrings her hands and departs. Drurie and Roger embrace one another; the Furies leap and embrace one another. [They sit down.] Whilst they sit down, Tragedy speaks.

TRAGEDY Here is the masque[201] unto this damned murder:
The Furies first; the devil leads the dance.
Next lawless Lust conducteth cruel Browne;   45
He doth seduce this poor deluded soul,
Attended by unspotted Innocence,[202]
As yet unguilty of her husband's death.
Next follows on that instrument of hell—
That wicked Drurie, the accursed fiend—   50
That thrusts her forward to destruction.
And last of all is Roger, Drurie's man,
A villain expert in all treachery,
One conversant in all her damnéd drifts[203]
And a base broker in this murderous act.   55
Here they prepare them to these lustful feasts,
And here they sit—all wicked Murder's guests.[204]

Tragedy standing to behold them awhile, till the show be done, again turning to the people.

A Warning for Fair Women 37

60   Thus sin prevails: she[205] drinks that poisoned draught,
       With which base thoughts henceforth infects her soul,
       And wins her free consent to this foul deed.[206]
       Now blood and Lust doth conquer and subdue,
       And Chastity is quite abandonéd.
65   Here enters murder into all their hearts,
       And doth possess them with the hellish thirst
       Of guiltless blood. Now will I wake my chime   [*hits a chime*]
       And lay this charming rod upon their eyes,[207]
       To make them sleep in their security.
70

       They sleep.

       Thus sits this poor soul, innocent of late,[208]   [*points to Anne*]
       Amongst these devils at this damnéd feast,
75   Won and betrayed to their detested sin,
       And thus with blood their hands shall be imbrued.

       Tragedy[209] sets down her blood and rubs their hands [with blood].

80   *To Browne*

       Thy hands shall both be touched for they alone
       Are the foul actors of this impious deed!

       To Drurie and Roger

85   And thine and thine, for thou didst lay the plot,
       And thou didst work this damnéd witch devise,
       Your hands are both as deep in blood as his.

       To Anne

90   Only thou dips a finger in the same,
       And here it is. Awake now when you will,
       For now is the time wherein to work your ill.

Here Browne starts up, draws his sword, and runs out.

TRAGEDY Thus he is gone whilst they are all secure,
　　Resolved to put these desperate thoughts to ure,[210]
　　They follow him, and them will I attend,
　　Until I bring them all unto their end.

Scene 5. Lombard Street, London

This scene snaps back to "reality" after the dumb show: George Sanders, finishing a business meeting/meal, says goodbye to his host, likely another merchant, while Browne and Roger wait for their victim to pass. The merchants' parting dialogue is much concerned with time: Sanders says he is "daily" a visitor; speakers note that it is getting dark (the host sends a torchbearer); and it looks as though Sanders will be coming home late again. Browne is poised to stab him, but along comes yet another gentleman/merchant who recognizes George Sanders and offers to walk along with him. Browne reacts like a cartoon villain in another soliloquy, where he is so angry that, he says, he could stab Night or himself.

Enter Sanders, and one or two with him [in the doorway of a town house].

SANDERS You see, sir, still I am a daily guest.   [*to the merchant/host*]
  But with so true friends as I hold yourself,
5   I had rather be too rude than too precise.[211]
GENTLEMAN 1 Sir, this house is yours; you come but to your own,
  And what else I call mine, is wholly yours.
  So much I to endear your love, sweet Master Sanders.
  A light. Ho, there.
10 SANDERS Well, sir, at this time I'll rather be unmannerly than
    ceremonious.
  I'll leave you, sir, to recommend my thanks
  Unto your kind respective wife.
GENTLEMAN 1 Sir, for your kind patience, she's much beholding to you
  And I beseech you remember me to Mistress Sanders.
15 SANDERS Sir, I thank you for her.
GENTLEMAN 1 Sirrah, ho, who's within there?   [*turning to call into
    the house*]
PRENTICE Sir.
GENTLEMAN 1 Light a torch there and wait on Master Sanders home.
SANDERS It shall not need sir; it is light enough.
20   Let it alone.
GENTLEMAN 1 Nay, I pray ye sir.
SANDERS I'faith, sir, at this time it shall not need.
  'Tis very light, the streets are full of people,
  And I have some occasion by the way that may detain me.[212]
25 GENTLEMAN 1 Sir, I am sorry that you go alone; 'tis somewhat late.
SANDERS 'Tis well, sir, God send you happy rest.
GENTLEMAN 1 God bless you sir; passion of me! I had forgot one
    thing,[213]
  I am glad I thought of it before we parted.
  Your patience for a little.   [*The merchant walks back into his house
    and returns again.*]

Here enters Browne speaking, casting one side of his cloak under his 30
arm [hiding his dagger]. While Master Sanders and [the gentleman]
are in busy talk one to the other, Browne steps to a corner.

BROWNE This way he should come, and a fitter place   *Aside*
　　The town affords not; 'tis his nearest way,
　　And 'tis so late, he will not go about.[214]
　　Then stand close, George, and with a lucky arm   35
　　Sluice out his life, the hinderer of thy love.[215]
　　O, sable Night, sit on the eye of heaven
　　That it discern not this black deed of darkness.
　　My guilty soul, burnt with lust's hateful fire,
　　Must wade through blood t'obtain my vile desire.   40
　　Be then my coverture, thick ugly night.[216]
　　The light hates me, and I do hate the light.
SANDERS Good night, sir.
GENTLEMAN 1 Good night, good Master Sanders.
　　Sir, I shall see you on the Exchange tomorrow.   45
SANDERS You shall, God willing. Sir, good night.
BROWNE I hear him coming fair unto my stand.[217]
　　Murder and Death, sit on my fatal hand.

Enters [at one door] a Gentleman with a [servant who carries] a   50
torch, [just as] Browne draws to strike.

GENTLEMAN 2 Who's there?
SANDERS A friend.
GENTLEMAN 2 Master Sanders? Well met.[218]
SANDERS Good even, gentle sir, so are you.   55
GENTLEMAN 2 Where have you been so late, sir?
BROWNE A plague upon't! A light and company,   *Browne aside.*
　　Even as I was about to do the deed!
　　See how the devil stumbles in the nick.
SANDERS Sir, here at a friend of mine in Lombard Street[219]   60

At supper, where I promise you
Our cheer and entertainment was so great
That we have past our hour.[220]
Believe me, sir, the evening's stolen away.
65 I see 'tis later than I took it for.
GENTLEMAN 2 Sirrah, turn there at the corner since 'tis late.   [*to his*
                servant]
I will go home with Master Sanders.
SANDERS No, I pray you, sir, trouble not yourself.
Sir, I beseech you.
70 GENTLEMAN 2 Sir, pardon me. Sirrah, go on now where we are.
My way lies just with yours.   [*to Sanders*]
SANDERS I am beholding to you.[221]   *Exeunt*

Browne commeth out alone.[222]
75

BROWNE Except by miracle, thou art delivered as was never man!
My sword unsheathed and with the piercing steel
Ready to broach his bosom, and my purpose
Thwarted by some malignant envious star![223]
80 Night, I could stab thee; I could stab myself!
I am so mad that he 'scaped my hands.
How like a fatal comet did that light,
With this portentous[224] vision fright mine eyes!
A masque[225] of devils walk alone with thee.
85 And thou, the torchbearer unto them all,
Thou fatal brand, ne'r mayest thou be extinct,[226]
Till thou hast set that damned house on fire,
Where he is lodged that brought thee to this place.
Sanders, this hand doth hold that death alone
90 And bears the seal of thy destruction!
Some other time shall serve till thou be dead.
My fortunes yet are ne'r accomplishéd.   *Exit*

Scene 6. Barnes's house, Woolwich

This scene in some ways reprises the opening of scene 4 when Sanders orders his man to do a difficult task for him (that is, to talk to his wife about money)—in this case, John Beane wants to stay home, but his master sends him on errands to Greenwich Palace and then to London, expecting Beane to return home again that night (a fourteen-mile journey round trip). This conversation concerns different places and times, including whether to travel along the Thames or overland, and the fact that it is Easter week (the day is Maundy Thursday, preceding Good Friday). Once Beane does set out, he trips and Barnes impatiently insults him. Along a path ("woody way") out of town, Beane meets his friends, Old John and John's helper, Joan, as they go about their tasks. Significantly, all three of them admit to having had disturbing dreams the night before. Beane and the pair of rustics eventually separate.

Enter Master Barnes and John Beane, his man.

BEANE Must I go first to Greenwich, sir?

BARNES What else?

5 BEANE I cannot go by water, for it ebbs.

The wind's at west, and both are strong against us.

BARNES My meaning is that you shall go by land,

And come by water, though the tide be late.[227]

Fail not to be at home again this night

10 With answer to those letters which ye have.

This letter give to Master Cofferer;[228]

If he be not at court when ye come there,

Leav't at his chamber in any case.

Pray Master Sanders to be here next week

15 About the matter at Saint Mary Cray.[229]

BEANE Me thinks, sir, under your correction,

Next week is ill appointed.

BARNES Why, I pray ye?

BEANE 'Tis Easter week, and every holiday[230]

20 Are sermons at the Spittle.

BARNES What of that?

BEANE Can Master Sanders then be spared to come?

BARNES Well said, John fool. I hope at afternoon

A pair of oars may bring him down to Woolwich.[231]

25 Tell him he must come down in any case.

BEANE What shall I bring from London?

BARNES A fool's head.[232]

BEANE A calf's head's better meat.

'Tis Maundy Thursday,[233] sir, and every butcher

30 Now keeps open shop.

BARNES Well, get ye gone, and hie ye home. How now?

Beane stumbles twice.

35 What art thou drunk? Canst thou not stand?

BEANE Yes sir, I did but stumble. God send me good luck.
I was not wont to stumble on plain ground.[234]
BARNES Look better to your feet then.   *Exit Barnes.*
BEANE Yea, forsooth, and yet I do not like it at my setting forth.
They say it does betoken some mischance.[235]   40
I fear not drowning if the boat be good.
There is no danger in so short a cut.
Betwixt Blackwall and Woolwich is the worst,
And if the watermen will watch the anchors,
I'll watch the catches and the hoyes myself.[236]   45
Well, I must go. Christ's cross, God be my speed.

Enter Old John and Joan, his maid. [They walk along together.]

Who comes there a God's name? This woody way   50
Doth harbor many a false knave, they say.
OLD JOHN False knaves, ha? Where be they? Let me
see them. Mass, as old as I am, and have little skill, I'll
hamper a false knave yet in my hedging bill![237] Stand,
thief or true man?   55
JOAN Master, it is John Beane.
JOHN Jesu! John Beane, why whither away by land?
What make you wand'ring this woody way?
Walk ye to Greenwich, or walk ye to Cray?
BEANE To Greenwich, father John. Good morrow, good morrow. 60
Good morrow, Joan; good morrow, sweet, to thee.
JOAN A thousand good morrows, gentle John Beane.[238]
I am glad I met ye for now I have my dream. I have been
so troubled with ye all this night, that I could not rest
for sleeping and dreaming: me thought you were grown   65
taller and fairer and that ye were in your shirt, and
me thought it should not be you and yet it was you. And
that ye were all in white, and went into a garden, and there
was the umberst[239] sort of flowers that ever I see, and me
thought you lay down upon a green bank, and I pinned   70

gilliflowers in your ruff.[240] And then me thought your nose
bled, and as I ran to my chest to fetch ye a handkercher,
me thought I stumbled and so waked. What does it betoken?[241]

BEANE Nay, I cannot tell, but I like neither thy

75   dream nor my own, for I was troubled with green meadows[242]
and bulls fighting and goring one another, and one of them,
methought, ran at me, and I ran away, that I sweat in my
sleep for fear.

OLD JOHN Tut, fear nothing, John Beane. Dreams are

80   but fancies. I dreamed myself last night that I heard
the bells of Barking[243] as plain to our own of Woolwich,
as if I had lain in the steeple. And that I should be
married, and to whom trowest[244] thou? But the fine gentle-
woman of London that was at your master's the last summer.[245]

85 BEANE Who? Mistress Sanders? I shall see her anon,
for I have an errand to her husband. Shall I tell her
ye dreamed of her?

OLD JOHN God forbid! No, she'll laugh at me, and
call me old fool. Art thou going to London?

90 BEANE Yea, when I have been at the Court at Greenwich.
Whither go you and your maid Joan?

OLD JOHN To stop a gap in my fence and to drive home
a cow and a calf that is in my close at Shooter's Hill
foot.[246]

95 BEANE 'Tis well done. Mass, I am merry since I met you
two. I would your journey lay along with mine.

JOAN So would I with all my heart. John, pray ye
bestow a groat for five pence of carnation ribbon[247] to
tie my smock sleeves; they flap about my hands too

100   bad, and I'll give you your money again.

BEANE That I will i'faith. Will you have nothing, father John?

OLD JOHN No God-amercy, son John, but I would
thou hadst my *aqua vita* bottle to fill at the Black Bull by
Battle Bridge.[248]

105 BEANE So would I. Well, here our ways part; you

must that way, and I this.   [*begins to walk off*]

[*Joan pouts or frowns to see Beane leave, and Old John steps in.*]

OLD JOHN Why, John Beane, canst part with thy love   110
   without a kiss?
BEANE Ye say true, father John; my business puts kissing
   out of my mind. Farewell, sweet Joan.   *Kiss[es] Joan.*
JOAN Farewell, sweet John; I pray ye have a care of
   yourself for my dream, and bless ye out of swaggerers'²⁴⁹   115
   company, and walk not too late. My master and I will
   pray for ye.
OLD JOHN That we will, i'faith, John Beane.
BEANE God be with ye both!
   I could e'n weep to   [*Aside*]   120
   see how kind they are unto me. There's a wench; well, if
   I live I'll make her amends.   *Exeunt [to separate doors].*

Scene 7. Drurie's house and a path along the Thames

The scene opens at Mistress Drurie's house, where she and Browne wait for Roger to return with information about where next to try to attack their victim. Browne recaps the initial failed murder attempt in the street, and Roger returns to report on George Sanders's business day: after an hour at a warehouse in "Cornhill" and another hour at the Exchange ("Burse"), he heads home at eleven for dinner, meeting along the way "a gentleman of the court," where he promises to come later. Roger overhears Sanders's plans for the rest of the day and continues to follow him from his house to Lion's (or Lyon's) Key, where he crosses the Thames to Greenwich. Roger learns that Sanders plans to return to London "by six," suggesting that as a good time and place to attack. After the trio confirm their contingency plan, the scene shifts to Anne Sanders and Beane walking along in hopes of meeting her husband, for whom Beane has the message from his master; Browne and Roger, who are hiding, then realize that they can't follow through with the murder since Anne is present. When Sanders lands and disembarks from the ferry, he briefly speaks with his wife and Beane, leaving Browne furious to have missed another chance, and Roger reassuring him that "the third time's a charm," as it were.

Enter Browne and Drurie.

BROWNE Nay, speak your conscience. Was't not strange fortune
    That at the instant when my sword was drawn,
5   And I had thought to have nailed him to a post,
    A light should come and so prevent my purpose?
DRURIE It was so, Master Browne. But let it pass;[250]
    Another time shall serve, never give o'er
    Till you have quite removed him out your way.
10 BROWNE And if I do, let me be held[251] a coward
    And no more worthy to obtain her bed,
    Than a foul Negro to embrace a Queen.[252]
DRURIE You need not quail for a doubt of your reward.[253]
    You know already she is won to this,
15   What, by my persuasion, and your own suit,
    That you may have her company when you will,
    And she herself is thoroughly resolved:
    None but George Browne must be her second husband.
BROWNE The hope of that makes me a' nights to dream
20   Of nothing but the death of wretched Sanders,
    Which I have vowed in secret to my soul
    Shall not be long before that be determin'd.
    But I do marvel that our scout returns not—
    Trusty Roger, whom we sent to dog him.[254]
25 DRURIE The knave's so careful (Master Browne) of you,
    As he will rather die than come again
    Before he find fit place to do the deed.
BROWNE I am beholding both to you and him,
    And, Mistress Drurie, I'll requite your loves.
30

Enter Roger.

DRURIE By the mass, see where the whoreson[255] comes,
    Puffing and blowing, almost out of breath.
35 BROWNE Roger, how now, where hast thou been all day?

ROGER Where have I been? Where I have had a jaunt,
    Able to tire a horse.
BROWNE But dost thou bring
    Any good news where I may strike the stroke,
    Shall make thyself and me amends[256] for all?   40
ROGER That gather by the circumstance: first know[257]
    That in the morning, till 'twas nine o'clock,
    I watched at Sanders's door till he came forth,
    Then followed him to Cornhill, where he stayed
    An hour talking in a merchant's warehouse.[258]   45
    From thence he went directly to the Burse,
    And there he walked another hour at least,
    And I at 's heels. By this, it struck eleven;
    Home then he comes to dinner.[259] By the way
    He chanced to meet a gentleman of the court,[260]   50
    With whom, as he was talking, I drew near,
    And at his parting from him heard him say,
    That in the afternoon without all fail,
    He would be with him at the court. This done,
    I watched him at his door till he had dined,   55
    Followed him to Lion's Key, saw him take boat,
    And in a pair of oars, as soon as he
    Landed at Greenwich,[261] where, ever since,
    I traced him to and fro, with no less care
    Than I had done before, till at the last   60
    I heard him call unto a waterman,
    And bade he should be ready, for by six
    He meant to be at London back again.
    With that away came I to give you notice,
    That as he lands at Lion's Key this evening,[262]   65
    You might dispatch him, and escape unseen.
BROWNE Hodge, thou has won my heart by this day's work.
DRURIE Beshrew me,[263] but he hath taken mighty pains.
BROWNE Roger come hither, there's for thee to drink   [*hands Roger*
    a small purse or some coins]

70   And one day I will do thee greater good.

ROGER I thank you sir, Hodge is at your command.

BROWNE Now Mistress Drurie, if you please, go home.

     'Tis much upon the hour of his return.

ROGER Nay, I am sure he will be here straitway.

75 DRURIE Well, I will leave you, for 'tis somewhat late.

     God speed your hand, and so, Master Browne, good night.

ROGER Mistress, I pray you spare me for this once.

     I'll be so bold[264] as stay with Master Browne.

DRURIE Do. And, Master Browne, if you prevail,

80   Come to my house; I'll have a bed for you.[265]   *Exit*

BROWNE You shall have knowledge if I chance to speed,

     But I'll not lodge in London for a while,

     Until the rumor shall be somewhat past.

     Come Roger, where is't best to take our standing?[266]   [*looking*

       around]

85 ROGER Marry, at this corner, in my mind.[267]

BROWNE I like it well; 'tis dark and somewhat close,[268]

     By reason that the houses stand so near.

     Beside, if he should land at Billingsgate,[269]

     Yet are we still betwixt his house and him.

90 ROGER You say well Master Browne; 'tis so indeed.

BROWNE Peace then, no more words for being spied.[270]

Enter Anne Sanders and John Beane [outside Anne's house].

95 ANNE I marvel, John, thou saw's him not at court.

     He hath been there ever since one o'clock.

BEANE Indeed, Mistress Sanders, I heard not of him.

ANNE Pray God that Captain Browne hath not been moved   *Aside*

     By some ill motion to endanger him.

100   I greatly fear it; he's so long away.

     But tell me, John, must thou needs home tonight?

BEANE Yes, of necessity, for so my master bade.

ANNE If it be possible, I pray thee stay

Until my husband come.

BEANE I dare not; trust me, 105
And I doubt[271] that I have lost my tide already.

ANNE Nay, that's not so; come I'll bring thee to the key.[272]
[*They begin to walk.*]
I hope we shall meet my husband by the way.

ROGER That should be Mistress Sanders, by her tongue.[273]

BROWNE It is my love. O, how the dusky night 110
Is by her coming forth made sheen and bright!
I'll know of her why she's abroad so late.

[*He starts to step out from the hiding place toward Anne, but Roger grabs his arm.*]

115

ROGER Take heed, Master Browne. See where Sanders comes.
[*whispers*]

BROWNE A plague upon't! Now am I prevented.
She being by, how can I murder him?   *Enter Sanders [and a Waterman].*

SANDERS Your fare's but eighteen pence; here's half a crown.[274]

WATERMAN I thank your worship. God give ye good night. 120

SANDERS Good night with all my heart.

ANNE O, here he is now!
Husband, y'are welcome home. Now, Jesu, man,
That you will be so late upon the water?

SANDERS My business, sweetheart, was such I could not choose.[275] 125

ANNE Here's Master Barnes's man hath stayed all day to speak
with you.

SANDERS John Beane, welcome, how is't?
How doth thy master and all our friends at Woolwich?

BEANE All in good health, sir, when I came thence.

SANDERS And what's the news, John Beane? 130

BEANE My master, sir, requests you, that upon Tuesday next you
would take the pains to come down to Woolwich about the
matter you wot[276] of.

SANDERS Well, John, tomorrow thou shalt know my mind.

BEANE Nay, sir, I must to Woolwich by this tide.

SANDERS What tonight? There is no such haste, I hope.

135 BEANE Yes, truly (with your pardon) it must be so.

SANDERS Well then, if, John, you will be gone, commend me to your
    master, and tell him, without fail on Tuesday some time of
    the day I'll see him, and so good night.

ANNE Commend me likewise to thy master, John.

BEANE I thank you, Mistress Sanders, for my cheer.[277]
    Your commendations shall be delivered.   [*Exit Sanders, Anne,*
    and Beane.]

140 BROWNE I would thyself and he were both sent hence[278]   [*Either*
    an aside or to Roger]
    To do a message to the devil of hell,
    For interrupting this my solemn vow!
    But—questionless—some power or else prayer
    Of some religious friend or other guards him,

145   Or else my sword's unfortunate. 'Tis so:
    This metal was not made to kill a man.

ROGER Good Master Browne, fret not yourself so much.
    Have you forgot what the old proverb is—
    "The third time pays for all"?[279] Did you not hear

150   That he sent word to Master Barnes of Woolwich,
    He would be with him as on Tuesday next?
    Twixt that and then lie you in wait for him
    And though he may have escaped your hand so oft,
    You may be sure to pay him home at last.[280]

155 BROWNE Fury had almost made me past myself.[281]
    'Tis well remembered, Hodge. It so shall be.
    Some place will I pick out as he does pass,
    Either in going or in coming back,
    To end his hateful life. Come, let's away,

160   And at thy mistress's house we'll spend this night
    In consultation how it may be wrought.   *Exeunt*

[Dumb show 2]

To introduce the second dumb show, Tragedy instructs the viewer to imagine or "suppose" offstage action ("Suppose [Sanders] now on the water for Woolwich"), and then she, as earlier, signals a new direction for the play: "and now the dreadful hour of death is come." The long stage directions, as earlier, read like choreography, and again music plays. But instead of a meal, there "suddenly riseth up a great tree" that, as Tragedy explains, "represents" Sanders. Anne Sanders is encouraged to chop it down, but she refuses, whereupon Lust gives Browne the axe to "cut down" the tree/rival that is in his way. Additionally, Chastity comes on the scene with "disheveled hair" (often shorthand for a sexual assault having taken place), leads Anne Sanders to view a portrait of her husband, and points to the tree. The remaining stage directions are clear and need no summary. Both dumb show 1 and 2 end with Browne exiting with his sword drawn.[282]

[*Enter Tragedy, speaking to audience.*]

TRAGEDY Twice (as you see) this sad distresséd man,
    The only mark whereat foul Murder shot
5   Just in the loose of envious eager death,
    By accidents strange and miraculous
    Escaped the arrow aimed at his heart.
    Suppose him on the water now for Woolwich,
    For secret[283] business with his bosom friend.
10   From thence, as fatal destiny conducts him
    To Mary Cray by some occasion called,
    Which by false Drurie's means made known to Browne.
    Lust, gain, and murder spurred this villain on,
    Still to pursue this unsuspecting soul.
15   And now the dreadful hour of death is come—
    The dismal morning when the Destinies,
    Do shear the laboring vital thread of life,[284]
    Whenas the lamb left in the woods of Kent,
    Unto this ravenous wolf becomes a prey.
20   Now of his death the general intent,
    Thus Tragedy doth to your eyes present.

[The following is the stage direction for the dumb show; Tragedy narrates and explicates this action in her speech that follows these lines.]

25   *The Music playing, enters Lust bringing forth Browne and Roger,*
    at one end. Mistress Sanders and Mistress Drurie at the other, they
    offering cheerfully to meet and embrace. Suddenly riseth up a great
    tree between them, whereat amazedly they step back, whereupon Lust
    bringeth an axe to Mistress Sanders, showing signs that she should cut
    it down, which she refuseth, albeit Mistress Drurie offers to help her.
    Then Lust brings the axe to Browne, and shows the like signs to him as
    before, whereupon he roughly and suddenly hews down the tree, and
    then they [Browne and Anne] run together and embrace. With that
    enters Chastity, with her hair disheveled, and taking Mistress Sanders

by the hand, brings her to her husband's picture hanging on the wall,
and pointing to the tree, seems to tell her that this is the tree so rashly
cut down. Whereupon she,[285] *wringing her hands, in tears departs.*
Browne, Drurie, Roger, and Lust, whispering, he [Browne] draws his
sword, and Roger follows him. Tragedy expressing that now he goes to
act the deed.

TRAGEDY Lust leads together this adulterous rout,
    But, as you see are hindered thus, before
    They could attain unto their foul desires.
    The tree springs up, whose body, whilst it stands,   30
    Still keeps them back when they would fain[286] embrace,
    Whereat they start, for fury evermore
    Is full replete with fear and envy.
    Lust giveth her the axe to cut it down,
    To rid her husband whom it represents,   35
    In which this damned woman would assist her.
    But though by them seducéd to consent,
    And had a finger in her husband's blood,[287]
    Could not be won to murder him herself.
    Lust brings the axe to Browne, who suddenly   40
    Doth give a fatal stroke unto the tree,
    Which being done, they then embrace together.   *[Browne and*
        Anne embrace.]
    The act performed, now Chastity appears
    And pointing to the picture and the tree,
    Unto her guilty conscience, shows her husband,   45
    Even so cut off by that vile murderer Browne.
    She wrings her hands repenting of the fact,
    Touched with remorse, but now it is too late.
    What's here expressed, in act is to be done:
    The sword is drawn; the murderer forth doth run;   50
    Lust leads him on; he follows him with speed.
    The only actor in this damned deed.[288]   *Exit*

Scene 8. A road near Shooter's Hill

This is the murder scene. Browne and Roger for the third time discuss where they should station themselves (as they did in the street in scene 5 and along the Thames in scene 7). Roger again reports on what he has seen and overheard, namely that John Beane is accompanying Sanders to London. Browne speaks two soliloquies that would suit later Shakespearean tragic heroes—someone like moody Hamlet—when Browne says that his "thoughts are studious and unsociable" before he kills Sanders, or Macbeth, when, after committing murder, he hears noises and fears judgment. Browne stabs Sanders and Beane, catches up with Roger, and the two flee the scene in different directions—Browne to Greenwich and on to Rochester and Roger back to London. Beane survives the attack and "creeps" along as Old John and Joan pass by. The dialogue between the pastoral characters is in prose, and Old John says that strange things are happening; the animals might be bewitched, and Joan notes it is a "dismal" day. They discover their dying friend, pick him up, and carry him home.

Enter Browne reading a letter, and Roger.

BROWNE Did I but waver, or were unresolved,
    These lines were able to encourage me.   [*pointing to the paper,*
       and speaking to it]
5   Sweet Nan, I kill in thy name, and for thy sake.
    What coward would not venture more than this?
    Kill him? Yea, were his life ten thousand lives,
    Not any spark or cinder of the same
    Should be unquenched in blood at thy request.
10   Roger, thou art assured he'll come this way?   [*snaps out of his*
       reverie to see Roger]
ROGER Assured, sir? Why I heard him say so.
    For having lodged at Woolwich all last night,
    As soon as day appeared, I got me up,
    And watched aloof at Master Barnes's door,
15   Till he and Master Sanders both came forth.
BROWNE Till both came forth? What, are they both together?[289]
ROGER No sir, Master Barnes himself went back again,
    And left his man to bear him company:
    John Beane. You know him; he was at London
20   When we last wait for him at Billingsgate.
BROWNE Is it that stripling?[290] Well, no more ado.
    Roger, go thou unto the hedge corner
    At the hill's foot. There stand and cast thine eye
    Toward Greenwich Park, see if Blackheath be clear,[291]
25   Lest by some passenger we be descried.
ROGER Shall ye not need my help, sir? They are twain.[292]
BROWNE No, were they ten, mine arm is strong enough,
    Even of itself to buckle[293] with them all,
    And e'r George Sanders shall escape me now,
30   I will not reck what massacre I make.[294]
ROGER Well, sir, I'll go and watch, and when I see
    Anybody coming, I'll whistle to you.   [*Exit Roger; stands on one*
       side of the stage.]

BROWNE Do so, I pray thee. I would be alone;
My thoughts are studious and unsociable,
And so's my body, till this deed be done.   35
But let me see; what time a day is't now?
It cannot be imagined by the sun,
For, why, I have not seen it shine today.
Yet as I gather by my coming forth,
Being then six, it cannot now be less   40
Than half an hour past seven. The air is gloomy.[295]
No matter—darkness best fits my intent.
Here will I walk, and after shroud myself
Within those bushes when I see them come.

                                                              45

Enter Master Sanders and John Beane.

SANDERS John Beane, this is the right way, is it not?
BEANE Aye, sir, would to God we were past this wood.
SANDERS Why art thou afraid? See yonder's company.[296]   [*pointing* 50
        to Browne across the stage]
BROWNE They have espied me, I will slip aside.
BEANE O God sir, I am heavy at the heart.
        Good Master Sanders, let's return back to Woolwich.
        Methinks I go this way against my will.   55
SANDERS Why so, I pray thee?
BEANE Truly, I do not like
        The man we saw; he slipped so soon away, behind the bushes.
SANDERS Trust me, John, nor I.
        But yet, God willing, we will keep our way.[297]   60
BEANE I pray you, sir, let us go back again.
        I do remember now a dream was told me.
        That might I have the world, I cannot choose
        But tremble every joint to think upon't.
SANDERS But we are men; let's not be so faint hearted,   65
        As to affright ourselves with visions.[298]
        Come on, in God's name.

Browne steps out and strikes up John's heels [that is, trips him].

70   BEANE O, we are undone.[299]

      SANDERS What seek you, sir?

      BROWNE Thy blood, which I will have.

      SANDERS O, take my money, and preserve my life.

      BROWNE It is not millions that can ransom thee,

75   Nor this base drudge,[300] for both of you must die.   *[Browne stabs*
        Beane.]

      SANDERS Hear me a word. You are a gentleman:

      Soil not your hands with blood of innocents.

      BROWNE Thou speakest in vain.   *[He stabs Sanders.]*

      SANDERS Then God forgive my sin.[301]

80   Have mercy on me, and upon thee too,

      The bloody author of my timeless death.[302]

      BROWNE Now will I dip my handkercher in his blood,

      And send it as a token to my love.[303]

      Look how many wounds my hand hath given him;   *[uses dagger*
        to stab at the cloth]

85   So many holes I'll make within this cloth.

      SANDERS Jesu, receive my soul into thy hands.   *[He dies.]*

      BROWNE What sound was that? It was not he that spoke.

      The breath is vanished from his nostrils.

      Was it the other? No, his wounds are such

90   As he is likewise past the use of speech.

      Who was it then that thundered in mine ears

      The name of Jesu? Doubtless, 'twas my conscience,

      And I am damned for this unhallowed deed.[304]

      O sin, how hast thou blinded me till now,

95   Promising me security and rest,

      But givest me dreadful agony of soul![305]

      What shall I do? Or whither shall I fly?

      The very bushes will discover me.

      See how their wounds do gape unto the skies,

100   Calling for vengeance.

Enter Roger.

ROGER How now, Master Browne?
　What have you done? Why so, let's away,　[*sees the bodies*]
　For I have spied some riding o'r the heath,　　　　　　　105
　Some half a dozen in a company.
BROWNE Away to London, thou; I'll to the court,
　And show myself, and, after, follow thee.
　Give this to Mistress Sanders. Bid her read
　Upon this bloody handkercher the thing　　　　　　　110
　As I did promise and have now performed.
　But were it, Roger, to be done again,
　I would not do it for a kingdom's gain.[306]
ROGER Tut! faint not now; come let us haste away.
BROWNE Oh I must fear, whatever thou dost say.　　　　115
　My shadow, if naught else, will me betray.[307]　*Exeunt [Roger and*
　　Browne through separate doors]

Beane left wounded, and for dead, stirs and creeps.[308]

BEANE Dare I look up, for fear he yet be near　　　　　120
　That thus hath martyred me? Yea, the coast is clear.[309]
　　[*He struggles to lift his head and looks around.*]
　For all these deadly wounds, yet lives my heart.
　Alack,[310] how loathe[311] poor life is from my limbs to part!
　I cannot go, ah no, I cannot stand.
　O God, that some good body were near hand[312]　　　125
　To help me home to Woolwich e'r I die.
　To creep that wayward, whilst I live, I'll try.
　O, could I crawl but from this cursèd wood
　Before I drown myself in my own blood.

　　　　　　　　　　　　　　　　　130

Enter Old John and Joan.

OLD JOHN Now, by my father's saddlc, Joan, I think we

135 are bewitched: my beasts were never wont to break out
so often. Sure as death, the harlotries are bespoken.[313]
But it is that heifer with the white back that leads
them all a gadding.[314] A good luck take her.

JOAN Is it not a dismal day, master? Did ye look
in the almanac?[315] If it be not, then 'tis either 'long[316] of
140 the brended[317] cow, that was ne'r well in her wits since the
butcher bought her calf, or 'long of my dream, or of my
nose bleeding this morning, for as I was washing my hands[318]
my nose bled three drops, then I thought of John Beane—
God be with him—for I dreamed he was married, and that
145 our white calf was killed for his wedding dinner. God
bless them both, for I love them both well.

Beane creeps.

150 OLD JOHN Marie,[319] amen, for I tell thee my heart is
heavy. God send me good luck: my eyes dazzle and I
could weep. Lord, bless us! What sight is this? Look,
Joan, and cross thyself.[320]

JOAN O, master, master, look in my purse for a piece of ginger.[321]
155 I shall sweb; I shall swoon. Cut my lace,[322]
and cover my face, I die else! It is John Beane—killed,
cut, slain! Master, if ye be a man, help.

OLD JOHN John Beane? Now, Gods forbid![323] Alack, alack,
good John, how came ye in this piteous plight? Speak,   [*Beane moans.*]
160 good John. Nay, groan not; speak. Who has done this deed?
Thou hast not fordone thyself, hast thou?[324]

BEANE Ah, no, no.

JOAN Ah no, no, he need not have done that, for,
God knows, I loved him as dearly as he loved me. Speak,
165 John, who did it?

BEANE One in a white doublet and blue breeches. He
has slain another too, not far off. O, stop my
wounds if ye can.

OLD JOHN Joan, take my napkin[325] and thy apron, and
    bind up his wounds, and cows go where they will till we   170
    have carried him home.
JOAN Woe worth him, John, that did this dismal deed.   [*She bends*
    down to comfort Beane.]
    Heartbreak be his mirth, and hanging be his mead.[326]
OLD JOHN Ah well-a-day,[327] see where another lies. A handsome
    comely
    ancient gentleman. What an age live we in?   175
    When men have no mercy of men more than of dogs,
    bloodier than beasts. This is the deed of some swaggering,
    swearing, drunken desperate Dick.[328] Call we them
    cavaliers? Mass, they be cannibals, that have the
    stab readier in their hands than a penny in their   180
    purse! Shame's death be their share. Joan, hast thou
    done?[329] Come, lend me a hand to lay this good man in
    some bush, from birds and from beasts, till we carry
    home John Beane to his master's, and raise all Woolwich
    to fetch home this man and make search. Lift there.   185
JOAN So, so.   *They carry out Sanders.*
BEANE Lord, comfort my soul, my body is past cure.
OLD JOHN Now let's take up John Beane: Softly, Joan, softly.[330]
JOAN Ah John, little thought I to have carried thee
    thus within this week, but my hope is aslope,[331] and my   190
    joy is laid to sleep.   *Exeunt [Joan and Old John carrying Beane].*

Scene 9. Greenwich Palace, the Queen's "buttery" or kitchen

This scene begins the relatively rapid movement toward discovery, arraignment, trials, and executions of the conspiring parties. Browne, having told Roger that he planned to use this visit to Greenwich as his alibi, arrives for a quick drink, pretending to be in a hurry to get back up to London, but really, he heads east to Rochester, planning to hide out. The yeoman of the buttery was like a steward, who handled provisions for occupants and guests, and Master James seems to be another court functionary (he is later appointed to investigate the murder). The three men have a drink together and James notices blood on Browne's socks, about which Browne invents a hunting story.[332]

Enter a yeoman of the buttery,[333] Browne, and Master James.

YEOMAN Welcome, Master Browne, what is't you'll drink, ale or beer?[334]

BROWNE Marry, ale, and if you please.

5   You see, sir, I am bold to trouble you.

YEOMAN No trouble sir at all, the Queen, our Mistress,

    Allows this bounty to all comers—much more

    To gentlemen of your sort: some ale there, ho.[335]

10   *Enter [servant] with a jack and a court dish [a liquor bottle and some food].[336]*

YEOMAN Here, Master Browne, thus much to your health.   [*He pours a small amount for a toast.*]

BROWNE I thank you sir. Nay, prithee fill my cup.   [*pointing to his cup*]

    Here, Master James, to you with all my heart.

15   How say you now sir? Was I not a-dry?[337]

YEOMAN Believe me, yes. Will't please ye mend[338] your draught?

BROWNE No more, sir, in this heat, it is not good.

JAMES It seems, Master Browne, that you have gone apace.[339]

    Came you from London that you made such haste?

20   But soft, what have I spied? Your hose is bloody.

BROWNE How, bloody? Where? Good sooth, 'tis so indeed.

YEOMAN It seems it is but newly done.

BROWNE No more it is:

    And now I do remember how it came:

25   Myself, and some two or three Gentlemen more

    Crossing the field this morning here from Eltham[340]

    Chanced by the way to start a brace of hares,[341]

    One of the which we killed; the other 'scaped.

    And pulling forth the garbage, this befell.   [*pointing to his stockings*]

30   But 'tis no matter; it will out again.[342]

YEOMAN Yes there's no doubt, with a little soap and water.

JAMES I would I had been with you at that sport.

BROWNE I would you had sir, 'twas good sport indeed.
　　Now, afore God, this blood was ill espied!　*Aside*
　　But my excuse I hope will serve the turn.　　　　　　35
　　Gentlemen, I must to London this forenoon,[343]
　　About some earnest business doth concern me.
　　Thanks for my ale, and your good companies.
BOTH Adieu, good Master Browne.
BROWNE Farewell unto you both.　*Exit*　　　　　　40
JAMES An honest proper gentleman as lives.
　　God be with you, sir, I'll up into the Presence.[344]

YEOMAN Y'are welcome, James, God be with ye, sir.　*Exeunt*

Scene 10. Sanders's house

The Annes and Roger meet after the murder to make a plan, and Anne
Sanders is inconsolable; she tries to injure herself.

*Enter Anne Sanders, Anne Drurie, and Roger. Drurie having the
bloody handkercher in her hand.*

ANNE Oh, show me not that ensign[345] of despair,
    But hide it, burn it, bury it in the earth!
5   It is a calendar[346] of bloody letters,
    Containing his, and yours, and all our shames.
DRURIE Good Mistress Sanders, be not so outrageous.[347]
ANNE What tell you me? Is not my husband slain?
    Are not we guilty of his cruel death?
10   Oh, my dear husband, I will follow thee!
    Give me a knife, a sword, or anything,   [*thrashing about, perhaps
        opening cabinets and drawers*]
    Wherewith I may do justice on myself.
    Justice for murder; justice for the death
    Of my dear husband, my betrothéd love.
15 ROGER These exclamations will bewray us all,[348]
    Good Mistress Sanders, peace.
DRURIE I pray you, peace.
    Your servants, or some neighbors else will hear.[349]
ANNE Shall I fear more my servants or the world
20   Than God himself? He heard our treachery,
    And saw our complot[350] and conspiracy!
    Our heinous sin cries in the ears of him,
    Louder than we can cry upon the earth!
    A woman's sin, a wife's inconstancy!
25   Oh God, that I was born to be so vile,
    So monstrous and prodigious[351] for my lust.
    Fie[352] on this pride of mine, this pampered flesh![353]
    I will revenge me on these 'ticing[354] eyes,
    And tear them out for being amorous. [*Anne begins to scratch at
        her own face.*]
30   Oh, Sanders, my dear husband, give me leave, [*Anne tries to stab
        herself.*]

Why do you hold me? Are not my deeds ugly?   [*Drurie and*
    Roger hold Anne's arm.]
    Let then my faults be written in my face.
DRURIE O, do not offer violence to yourself.
ANNE Have I not done so already? Is not
    The better part of me by me misdone?[355]   35
    My husband, is he not slain? Is he not dead?
    But since you labor to prevent my grief,
    I'll hide me in some closet[356] of my house,
    And there weep out mine eyes, or pine to death,
    That have untimely stopped my husband's breath.   *Exit*   40
DRURIE What shall we do, Roger? Go thou and watch
    For Master Browne's arrival from the Court,
    And bring him hither. Haply his presence
    Will be a means to drive her from this passion.[357]
    In the mean space I will go after her,   45
    And do the best I can to comfort her.
ROGER I will. Take heed she do not kill herself.

DRURIE For God's sake, haste thee, and be circumspect.[358]

Scene 11. Sanders's house, the street or stoop outside

This is the third encounter in this liminal space, where in scene 2, Browne had first accosted Anne, and in scene 4, whence Sanders leaves for the Exchange. Now, the Sanders boy and his friend enter first and start to play a coin-toss game that involves betting, and then Roger and Browne, newly returned to London from Greenwich, walk along, apparently going to meet the women there. As Roger tells the captain about Anne's disturbing reaction to the murder, Browne spies her son and "swoons" or nearly faints from his sense of guilt and fear, begging Roger to send the boys out of his sight. Finally, the third pair of characters arrives—Anne and Drurie. This gathering is the last time that the lovers meet, and it does not go well.

Enter Sanders's young son and another boy coming from school.

YOUNG SANDERS Come, Harry, shall we play a game?

HARRY At what?

5 YOUNG SANDERS Why, at cross and pile.[359]

HARRY You have no counters.[360]

YOUNG SANDERS Yes, but I have as many as you.

HARRY I'll drop with you, and he that has most, take all.

YOUNG SANDERS No sir, if you'll play a game, 'tis not yet twelve by half an hour. I'll set you like a gamester.[361]

10 HARRY Go to, where shall we play?

YOUNG SANDERS Here at our door.

HARRY What? And if your father find us?

YOUNG SANDERS No he's at Woolwich, and will not come home tonight.[362]

HARRY Set me then, and here's a good.[363]

15

Enter Browne and Roger.

BROWNE Is she so out of patience[364] as thou sayest?

ROGER Wonderful, sir, I have not seen the like.

20 BROWNE What does she mean by that? Nay, what mean I
    To ask the question? Has she not good cause?
    Oh yes, and we have every one of us just cause
    To hate and be at variance[365] with ourselves.
    But come, I long to see her.   *[Browne] spies the boy [and staggers
        as if fainting].*

25 ROGER How now, Captain?
    Why stop you on the sudden? Why go you not?
    What makes you look so ghastly[366] toward the house?

BROWNE Is not the foremost[367] of those pretty boys
    One of George Sanders's sons?

30 ROGER Yes, 'tis his youngest.

BROWNE Both young'st and eld'st are now made fatherless
    By my unlucky[368] hand. I prithee go

And take him from the door; the sight of him
Strikes such a terror to my guilty conscience,
As I have not the heart to look that way,   35
Nor stir my foot until he be removed.
Methinks in him I see his father's wounds
Fresh bleeding in my sight.[369] Nay, he doth stand
Like to an angel with a fiery sword
To bar mine entrance at that fatal door.   40
I prithee, step, and take him quickly thence.
ROGER Away, my pretty boy, your master comes   [*Walks up to the*
     boys, speaking to Harry]
And you'll be taken playing in the street.[370]
What? At unlawful games? Away, be gone,
'Tis dinner time, young Sanders; you'll be jerked.[371]   45
Your mother looks for you before this time.
YOUNG SANDERS Gaffer,[372] if you'll not tell my master of me,
     I'll give you this new silk point.[373]
ROGER Go to, I will not.
HARRY Nor of me, and there's two counters, I have won no more. 50
ROGER Of neither of you, so you will be gone.
YOUNG SANDERS God be with you, ye shall see me no more.
HARRY Nor me, I mean playing at this door.   [*Exit boys, running in*
     different directions.]
ROGER Now, Captain, if you please, you may come forward.
     But see where Mistress Sanders and my mistress   55
     Are coming forth to meet you on the way?

[*Enter Drurie and Anne.*]

DRURIE See where Master Browne is; in him take comfort,   60
     And learn to temper your excessive grief.
ANNE Ah, bid me feed on poison and be fat,
     Or look upon the basilisk[374] and live,
     Or surfeit[375] daily and still be in health,
     Or leap into the sea and not be drowned: 65

A Warning for Fair Women   79

All these are even as possible as this,
That I should be recomforted[376] by him,
That is the author of my whole lament.[377]

BROWNE Why Mistress Anne, I love you dearly,
70   And but for your incomparable beauty,
My soul had never dreamt of Sanders's death!
Then give me that which now I do deserve—
Yourself, your love, and I will be to you
A husband so devote, as none more just,
75   Or more affectionate shall tread this earth.

ANNE If you can carve it of me with a tongue
That hath not been profaned with such wicked vows,
Or think it in a heart did never harbor
Pretense of murder, or put forth a hand
80   As not contaminate with shedding blood,
Then I will willingly grant your request.
But, oh, your hand, your heart, your tongue, and eye
Are all presenters of my misery.

BROWNE Talk not of that, but let us study[378] now
85   How we may salve[379] it and conceal the fact.

ANNE Mountains will not suffice to cover it,
Cimmerian darkness cannot shadow it,[380]
Nor any policy[381] wit hath in store,
Cloak it so cunningly, but at the last
90   If nothing else, yet will the very stones
That lie within the streets cry out for vengeance,
And point at us to be the murderers.[382]   *Exeunt*

1. Melpomene, the goddess of Tragedy. Courtesy Creative Commons.

37. *Iunonis ad Furias alloquium.*

2. The Furies. From Antonio Tempesta, "Juno with the Furies at the Gate of Hell," in *The Metamorphoses of Ovid* by Wilhelm Janson (plate 13). 1606. Courtesy Creative Commons.

3. *(top)* Tragedy (played by Catie Osborn) wields her whip with Furie (Ind. *77*) in the background: "I'll scourge and lash you both from off the stage!" (Ind.). Resurgens Theatre production, November 2018. Reproduced with kind permission from the Resurgens Theatre Company.

4. *(bottom)* Comedy (played by Ash Anderson) and History (Matthew Trautwein) talk back: "And Tragedy, although today thou reign, / Tomorrow here I'll domineer again" (Ind.). Resurgens Theatre production, November 2018. Reproduced with kind permission from the Resurgens Theatre Company.

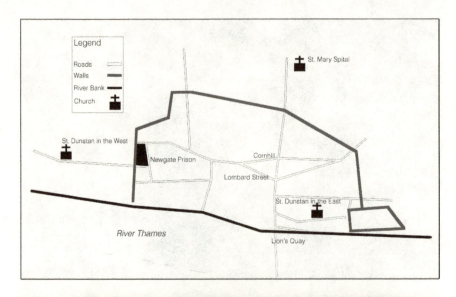

5. (*top*) Map of *A Warning*'s London. Cartographer Claude Willen, 2020.

6. (*bottom*) Mistress Drurie (played by Ash Anderson) counsels Captain Browne (Tamil Periasamy): "I'faith, have I found you; are ye such one?" (sc. 1). Resurgens Theatre production, November 2018. Reproduced with kind permission from the Resurgens Theatre Company.

7. The Royal Exchange. Wenceslaus Hollar, *Byrsa Londinensis vulgo The Royal Exchange* (London, England s.n., 1647?). Call no. 34648. Courtesy Folger Shakespeare Library.

8. Anne Sanders (Sims Lamason) sits with her child (played by Teagan Williams): "I pray God bless thee; th'art a very wag" (sc. 2). Resurgens Theatre production, November 2018. Reproduced with kind permission from the Resurgens Theatre Company.

9. (*top*) Anne Sanders (Sims Lamason) refuses the approach of Captain Browne (Tamil Periasamy): "Resolve your doubt, and trouble me no more" (sc. 2). Resurgens Theatre production, November 2018. Reproduced with kind permission from the Resurgens Theatre Company.

10. (*bottom*) Mistress Drurie (Ash Anderson) reads the palm of Anne Sanders (Sims Lamason). "Have you such knowledge then in palmistry?" (sc. 4). Resurgens Theatre production, November 2018. Reproduced with kind permission from the Resurgens Theatre Company.

11. A French hood. Hans Holbein, *Portrait of a Lady, Probably a Member of the Cromwell Family*, ca. 1535–40. Toledo Museum of Art, eMuseum. Public domain.

12. (*opposite top*) "Enter Tragedy with a bowl of blood in her hand" (Dumb show 1, stage direction). Catie Osborn, Resurgens Theatre production, November 2018. Reproduced with kind permission from the Resurgens Theatre Company.

13. (*opposite bottom*) Adolph von Menzel, *Study of a Man with a Ruff Collar*, ca. 1850. National Museum in Warsaw. Accession no. 186077. Public domain.

14. (*above*) Captain Browne (Tamil Periasamy) holds "a token to [his] love": "Give this to Mistress Sanders. Bid her read / Upon this bloody handkercher the thing / As I did promise and have now performed" (sc. 8). Resurgens Theatre production, November 2018. Reproduced with kind permission from the Resurgens Theatre Company.

15. (*opposite top*) Beane (played by Bob Lanoue) is left for dead; Old John (Richard Herren) orders his maidservant Joan (Catherine Thomas) to "take my napkin and thy apron, and / bind up his wounds, and cows go where they will till we / have carried him home" (sc. 8). Resurgens Theatre production, November 2018. Reproduced with kind permission from the Resurgens Theatre Company.

16. (*opposite bottom*) Anne Sanders (Sims Lamason) swears an oath with a white rose, "in token of my spotless innocence" (sc. 17). Resurgens Theatre production, November 2018. Reproduced with kind permission from the Resurgens Theatre Company.

17. (*above*) "Pillory." Geoffrey Whitney, *A Choice of Emblems* (1586) STC 25437.8. Courtesy Folger Shakespeare Library.

18. Anne Sanders (Sims Lamason), standing at the grate of her prison cell, sings the ballad "The Lamentation of Mistress Anne Sanders" to Mistress Drurie (Ash Anderson) (sc. 21). Resurgens Theatre production, November 2018. Reproduced with kind permission from the Resurgens Theatre Company.

Scene 12. Greenwich Palace

The initial investigation begins. Lords and Master James meet to process information from a letter; more news arrives, along with witnesses, the Waterman and a Page.

Enter three Lords, Master James, and two Messengers with their
boxes,[383] *one Lord reading a letter.*

FIRST LORD 'Fore God (my Lords) a very bloody act.   *This [Lord]*
   hath the letter.
SECOND LORD Yea, and committed in eye of court
5   Audaciously, as who should say, he durst
   Attempt a murder in despite of law.[384]
THIRD LORD Pray ye let's see your letter, good my Lord.

He takes and reads the letter.

10

   Ten wounds at least, and deadly ev'ry wound,
   And yet he lives and tells marks[385] of the man.
   Ev'n at the edge of Shooter's Hill, so near?
FIRST LORD We shall not need to send these messengers,
15   For hue and cry[386] may take the murderers.

Enter a fourth Lord with a Waterman and a Page.

FOURTH LORD Nay, sirrah, you shall tell this tale again   [*speaking to*
   the Waterman]
20   Before the Lords; come on. My Lords, what news?
FIRST LORD Bad news, my Lord. A cruel murder's done,
   Near Shooter's Hill, and here's a letter come
   From Woolwich, from a gentleman of worth,
   Noting the manner, and the marks of him,
25   (By likelihood) that did that impious deed.
FOURTH LORD 'Tis noised[387] at London that a merchant's slain,
   One Master Sanders dwelling near Thames Street,
   And that George Browne, a man whom we all know,
   Is vehemently suspected for the fact,
30   And fled upon't, and this same waterman
   That brought me down says he rowed him up,
   And that his hose were bloody, which he hid

Still with his hat sitting bare head in the boat,
And sighed and stared as one that was afraid.
How sayest thou, sirrah, was't not so he did? 35
WATERMAN Yes, and't please your Lordship, so it was.
FIRST LORD What did he wear?[388]
WATERMAN A doublet of white satin
And a large pair of breeches of blue silk.
SECOND LORD Was he so suited when you drank with him, 40
[to Master James]
Here in the buttery?[389]
JAMES Yea my Lord he was.
THIRD LORD And his hose bloody?
JAMES Just as he affirms.
THIRD LORD Confirm the marks the wounded fellow tells with 45
these reports. [hands papers to First Lord]
FIRST LORD The man that did the deed   Reads
Was "fair and fat, his doublet of white silk,
His hose of blue." I am sorry for George Browne.   Looks off
'Twas he, my Lords. 50
FOURTH LORD The more accursed man.
Get warrants drawn, and messengers attend:
Call all your fellows; ride but every way.
Post to the ports! Give charge that no man pass
Without our warrant. One take boat to London, 55
Command the sheriffs make wise and speedy search.[390]
Decipher[391] him by all the marks you can.
Let blood be paid with blood in any man.
FIRST LORD We were to blame else.[392] Come my Lords, let's in,
To sign our warrants and to send them out.   Exeunt omnes. 60

Scene 13. Drurie's house

In the aftermath of the crime, the conspirators experience infighting. Roger has been sent to pawn some of the women's "plate," i.e., gold or silver vessels and utensils, to raise money for Browne's flight. Drurie and Roger discuss selling these household items. (Anne Sanders later denies this and accuses Roger of theft.) Here, Drurie blames Browne, who in turn blames her and also Anne.

Enter Drurie and Roger with a bag.

DRURIE Why Roger, canst thou get but twenty pound
   For all the plate[393] that thou hadst from us both?
5   My own's worth twenty. What hadst thou of her?
ROGER Two bowls and spoons; I know not what myself.
   'Tis in a note, and I could get no more
   But twenty pound.   [*He hands her a paper receipt.*]
DRURIE Alas, 'twill do no good,
10   And he must thence. If he be ta'n[394] he dies.
   On his escape thou knowest our safety lies.
ROGER That's true. Alas, what will ye have me do?
DRURIE Run to Nan Sanders; bid her make some shift.[395]
   Try all her friends to help at this dead lift[396]
15   For all the money that she can devise.[397]
   And send by thee with all the haste she may.
   Tell her we die if Browne make any stay.
ROGER I will. I will.   *Exit Roger.*
DRURIE Thou wilt; thou wilt. Alas!
20   That ere this dismal deed was brought to pass,
   But now 'tis done, we must prevent the worst.   *Enter Browne.*
   And here comes he that makes us all accursed.[398]
   How now, George Browne?
BROWNE By Nan Drurie now undone.
25   Undone by that thou hast made me do.
DRURIE I made ye do it? Your own love made ye do it.
BROWNE Well, done it is! What shall we now say to't?
   Search is made for me. Be I ta'n, I die,
   And there are others as far in as I.
30   I must beyond sea; money I have none,
   Nor dare I look for any of mine own.[399]
DRURIE Here's twenty pound I borrowed[400] of my plate,
   And to your Mistress I have sent for more   *Enter Roger.*
   By Hodge my man. Now, Roger, hast thou sped?
35 ROGER Yea, of six pound. 'Tis all that she can make.

She prays ye take't in worth, and be gone.[401] 40
She hears the sheriffs will be there anon
And at our house. A thousand commendations
She sends you, praying you to shift for yourself.
BROWNE Even as I may. Roger, farewell to thee.
  If I were richer, then thou shouldst go with me, 45
  But poverty parts company.[402] Farewell, Nan.[403]
  Commend me to my Mistress if you can.
DRURIE Step thither yourself; I dare not come there.
  I'll keep my house close, for I am in fear.[404]
ROGER God be with you, good Captain. 50
BROWNE Farewell, gentle Hodge.   [*Exit Roger.*]
  Oh, Master Sanders, wert thou now alive,
  All London's wealth thy death could not contrive.[405]
  This heat of love and hasty climbing breeds.
  God bless all honest, tall men from such deeds.[406]   [*Exit all.*] 55

[Dumb show 3]

The third and shortest dumb show comes between the murder and the trials and introduces new allegorical figures—Justice, Mercy, and Diligence—in a courtroom setting, where Justice falls asleep as Chastity silently "utter[s] her grief" to Mercy, who awakens Justice, who, in turn, sends for officers to bring in the merchant's dead body. Anne Sanders, Drurie, and Roger enter, and Diligence is sent to fetch Browne.

Enter Tragedy before the show.

TRAGEDY Prevailing Sin, having by three degrees,
　　　Made his ascension to forbidden deeds—
5　　As first, alluring their unwary minds
　　　To like what she proposed; then practicing
　　　To draw them to consent. And last of all
　　　Minist'ring fit means and opportunity[407]
　　　To execute what she approved good.
10　　Now she unveils their sight and lets them see
　　　The horror of their foul immanitie.[408]
　　　And Wrath, that all this while hath been obscured,[409]
　　　Steps forth before them in a thousand shapes
　　　Of ghastly thoughts and loathing discontents,
15　　So that the rest was promised, now appears
　　　Unrest and deep affliction of the soul.
　　　Delight proves danger; confidence despair,
　　　As by this following show shall more appear.

20　[As in previous dumb shows, this is acted out silently as Tragedy narrates. It is staged as if a court trial.]

　　　Enter Justice and Mercy. When they've taken their seats, Justice
　　　falls into a slumber. Then enters wronged Chastity, and in dumb
　　　action uttering her grief to Mercy, is put away,[410] whereon she
　　　[Mercy] wakens Justice, who listening [to] her attentively, starts up,
　　　commanding his officers to attend her. Then go they with her, and fetch
　　　forth Master Sanders's body; Mistress Sanders, Drurie, and Roger, led
　　　after it, and being shown it, they all seem very sorrowful, and so are led
　　　away. But Chastity shows that the chief offender [Browne] is not as yet
　　　taken, whereon Justice dispatcheth his servant Diligence to make further
　　　enquiry after the murderer, and so they depart the stage with Chastity.

　　　TRAGEDY Thus lawless actions and prodigious crimes
25　　Drink not the blood alone of them they hate,

But even their ministers,[411] when they have done
All that they can, must help to fill the scene
And yield their guilty necks unto the block.
For which intent, the wronged Chastity
Prostrate[412] before the sacred throne of Justice,   30
With wringing hands, and cheeks besprent[413] with tears,
Pursues the murderers. And being heard
Of Mercy first, that in relenting[414] words
Would fain persuade her to humility,
She turns from her, and with her tender hand   35
Wakes slumbering Justice. When her tale being told,
And the dead body brought for instance[415] forth,
Straight inquisition[416] and search is made,
And the offenders as you did behold,
Discover'd where they thought to be unseen.   40
Then trial now remains as shall conclude:
Measure for measure, and lost blood for blood.[417]   [*Exit all.*]

Scene 14. A butcher's shop, Rochester

Captain Browne arrives to a Rochester butcher shop owned by a man named Browne, to whom the captain pretends to be related and from whom he claims to need a place to hide out from a debt collector. The butcher is sure this fine captain and he are not related, but he treats his higher-class visitor well anyway. The Mayor of Rochester, Master James, and officers arrive to apprehend Browne on suspicion of murder, which charge Browne denies. James explains that the Privy Council enlists the Mayor to escort the accused to Woolwich, and they all exit with the alleged felon Browne.

Enter George Browne and one Browne a Butcher in Rochester.

BUTCHER 'Tis marvel,[418] cousin Browne, we see you here,
And thus alone without all company!
5   You were not wont to visit Rochester,
But you had still some friend or other with you.
BROWNE Such is th'occasion, cousin, at this time,
And for the love I bear you, I am bold
To make myself your guest, rather than lie
10   In any public inn because indeed
The house where I was wont to host is full
Of certain Frenchmen[419] and their followers.
BUTCHER Nay, cousin Browne, I would not have you think
I do object thus much as one unwilling
15   To show you any kindness that I can.
My house though homely,[420] yet such as it is,
And I myself will be at your command.
I love you for your namesake, and trust me sir,
Am proud that such a one as you will call me cousin,
20   Though I am sure we are no kin at all.
BROWNE Yes, cousin, we are kin. Nor do I scorn
At any time to acknowledge as much
Toward men of baser calling than yourself.[421]
BUTCHER It may be so, sir, but to tell you truth,
25   It seemed somewhat strange to me at first
And I was half afraid some ill[422] had happened
That made you careful whom you trusted to.
BROWNE Faith, cousin, none but this: I owe some money,
And one I am indebted to of late
30   Hath brought his action to an outlawry
And seeks to do me all extremity.[423]
But that I am not yet provided for him,
And that he shall not have his will of me,
I do absent me,[424] till a friend of mine
35   Do see what order he may take with him.

BUTCHER How now who's this?   [*The sound of loud knocking.*]

Enter Master Mayor [of Rochester], Master James, with a
Pursuivant,[425] *and others.*

MAYOR OF ROCHESTER Where are you, neighbor Browne?   40
BUTCHER Master Mayor, y'are welcome, what's the news, sir?
   You come so guarded; is there aught amiss?
BROWNE Heaven will have justice shown; it is even so.   [*Aside*]
JAMES I can assure you 'tis the man we seek.
   Then do your office, Master Mayor.[426]   45
MAYOR OF ROCHESTER George Browne,
   I do arrest you in her Highness's name
   As one suspected to have murdered George Sanders, Citizen of
      London.
BROWNE Of murder, sir? There lives not in this land
   Can touch me with the thought of murder.[427]   50
MAYOR OF ROCHESTER Pray God it be so. But you must along
   Before their honors there to answer it.
   Here's a commission that commands it so.   [*pointing to a paper*]
BROWNE Well, sir, I do obey and do not doubt
   But I shall prove me innocent therein.   55
JAMES Come, Master, it is the Council's pleasure[428]   [*speaking to*
      the Mayor]
   You must assist us till we come to Woolwich,
   Where we have order to confer at large
   With Master Barnes concerning this mishap.[429]
MAYOR OF ROCHESTER With all my heart. Farewell, good neighbor   60
      Browne.
BUTCHER God keep you, Master Mayor, and all the rest,
   And, Master Browne, believe me I am sorry
   It was your fortune to have no more grace.
BROWNE Cousin, grieve not for me; my case is clear.
   Suspected men may be, but need not fear.   *Exeunt*   65

Scene 15. Barnes's house, Woolwich

This is the scene when the murderer is brought before his victim, John Beane, who is clearly dying; his wounds begin to bleed anew, which is taken as a sign that Browne was the guilty party. The Mayor of Rochester explains to Barnes how he came to apprehend and transport Browne that day, and Barnes and James exchange compliments about the other's service to the state and potential for reward. Browne, shocked to see Beane still alive, speaks in an aside. Beane correctly identifies him and then "sinks down" to die. The Mayor of Rochester sends the officers ahead, then he, James, and Barnes share stories of other cases of "murder will out," that is, anecdotes of guilty parties being discovered or confessing through strange or miraculous means including plays about murder.

Enter John Beane brought in a chair, Master Barnes, and Master James.

BARNES Sir, how much I esteemed this Gentleman,[430]
    And in how high respect I held his love,
5   My griefs can hardly utter.
JAMES It shall not need.
    Your love after his death expresses it.
BARNES I would to God it could. And I am very glad
    My Lords of her most honorable Council
10   Have made choice of yourself, so grave[431] a gentleman
    To see the manner[432] of this cruel murder.
JAMES Sir, the most unworthy I of many men,
    But that in the high bounty of your kindness, so you term me.
    But trust me, Master Barnes, amongst the rest
15   That was reported to them of the murder,
    They hardly were induced to believe,
    That this poor soul having so many wounds   *Laying his hand*
        upon him
    And all so mortal as they were reported,
    Why, it is past belief.
20 BARNES Sir it is so, your worthy self can witness.
    As strange to us that look upon the wretch,[433]
    As the report thereof unto their wisdoms.
JAMES More fearful wounds, nor hurts more dangerous,
    Upon my faith I have not seen.
25 BEANE Hey ho, a little drink. O, my head.
BARNES Good John, how dost thou?
BEANE Who's that? Father John?[434]
BARNES Nay John, thy master.
BEANE O Lord, my belly.
30 JAMES He spends more breath that issues through his wounds than
        through his lips.
BEANE I am dry.[435]
BARNES John, dost thou know me?

JAMES See where thy master is. Look, dost thou know him?
BARNES Sir, he never had his perfect memory since the first hour.[436]
JAMES Surely, he cannot last.   35
BARNES And yet, sir, to our seeming I assure you,
   He sat not up so strongly[437] as you see him
   Since he was brought into this house as now.
JAMES 'Tis very strange.

                                                                                40

Enter the Mayor of Rochester with Browne, and Officers.

BARNES As I take it, Master Mayor of Rochester?
MAYOR OF ROCHESTER The same, good Master Barnes.
BARNES What happy fortune sent you here to Woolwich   45
   That yet your company may give us comfort in this sad time?
MAYOR OF ROCHESTER Believe me, sad indeed, and very sad.
   Sir, the Council's warrant lately[438] came to me
   About the search for one Captain George Browne,
   As it should seem suspected for this murder,   50
   Whom in my search I hap't to apprehend.
   And hearing that the bodies of the murdered
   Remained here, I thought it requisite[439]
   To make this in my way unto the Court,
   Now going thither with the prisoner.[440]   55
BARNES Believe me, sir, ye have done right good service,
   And shown yourself a painful gentleman,[441]
   And shall no doubt deserve well of the state.
JAMES No doubt you shall, and I durst assure you so,
   The Council will accept well of the same.   60
BARNES Good Master Mayor, this wretched man of mine,
   Is not yet dead. Look you where he sits,
   But past all sense, and laboring to his end.
MAYOR OF ROCHESTER Alas, poor wretch.
BARNES Is this that Browne that is suspected to have done   65
   The murder? A goodly man, believe me:
   Too fair a creature for so foul an act.

BROWNE My name is Browne, sir.

JAMES I know you well; your fortunes have been fair

70   As any gentleman of your repute.

    But Browne, should you be guilty of this fact,

    As this your flight hath given shrewd suspicion.

    O Browne, your hands have done the bloodiest deed

    That ever was committed.

75 BROWNE He doth not live dare charge me with it.

JAMES Pray God there be not.

MAYOR OF ROCHESTER Sergeants, bring him near. See if this poor soul

    know him.   [*Officers escort Browne toward Beane.*]

BARNES It cannot be! These two days space

80   He knew no creature.   [*Beane sits up and reacts to seeing Browne*

    by gasping or pointing to him.]

BROWNE 'Swounds,[442] lives the villain yet?   *Aside*

    O how his very sight affrights my soul!

    His very eyes will speak had he no tongue,

    And will accuse me.

85 BARNES See how his wounds break out afresh in bleeding.   [*Beane's*

    wounds suddenly bleed.][443]

JAMES He stirs himself.

MAYOR OF ROCHESTER He openeth his eyes.

BARNES See how he looks upon him.

BROWNE I gave him fifteen wounds,   *Aside*

90   Which now be fifteen mouths that do accuse me.

    In ev'ry wound there is a bloody tongue,[444]

    Which all speak. Although he hold his peace,

    By a whole jury I shall be accused.

BARNES John, dost thou hear? Knowest thou this man?

95 BEANE Yea, this is he that murdered me and Master Sanders.   *He*

    sinks down.

JAMES O, hold him up.

MAYOR OF ROCHESTER John, comfort thyself.

JAMES Bow[445] him, give him air.

BARNES No, he is dead.

BROWNE Methinks he is so fearful in my sight,   100
    That were he now but where I saw him last,
    For all this world I would not look on him.

BARNES The wondrous work of God—that the poor
    creature, not speaking for two days, yet now
    should speak to accuse this man, and presently   105
    yield up his soul!

JAMES 'Tis very strange, and the report thereof
    Can seem no less unto the Lord's.[446]

MAYOR OF ROCHESTER Sergeants, away, prepare you for the court,
    And I will follow you immediately.   110

BARNES Sure, the revealing of this murder's strange.

JAMES It is so, sir; but in the case of blood,
    God's justice hath been still miraculous.

MAYOR OF ROCHESTER I have heard it told, that digging up a grave,
    Wherein a man had twenty years been buried,   115
    By finding of a nail knocked in the scalp,
    By due inquiry who was buried there,
    The murder yet at length did come to light.

BARNES I have heard it told that once a traveler,
    Being in the hands of him that murdered him,   120
    Told him, the fern that then grew in the place—
    If nothing else—yet that would sure reveal him.
    And seven years after, being safe in London,
    There came a sprig of fern borne by the wind
    Into the room where as the murderer was.   125
    At sight whereof he suddenly start up,
    And then revealed the murder.

JAMES I'll tell you, sir, one more to 'quite[447] your tale:
    A woman that had made away her husband
    And sitting to behold a tragedy   130
    At Lynn, a town in Norfolk,[448]
    Acted by Players traveling that way,
    Wherein a woman that had murdered hers

Was ever haunted with her husband's ghost.
135   The passion, written by a feeling pen
        And acted by a good Tragedian,
        She was so moved with the sight thereof,
        As she cried out, the play was made by her,
        And openly confessed her husband's murder.[449]
140   BARNES How ever theirs, God's name be praised for this.[450]
        You, Master Mayor, I see must to the Court.
        I pray you do my duty to the Lords.[451]
        MAYOR OF ROCHESTER That will I sir.

145   JAMES Come, I'll go along with you.   *Exeunt*

Scene 16. Greenwich Palace

More news arrives at court about Browne's apprehension that various Lords gather to discuss. The Mayor of Rochester enters with some others and Browne, who, upon interrogation, admits his own guilt, but refuses to implicate Anne Sanders. Another letter is delivered from the Sheriffs of London, which seems to contain Drurie's and Roger's confessions that indict Anne Sanders. A Lord orders the trial to be set up.

Enter the [four] Lords at the Court, and [two] Messengers.

1 LORD Where was Browne apprehended, Messenger?

MESSENGER 2 At Rochester, my Lord, in a Butcher's house

5   of his own name, from thence brought up to Woolwich.

4 LORD And there the fellow he left for dead

with all those wounds affirmed that it was he.

1 MESSENGER He did, my Lord, and with a constant voice,

Prayed, God forgive Browne, and receive his soul, and

10   so departed.

1 LORD 'Tis a wondrous thing,

But that the power of heaven sustained him—

A man with nine or ten such mortal wounds,

Not taking food, should live so many days,

15   And then, at sight of Browne, recover strength,

And speak so cheerily[452] as they say he did.

4 LORD Aye, and soon after he avouched[453] the fact

Unto Browne's face then to give up the ghost.[454]

2 LORD 'Twas God's good will it should be so, my Lord.

20   But what said Browne? Did he deny the deed?

1 MESSENGER Never my Lord, but did with tears lament,

(As seemed to us) his heinous cruelty.

1 LORD When will they come?[455]

1 MESSENGER Immediately my Lord,

25   For they have wind, and tide, and boats do wait.

Enter Master Mayor, Master James, &c.[456]

JAMES My Lords, the Mayor of Rochester is come

30   with Browne.

4 LORD Let him come in. You, messenger,

Haste you to London to the Justices.

Will[457] them from us see an indictment drawn

Against George Browne for murdering of George Sanders.

Enter Mayor [of Rochester], Browne, a Messenger, another, and   35
Master Humphries.[458]

1 LORD Welcome, good Master Mayor of Rochester.

MAYOR OF ROCHESTER I humbly thank your honors.

4 LORD We thank you

    For your great care and diligence in this,   40

    And many other faithful services.

    Now, Master Browne, I am sorry it was your hap[459]

    To be so far from grace and fear of God,

    As to commit so bloody a murder,

    What say ye? Are ye not sorry for it?   45

BROWNE Yes, my Lord, and were it now to do,

    All the world's wealth could not entice me to't.

1 LORD Was there any ancient quarrel, Browne,

    Betwixt yourself and Master Sanders?

BROWNE No.   50

2 LORD Was't for the money that he had about him?

BROWNE No, my good Lord; I knew of none he had.

4 LORD No, I heard an inkling of the cause:

    You did affect[460] his wife, George Browne, too much.

BROWNE I did my Lord, and God forgive it me.   55

3 LORD Then she provok'd ye to dispatch[461] him?

BROWNE No.

4 LORD Yes. And promised you should marry her.

BROWNE No. I will take it upon my death.

1 LORD Some other were confederate[462] in the fact,   60

    Confess then, Browne, discharge thy conscience.

BROWNE I will, my Lord, at hour of my death.

2 LORD Nay, now, that they with thee may die for it.   *Master James*

    delivers a letter.

4 LORD From whom is this letter?   *Opens and reads it*

JAMES From the Sheriffs of London.   65

4 LORD I told ye: Mistress Sanders's hand was in.

    The act's confessed by two, that she knew on't.[463]

BROWNE They do her wrong, my Lords, upon my life.

4 LORD Why, Drurie's wife and Roger do affirm[464]
70   Unto her face, that she did give consent.

BROWNE God pardon them; they wrong the innocent.
    They both are guilty and procured the deed,
    And gave me money since the deed was done—
    Twenty-six pound to carry me away,
75   But Mistress Sanders—as I hope for heaven—
    Is guiltless, ignorant how it was done.
    But Drurie's wife did bear me still in hand,
    If he were dead she would affect the marriage,
    And Trusty Roger, her base apple-squire,[465]
80   Haunted me like a sprite[466] till it was done,
    And now like devils accuse that harmless soul.

1 LORD Well, Master Browne, w'are sorry for your fall.
    You were a man respected of us all
    And noted fit for many services,[467]
85   And, fie, that wanton lust should overthrow
    Such gallant parts in any gentleman.
    Now all our favors cannot do ye good.
    The act's too odious to be spoken of.
    Therefore, we must dismiss ye to the Law.

90 4 LORD Expect no life, but meditate of death,
    And for the safeguard of thy sinful soul,
    Conceal no part of truth for friend or foe.
    And, Master Mayor, as you have taken pains,
    So finish it, and see him safe conveyed
95   To the justices of the Bench at Westminster.[468]
    Will them from us to try him speedily.
    That Gentleman shall go along with you   [pointing to one of the
        Lords]
    And take in writing his confession.

2 LORD Farewell, George Browne. Discharge thy conscience.[469]
100

BROWNE I do, my Lord—that Sanders's wife is clear.   *Exeunt omnes.*

Scene 17. Westminster Palace, a room
set up as a courtroom

At first, two court officers jokingly chat as they set up the room for the official business to follow—the arraignment of all four of the conspirators. The Lord Mayor of London, Justice, and Lords enter and a Clerk reads the charges to Browne, who pleads guilty, and as he is "led out," Anne Sanders and Drurie enter—this is the last, silent encounter among them. The Clerk reads charges against both Annes at once and they both plead "not guilty." Then Roger is questioned about Mistress Sanders's knowledge of the plot. Certain evidence is discussed: the letter from Browne and the bloody handkerchief. The Lord Chief Justice advises them to confess their sins and lectures them about what will happen next. Anne refuses to admit her guilt, claiming to be as innocent as the white rose she wears like a corsage, but amazingly it changes color, to red or perhaps to black.

*Enter some [two officers] to prepare the judgment seat to the Lord
Mayor [of London], Lord Justice, and the four Lords, and one Clerk,
and a Sheriff, who being set [once they are all seated], command
Browne to be brought forth.*

OFFICER 1 Come, let's make haste, and well prepare this place.

OFFICER 2 How well I pray you? What haste more then was wont?

5 OFFICER 1 Why, diverse[470] lords are come from court today,

To see th'arraignment of this lusty[471] Browne.

OFFICER 2 Lusty? How lusty? Now he's tame enough[472]

And will be tamer. Oh, a lusty youth,

Lustily fed, and lustily appareled,

10 Lusty in look, in gait, in gallant talk,

Lusty in wooing, in fight and murdering,

And lustily hanged, there's th'end of lusty Browne.

OFFICER 1 Hold your lusty peace, for here come the Lords.

15 *Enter all as before. [They walk to their seats and sit.]*

MAYOR OF LONDON Please it your honors, place yourselves, my lords.

JUSTICE Bring forth the prisoner and keep silence there.   [*onstage
auditors whispering*]

Prepare the indictment that it may be read.

20

Browne is brought in.

CLERK To the bar,[473] George Browne, and hold up thy hand.

[*Browne stands before the court and holds up his right hand.*]

Thou art here indicted by the name of George Browne, late

25 of London, Gentleman, for that thou upon the twenty-fifth day of

March in the fifteenth year of the reign of her sacred

Majesty (whom God long preserve) between the hours of

seven and eight 'clock in the forenoon of the same

day, near unto Shooter's Hill, in the county of Kent,

30 lying in wait of purpose and pretended malice, having

no fear of God before thine eyes, the persons of George
Sanders, Gentleman, and John Beane, yeoman, then and there
journeying in God's peace and the prince's, feloniously
did assault, and with one sword (price—six shillings)—
mortally and willfully, in many places did'st wound unto   35
death against the peace, crown, and dignity of her
Majesty. How sayest thou to these felonious murders?
Art thou guilty or not guilty?

BROWNE Guilty.

JUSTICE The Lord have mercy upon thee.   40
Master Sheriff, ye shall not need to return any jury to
pass upon him, for he hath pleaded guilty, and stands
convict at the bar attending his judgment. What canst
thou say for thyself, Browne, why sentence of death
should not be pronounced against thee?   45

BROWNE Nothing, my Lord, but only do beseech
Those noble men, assistants on that bench,
And you, my Lord who are to justice sworn,
As you will answer at God's judgment seat,
To have a care to save the innocent,   50
And (as myself) to let the guilty die—
That's Drurie's wife and her man Trusty Roger.
But if Anne Sanders die, I do protest
As a man dead in law, that she shall have
The greatest wrong that e'r had guiltless soul.[474]   55

JUSTICE She shall have justice, and with favor, Browne.[475]

4 LORD Assure yourself, Browne, she shall have no wrong.

BROWNE I humbly thank your Lordships.

2 LORD Hark ye, Browne,
What countryman are ye borne?   60

BROWNE Of Ireland, and in Dublin.

JUSTICE Have you not a brother called Anthony Browne?

BROWNE Yes, my Lord, whom (as I hear)
Your Lordship keeps close prisoner now in Newgate.[476]

JUSTICE Well, two bad brothers. God forgive ye both.   65

BROWNE Amen, my Lord, and you, and all the world.

JUSTICE Attend your sentence.

BROWNE Presently, my Lord.

But I have one petition first to make

70 Unto these noblemen, which on my knees

I do beseech them may not be denied.

4 LORD What is't, George Browne?

BROWNE I know the Law

Condemns a murderer to be hanged in chains.

75 O, good my Lords, as you are noble men

Let me be buried so soon as I am dead.[477]

1 LORD Thou shalt, thou shalt. Let not that trouble thee.

But hear thy judgment.

JUSTICE Browne, thou art here by Law condemned to die,

80 Which, by thine own confession, thou deserv'st.

All men must die, although by diverse means.

The manner how is of least moment, but

The matter why, condemns or justifies.

But be of comfort: though the world condemn,

85 Yea, though thy conscience sting thee for thy fact,

Yet God is greater than thy conscience,

And he can save whom all the world condemns,

If true repentance turn thee to his grace.

Thy time is short; therefore, spend this thy time

90 In prayer and contemplation of thy end.

Labor to die better than thou hast lived.[478]

God grant thou mayest. Attend thy judgment now:

Thou must go from hence to the place from where thou cam'st;

From thence to th'appointed place of execution,

95 And there be hanged until thou be dead,

And thy body after the Prince's pleasure.

And so, the Lord have mercy upon thee, Browne.

Master Sheriff, see execution, and now take him hence,

And bring those other prisoners that you have.

100 BROWNE My Lords, forget not my petitions—

Save poor Anne Sanders for she's innocent.
And, good my Lords, let me not hang in chains!

Browne is led out, and Anne Sanders, and Drurie brought in.

4 LORD Farewell. Let none of these things trouble thee.
1 LORD See how he labors to acquit Anne Sanders?
4 LORD What hath his brother that is in Newgate done?
JUSTICE Notorious felonies in Yorkshire, my Lord.
 Here come the prisoners: bring them to the bar.
 Read their indictment. Master Sheriff, prepare
 Your jury ready. Command silence there. [*Some noises, shifting*
  in seats, and murmurs in the court, as earlier]

Anne Sanders hath a white rose in her bosom.

CLERK Anne Sanders and Anne Drurie,
 To the bar and hold by your hands. [*They hold up their right*
  hands to swear.]
 You are here jointly and severally[479] indicted in form following, viz.[480]
 that you Anne Sanders, and Anne Drurie, late of London,
  spinsters,[481]
 and thou Roger Clement, late of the same, yeoman, and every of
  you, jointly
 and severally, before and after the twenty-fifth day of March last
  past, in
 the fifteenth year of the reign of her sacred Majesty,[482] whom
 God long preserve, having not the fear of God before your
 eyes, did maliciously conspire and conclude with one George
 Browne, Gentleman, the death of George Sanders, late husband to
 you, Anne Sanders, and did entice, animate, and procure the
 said George Browne to murder the said Master Sanders.
 And also, after the said heinous murder committed, did
 with money and other means, aid, relieve, and abet the said
 Browne, knowing him to have done the deed, whereby you

are all accessories both before and after the fact, contrary to the peace, crown,

and dignity of our Sovereign Lady, the Queen. How say ye severally? Are

ye guilty or not guilty, as accessories both before and after to this felony and murder?

ANNE Not guilty.

135 DRURIE Not guilty.

CLERK How will ye be tried?

BOTH By God and by the Country.

JUSTICE Bring forth Trusty Roger there,

Roger, what sayest thou to this letter?

140 Who gave it thee to come unto Browne?

ROGER My mistress gave it me,

And she did write it on Our Lady's Eve.[483]

JUSTICE Did Mistress Sanders know thereof, or no?

ROGER She read it twice before the same was sealed.

145 ANNE Did I, thou wicked man?

This man is hired to betray my life. *[thrusting her finger at Roger and speaking to Lords]*

2 LORD Fie, Mistress Sanders, you do not well

To use such speeches when ye see the case

Is too, too manifest.[484] But I pray ye,

150 Why do you wear that white rose in your bosom?[485]

ANNE In token of my spotless innocence:

As free from guilt as is this flower from stain.

2 LORD I fear it will not fall out so.

JUSTICE Roger, what money carried you to Browne

155 After the deed to get him gone withal?

ROGER Twenty-six pounds, which coin was borrowed

Part of my mistress's plate, and some of Mistress Sanders's.

JUSTICE How say ye to that, Mistress Sanders?

ANNE Indeed, I grant I miss some of my plate,

160 And now I am glad I know the thief that stole it.

ROGER O, God forgive ye; you did give it me!

And God forgive me; I did love you all
Too well, which now I dearly answer for.
1 LORD Anne Drurie, what say you—was not the plate
Part of it yours, and the rest Mistress Sanders's,   165
According as your man hath there confessed
With which he borrowed twenty pound for Browne?
DRURIE My Lord, it was.
2 LORD And you and she together,
Were privy of the letter, which was sent.   170
Was it so or no? Why do you not speak?
DRURIE It was, my Lord, and Mistress Sanders knew
That Roger came that morning ere he went,
And had a token from her to George Browne,
A handkercher, which after was sent back   175
Imbued[486] in Sanders's blood.
JUSTICE Who brought that handkercher?
DRURIE That did my man.
1 LORD To whom did you deliver it, sirrah?
ROGER To Mistress Sanders at her house, my Lord.   180
ANNE O God, my Lords, he openly belies[487] me!
I kept my childbed chamber[488] at that time,
Where 'twas not meet[489] that he or any man
Should have access.
JUSTICE Go to, clog not your soul   185
With new additions of more heinous sin.
'Tis thought, beside conspiring of his death,
You wronged your husband with unchaste behavior,[490]
For which the justice of the righteous God,
Meaning to strike you, yet reserves a place   190
Of gracious mercy, if you can repent—
And therefore bring your wickedness to light—
That suffering for it in this world, you might,
Upon your hearty[491] sorrow, be set free,
And fear no further judgment in the next.   195
But, if you spurn at his affliction,

And bear his chastisement with grudging minds,
Your precious soul as well as here your bodies
Are left in hazard of eternal death.

200 Be sorry, therefore; 'tis no petty sin,
But murder most unnatural of all,[492]
Wherewith your hands are tainted, and in which,
Before and after the accursed fact,
You stand as accessory. To be brief—

205 You shall be carried back unto the place,
From whence you came, and so from thence at last,
Unto the place of execution, where
You shall all three be hanged till you be dead.
And so the Lord have mercy on your souls.

210 ANNE Ah, good my Lords, be good unto Anne Sanders,
Or else you cast away an innocent.

[The rose changes color—to black or red.][493]

215 2 LORD It should not seem so by the rose you wear!
His color is now of another hue.
ANNE So you will have it. But my soul is still
As free from murder as it was at first.
JUSTICE I think no less. Jailer, away with them.

220 ANNE Well, well, Anne Drurie, I may curse the time
That ere I saw thee; thou brought'st me into this.
ROGER I will not curse, but God forgive ye both,
For had I never known nor you nor her,
I had not come unto this shameful death.   *Exeunt*

Scene 18. London, a street, the scaffold

The Sheriff leads Browne to the scaffold in a crowd of onlookers, when they suddenly stop. The Sheriff reports that Browne's brother has also been arrested and convicted of murder and has permission to speak to Captain Browne. The brothers reunite, briefly comparing notes on their crimes and apprehension and so on. Captain Browne is offered one last chance to come clean and implicate Anne Sanders, and he weighs the pros and cons of doing so in an aside. Eventually deciding to keep the truth to himself about Anne's role in the plot, Browne delivers a long confession and then "leap[s] off" the scaffold to hang himself.

*Enter Master Browne to execution with Sheriff and Officers. [They
walk across the stage and stop.]*

BROWNE Why do you stay me, in the way of death?[494]
　　The people's eyes have fed them with my sight;
5　　The little babies in the mothers' arms
　　Have wept for those poor babies—seeing me—
　　That I by my murder have left fatherless—[495]
　　And shrieked and started when I came along
　　And sadly sighed, as when their nurses use
10　　To fright them with some monster when they cry.
SHERIFF You have a brother, Browne, that for a murder
　　Is lately here committed unto Newgate
　　And hath obtained he may speak with you.
BROWNE Have I a brother that hath done the like?
15　　Is there another Browne hath killed a Sanders?
　　It is my other self hath done the deed.
　　I am a thousand! Every murderer is my own self!
　　I am at one time in a thousand places
　　And I have slain a thousand Sanderses.
20　　In every shire, each city, and each town,
　　George Sanders still is murdered by George Browne!　*Browne's
　　　　brother is brought forth.*
BROWNE'S BROTHER Brother.
BROWNE Dost thou mean me?
　　Is there a man will call me brother?
25 BROWNE'S BROTHER Yes, I will call thee so, and may do it,
　　That have a hand as deep in blood as thou.
BROWNE Brother, I know thee well; of whence was thine?[496]
BROWNE'S BROTHER Of York he was.
BROWNE Sanders of London mine.
30　　Then see I well England's two greatest towns
　　Both filled with murders done by both the Brownes.
BROWNE'S BROTHER Then may I rightly challenge thee a brother.
　　Thou slewest one in the one, I one in th'other.

BROWNE When didst thou thine?

BROWNE'S BROTHER A month or five weeks past. 35

BROWNE Hardly to say then which was done the last.
　　Where shalt thou suffer?

BROWNE'S BROTHER Where I did the fact.⁴⁹⁷

BROWNE And I here, brother, where I laid my act.
　　Then I see well that be it near or further, 40
　　That heaven will still take due revenge on murder.

BROWNE'S BROTHER Brother, farewell. I see we both must die—
　　At London you this week, next at York, I.

BROWNE Two luckless brothers sent both at one hour,
　　The one from Newgate, th'other from the Tower. *Exit Brot[her].* 45

SHERIFF Browne, yet at last to satisfy the world,
　　And for a true and certain testimony
　　Of thy repentance for this deed committed,
　　Now at the hour of death, as thou dost hope
　　To have thy sins forgiven at God's hands, 50
　　Freely confess what yet unto this hour
　　Against thy conscience, Browne, thou hast concealed—
　　Anne Sanders's knowledge of her husband's death.

BROWNE Have I not made a covenant⁴⁹⁸ with her, *Aside*
　　That for the love that I ever bore to her 55
　　I will not sell her life by my confession?
　　And shall I now confess it? I am a villain.
　　I will never do it. Shall it be said Browne proved
　　A recreant? And yet I have a soul.⁴⁹⁹
　　Well, God the rest reveal: 60
　　I will confess my sins, but this conceal.
　　Upon my death, she's guiltless of the fact. [*to the Sheriff*]
　　Well, much ado I had to bring it out, *Aside*
　　My conscience scarce would let me utter it,
　　I am glad 'tis past. 65

SHERIFF But, Browne, it is confessed by Drurie's wife
　　That she is guilty, which doth fully prove
　　Thou hast no true contrition,⁵⁰⁰ but conceal'st

Her wickedness, the bawd unto her sin.

70 BROWNE Let her confess what she thinks good.

Trouble me no more, good master Sheriff.

SHERIFF Browne, thy soul knows.

BROWNE Yea, yea, it does. Pray you be quiet, sir.

Vile world, how like a monster come I soiled from thee![501]

    [addressing the theater audience]

75 How have I wallowed in thy loathsome filth,

Drunk and besmeared with all thy bestial[502] sin?

I never spoke of God, unless when I

Have blasphemed his name with monstrous oaths.

I never read the scriptures in my life,

80 But did esteem them worse than vanity;

I never came in Church where God was taught,

Nor ever to the comfort of my soul

Took benefit of Sacrament or Baptism.

The Sabbath days I spent in common stews,[503]

85 Unthrifty gaming,[504] and vile perjuries.[505]

I held no man once worthy to be spoke of

That went not in some strange disguised[506] attire,

Or had not fetched some vile monstrous fashion,

To bring in odious detestable pride.

90 I hated any man that did not do

Some damned or some hated filthy deed

That had been death for virtuous men to hear.

Of all the worst that live, I was the worst.

Of all the cursed, I the most accursed.

95 All careless men be warnéd by my end,

And by my fall your wicked lives amend.[507] *He leaps off [the*

    scaffold to hang himself].

Enter a Messenger.

MESSENGER It is the Council's pleasure, Master Sheriff,
    The body conveyed to Shooter's Hill,
    And there hung up in chains.[508]

SHERIFF It shall be done.

Scene 19. Newgate Prison, inside, and the street outside

Meanwhile, back inside the prison, Master James interrogates the Minister who is protecting Anne. (This is the first and only time we see this Minister.) James accuses him of collusion in trying to save Anne in hopes of marrying her. This situation is not developed in the play but was part of the records. James tells the Minister that he will be pilloried or set in the stocks as his punishment.

JAMES Why, then you are persuaded certainly
   That Mistress Sanders is mere innocent?[510]
5 MINISTER That I am, sir, even in my very soul.
   Compare but all the likelihoods thereof:[511]
   First, her most firm denial of the fact;
   Next, Mistress Drurie's flat confession,
   That only she and Roger did contrive
10 The death of Master Sanders. Then, yourself
   Cannot but be of mine opinion.
JAMES Then all you labor for,
   Is that I should procure her pardon?
MINISTER To save an innocent,
15 Is the most Christian work that man can do.
   Beside, if you perform it, sir, sound recompense,
   Shall quit[512] your pains so well employed herein.
JAMES Now let me tell ye that I am ashamed
   A man of your profession should appear
20 So far from grace and touch of conscience,
   As making no respect of his own soul,
   He should with such audaciousness presume
   To baffle Justice, and abuse the seat
   With your fond overweening[513] and sly fetch.[514]
25 Think you the world discerneth not your drift?[515]
   Do not I know that if you could prevail
   By this far-fetched insinuation,
   And Mistress Sanders's pardon thus obtained,
   That your intent is then to marry her?
30 And thus you have abused her poor soul
   In trusting to so weak and vain a hope.
   Well, sir, since you have so forgot yourself
   And—shameless—blush not at so bold offense,
   Upon their day of execution
35 And at the self-same place, upon a pillory[516]

There shall you stand, that all the world may see
  A just desert for such impiety.
MINISTER Good sir, hear me.
JAMES I will not hear thee. Come and get thee hence,
  For such a fault, too mean a recompense.[517]   *Exeunt*   40

Scene 20. A street outside Newgate Prison

This short scene between two old friends offers a workingman's view of the executions and sets the stage (literally) for the public spectacle that is to take place. From the perspective of the gallows maker, Tom Peart, we learn that all three of the remaining conspirators are meant to hang that day and that Smithfield is crowded (as the sources also report). This conversation lends a sort of mundane cast to the drama, as if it's "all in a day's work"; the men head off to a tavern for a beer while life and death decisions happen to their betters.

Enter two Carpenters[518] under Newgate [i.e., near the prison; Anne visible from a window[519]].

WILL Tom Peart, my old companion? Well met.

TOM Good morrow, Will Crow, good morrow, how dost?
5   I have not seen thee a great while.

WILL Well, I thank God; how dost thou? Where hast
thou been this morning so early?

TOM Faith, I have been up ever since three o'clock.

WILL About what, man?

10 TOM Why, to make work for the hangman. I and
another have been setting up a gallows.

WILL O, for Mistress Drurie; must she die today?

TOM Nay I know not that, but when she does, I am
sure there is a gallows big enough to hold them both.

15 WILL Both whom? Her man and her?

TOM Her man, and her, and Mistress Sanders, too. 'Tis a
swinger,[520] i'faith. But come, I'll give thee a pot[521] this
morning, for I promise thee I am passing dry after
my work.

20 WILL Content, Tom, and I have another for thee, and
afterward I'll go see the execution.

TOM Do as thou wilt for that.

WILL But dost thou think it will be today?

TOM I cannot tell; Smithfield is full of people, and
25   the Sheriff's man that set us a work told us it would
be today. But, come, shall we have this beer?[522]

WILL With a good will; lead the way. *Exeunt*

Scene 21. Newgate Prison, Anne Sanders's cell and outside

Anne has overheard the previous conversation through her prison window, which causes more urgent fears for her death. She calls for Drurie to visit her cell, and as the two women talk, Anne suddenly has a change of heart: "Even at this instant, I am strangely changed." The Doctor, a kind of spiritual counselor, arrives just then and she makes her confession. Anne's children are brought to her and she says goodbye to them, apologizes to her family, and bequeaths the children copies of a book of meditations or prayers. The Sheriff enters with Roger, guarded, and Anne kisses her children.

Enter Anne Sanders and her keeper following her.

KEEPER Called you, Mistress Sanders?

ANNE Keeper, I did.

5   I prithee fetch up Mistress Drurie to me.

       I have a great desire to talk with her.

KEEPER She shall be brought unto you presently.   *Exit*

       ANNE O, God, as I was standing at a grate   [*alone*]

       That looks into the street, I heard men talk—

10   The execution should be done today,

       And what pair of gallows were set up,

       Both strong and big enough to hold us all!—

       Which words have struck such terror to my soul

       As I cannot be quiet till I know

15   Whether Nan Drurie be resolved still

       To clear me of the murder as she promised.

       And here she comes. I prithee, gentle Keeper,   [*Enter Drurie*

          with Keeper.]

       Give us a little leave we may confer

       Of things that nearly do concern our souls.

20 KEEPER With all my heart; take time and scope[523] enough.   *Exit*

DRURIE Now, Mistress Sanders, what's your will with me?[524]

ANNE O, Mistress Drurie, now the hour is come

       To put your love unto the touch, to try

       If it be current or it be counterfeit.[525]

25   This day it is appointed we must die.

       How say you then—are you still purposed

       To take the murder upon yourself?

       Or will you now recant your former words?[526]

DRURIE Anne Sanders, Anne; 'tis time to turn the leaf,[527]

30   And leave dissembling.[528] Being so near my death,

       The like I would advise yourself to do.

       We have been both notorious vile transgressors,[529]

       And this is not the way to get remission,

       By joining sin to sin, nor doth't agree

With godly Christians but with reprobates,[530]   35
And such as have no taste of any grace.
And therefore (for my part) I'll clear my conscience
And make the truth apparent to the world.
ANNE Will you prove then inconstant to your friend?
DRURIE Should I, to purchase safety for another,   40
Or lengthen out another's temporal life,
Hazard mine own soul everlastingly,
And lose the endless joys of heaven,
Prepared for such as will confess their sins?
No, Mistress Sanders. Yet there's time of grace,   45
And yet we may obtain forgiveness,
If we will seek it at our Savior's hands.
But if we willfully shut up our hearts
Against the Holy Spirit that knocks for entrance,
It is not this world's punishment shall serve,   50
Nor death of body, but our souls shall live
In endless torments of unquenchéd fire.[531]
ANNE Your words amaze me, and although I'll vow
I never had intention to confess
My heinous sin that so I might escape   55
The world's reproach, yet God—I give him thanks—
Even at this instant, I am strangely changed
And will no longer drive repentance off,
Nor cloak my guiltiness before the world.
And in good time. See where the Doctor comes,[532]   60
By whom I have been seriously instructed.
DOCTOR Good morrow, Mistress Sanders, and soul's health
Unto you both. Prepare yourselves for death;
The hour is now at hand, and, Mistress Sanders,
At length acknowledge and confess your fault,   65
That God may be propitioner[533] to your soul.
ANNE Right reverend sir, not to delude the world,[534]
Nor longer to abuse your patience,
Here I confess I am a grievous sinner,

70 And have provoked the heavy wrath of God,
   Not only by consenting to the death
   Of my great husband, but by wicked lust
   And willful sin, denying of the fault.
   But now I do repent and hate myself,
75 Thinking the punishment prepared for me
   Not half severe enough for my deserts.[535]
   DOCTOR Done like a Christian and a child of grace:
   Pleading to God, to angels, and to men,
   And doubt not but your soul shall find a place
80 In Abraham's bosom,[536] though your body perish.
   And, Mistress Drurie, shrink not from your faith,
   But valiantly prepare to drink this cup
   Of sour affliction,[537] 'twill raise up to you
   A crown of glory in another world.
85 DRURIE Good Doctor, I am bound to you.
   My soul was ignorant, blind, and almost choked
   With this world's vanities, but, by your counsel,
   I am as well resolved to go to death
   As if I were invited to a banquet.
90 Nay such assurance have I in the blood
   Of him that died for me, as neither fire,
   Sword, nor torment could retain me from him.[538]
   DOCTOR Spoke like a champion of the Holy Cross.
   Now, Mistress Sanders, let me tell to you:
95 Your children, hearing this day was the last
   They should behold their mother on the earth,
   Are come to have your blessing ere you die,
   And take their sorrowful farewell of you.
   ANNE A sorrowful farewell 'twill be indeed
100 To them (poor wretches) whom I have deprived
   Of both the natural succors[539] of their youth.
   But call them in, and, gentle Keeper, bring me
   Those books that lie within my chamber window.
   Oh, master Doctor, were my breast transparent,

That what is figured[540] there, might be perceived,   105
Now should you see the very image of poor
And tottered ruins, and a slain conscience.
Here, here they come behind mine eyes with tears,
And soul and body now asunder part.
                                                                        110

[*The children enter.*]

ALL THE CHILDREN O, mother, mother.
ANNE O, my dear children!
    I am unworthy of the name of Mother.   115
ALL Turn not your face from us, but ere you die,
    Give us your blessing.[541]
ANNE Kneel not unto me.
    'Tis I that have deserved to kneel to you.
    My trespass hath bereft you of a father,   120
    A loving father, a kind, careful father,
    And by that self-same action, that foul deed
    Your mother likewise is to go from you,
    Leaving you (poor souls) by her offense,
    A corasie[542] and a scandal to the world.   125
    But could my husband and your father hear me,
    Thus humbly at his feet I would fall down
    And plentiful in tears bewail my fault.
    Mercy I ask of God, and him, and you,
    And of his kindred which I have abused,[543]   130
    And of my friends and kindred which I have abused,
    Of whom I am ashaméd and abashed,
    And of all men and women in the world,
    Whom by my foul example I have grieved.
    Though I deserve no pity at their hands,   135
    Yet I beseech them all to pardon me,
    And God I thank that hath found out my sin,
    And brought me to affliction[544] in this world,
    Thereby to save me in the world to come.

140 O, children, learn, learn by your mother's fall[545]
To follow virtue, and beware of sin,
Whose baits[546] are sweet and pleasing to the eye,
But being tainted, more infect than poison,
And are far bitterer than gall[547] itself.
145 And lived in days where you have wealth at will,
As once I had and are well matched beside.[548]
Content yourselves, and surfeit[549] not on pride.

Enter Sheriff, bringing in Trusty Roger with halberds.
150

SHERIFF What, Doctor, have you made an end?[550]
The morning is far spent; 'tis time to go.
DOCTOR Even when you will, Sheriff, we are ready.
ANNE Behold, my children, I will not bequeath
155 Or gold or silver to you; you are left
Sufficiently provided in that point,
But here I give each of you a book
Of holy meditations, *Bradford's Works*,[551]
That virtuous chosen servant of the Lord.
160 Therein you shall be richer than with gold,
Safer than in fair buildings, happier
Than all the pleasures of this world can make you.
Sleep not without them when you go to bed,
And rise a'mornings with them in your hands.
165 So God send down his blessing on you all:
Farewell, farewell, farewell, farewell, farewell.[552]

She kisses them one after another. [The children weep and cling to her.]

170 Nay, stay not to disturb me with your tears.
The time is come, sweethearts, and we must part.
That way go you; this way my heavy heart. [*Anne points to the
scaffold.*] *Exeunt*

132 *A Warning for Fair Women*

Epilogue

Tragedy closes the play in an epilogue, a device that Shakespeare uses, for example, in *A Midsummer Night's Dream* when Puck begs for applause. Her speech returns us to the opening fight among the three dramatic genres. Her claim that the play is a "true and home-borne Tragedy, / Yielding so slender argument and scope" is in part a rhetorical device like a poet's envoy or dedication—a pose of humility. At the same time, the line locates the plot at "home" in London and asserts its relatively small ("slender") scope as a new and legitimate tragic genre. Recall Tragedy's opening lament that the story was "too well known."

Tragedy enters to conclude.

TRAGEDY Here are the lances that have sluiced forth sin,[553]

5   *[She points to the tableau behind her on the scaffold, or perhaps to the*
black curtains that signify tragedy.]

And ripped the venomed ulcer of foul lust,
Which, being by due vengeance qualified,
Here, Tragedy of force must needs conclude.
10   Perhaps it may seem strange unto you all,
That one hath not revenged another's death[554]
After the observation of such course.
The reason is, that now of truth I sing,
And should I add, or else diminish aught,
15   Many of these spectators then could say,
I have committed error in my play.
Bear with this true and home-borne Tragedy,
Yielding so slender argument and scope,[555]
To build a matter of importance on,
20   And in such form[556] as haply[557] you expected.
What now hath failed, tomorrow you shall see,
Performed by History or Comedy.   *Exit*
FINIS

Appendix

Arthur Golding's *A briefe discourse of the late*
Murther of master George Sanders

Arthur Golding (1535/6–1606) attended Jesus College Cambridge
and is best known today for his verse translation from Latin of
Ovid's *Metamporhoses* (Golding published the first four books
in 1565 and the full fifteen books in 1567). Allusions to Golding's
Ovid appear in Edmund Spenser's *Faerie Queene*, Christopher
Marlowe's *Tamburlaine* and *Edward II*, and Shakespeare's *A
Midsummer Night's Dream* and *The Tempest* and other works. As
the editor of the entry on Golding in the *Oxford Dictionary of
National Biography* clarifies, though: "His work on Ovid is an
anomaly in Golding's career: all his other translations were of
religious or factual works."[1] Golding translated commentaries
on the New Testament and other work by Protestant writers,
including John Calvin's writings: *A Little Booke of John Calvines
Concernynge Offences* (1567), Calvin's commentaries on the Psalms
(1571), and his sermons on Job and Galatians (1574), Ephesians
(1577), and Deuteronomy (1583). Other major secular translations
include Seneca's *De beneficiis* (1578) and Caesar's "Commentaries."
Along with the account of the murder of George Sanders (1573),
he published only one other original book, which was another
moral news story, "Discourse upon the Earthquake that hapned
throughe this realme of England and other places of Christendom,
the first of April 1580," published both by itself and also "as an
appendix to a special prayer, occasioned by the earthquake, which
was circulated in 1580 for use in all parish churches," according
to John Considine. Golding had influential patrons and dedi-
catees, among them Sir William Cecil, Sir Christopher Hatton,

the Earls of Leicester and Essex, and Sir William Mildmay; Sir Philip Sidney was his friend. With his wife Ursula he had four daughters and four sons; he inherited property and spent time in debtors' prison, too. Golding enjoyed renown and his contemporaries regarded his work highly. (From Arthur Golding, *A briefe discourse of the late Murther of master George Sanders, a worshipful citizen of London and of the apprehension, arreignement, and execution of the principall and accessaries of the same. Seene and allowed.* London: Henrie Bynnyman, 1577.)

Forasmuch as the late murder of Master Saunders, Citizen and Merchant tailor of this city ministered great occasion of talk among all sorts of men, not only here in the town, but also far abroad in the country, and generally through the whole realm, and the sequels and accidents ensuing thereupon, breed much diversity of reports and opinions, while some do justly detest the horribleness of the ungracious fact, some lament the grievous loss of their dear friends; some rejoice the commendable execution of upright justice; the godly bewail the immeasurable inclination of human nature to extreme wickedness, and therewith magnify God's infinite mercy in revoking of forlorn sinners to final repentance; many to hear and tell news, without respect of the certainty of the truth or regard of due humanity, every man debating the matter as occasion or affection leadeth him, and few folk turning the advised consideration of God's open judgments to the speedy reformation of their own secret faults, it is thought convenient (gentle reader) to give thee a plain declaration of the whole matter, according as the same is come to light by open trial of Justice and voluntary confession of the parties, that thou mayest know the truth to the satisfying of thy mind, and the avoiding of discredit, and also use the example to the amendment of thy life.[2]

Notwithstanding, thou shalt not look for a full discovery of every particular by-matter appendant[3] to the present case, which might serve to feed the fond humor of such curious appetites as are more inquisitive of other folks' offences than hasty to redress their own, for that were neither expedient nor necessary. And men's misdoings are to be prosecuted no further with open detestation than till the parties be either reclaimed by reasonable and godly persuasion or punished by orderly and lawful execution, according to the quality of their offence. When law has once passed upon them and given them the wages of their wicked deserts, then Christian charity wills men either to bury the faults with the offenders in perpetual silence or else so to speak of them as the vices and not the parties themselves may seem to be any more touched.[4]

But hereof shall more be spoken (God willing) in the winding up of this matter. Now I will set down, first the murdering of Master Saunders by George Browne with Browne's apprehension, trial and execution; then, the trial and execution of Anne Saunders, the wife of the said George Saunders, of Anne Drurie, Widow, and of Roger Clement, called among them Trusty Roger, the servant of the said Anne Drurie; and lastly, a brief rehearsal of certain sayings and dealings of the parties convicted, between the time of their apprehensions and the time of their execution, which are not things proper and peculiar to the very body of the case, but yet incident, and therefore necessary for the hearer, as whereby will appear the very original cause, and first ground of this ungodly deed; and this rehearsal shall be shut up and concluded with a short admonition [about] how we ought to deal in this and all other such cases.

The Tuesday in Easter week last past (which was the 23rd day of March [1573]) the said George Browne, receiving secret intelligence by letter from Mistress Drurie that Master Saunders should lodge the same night at the house of one Master Barnes in Woolwich and from thence go on foot to Saint Mary Cray the next morning, met him by the way a little from Shooter's Hill, between seven and eight of the clock in the forenoon, and there slew both him, and also one John Beane, the servant of the said Master Barnes.

As soon as Master Saunders felt himself to have his death's wound (for he was stricken quite and clean through at the first blow) he kneeled down, and lifting up his hands and eyes unto heaven, said, "God have mercy on me, and forgive me my sins, and thee too" (speaking to Browne, whom indeed he knew not—whatsoever report hath been made of old acquaintance betwixt them[5]), and with that word he gave up the Ghost. And Browne (as he himself confessed afterward) was thereat stricken with such a terror and agony of heart, as he [knew] not what to do, but was at the point to have fainted even then and oftentimes else that day, and could brook neither meat nor drink that he received of all that day after. He was so abashed afterward at the sight of one of Master Saunders's little young children, as he had much ado to forbear from swooning in the street, a notable example of the secret working of God's terrible wrath in a guilty and bloody conscience. But Master Barnes's man having ten or eleven deadly wounds, and being left for dead, did by God's wonderful Providence revive again, and creeping a great way on all four[s] (for he could neither go nor stand), was found by an old man and his maiden[6] that went that way to seek their kine,[7] and conveyed to Woolwich, where he gave evident tokens and marks of the murderer,[8] and so continuing still alive till he had been apprehended and brought unto him, died the next Monday after. Immediately upon the deed doing, Browne sent Mistress Drurie word thereof by Trusty Roger; he himself repaired forthwith to the Court at Greenwich, and anon[9] after him came thither the report of the murder also. Then departed he thence unto London straight away and came to the house of Mistress Drurie, howbeit[10] he spoke not personally with her. But after conference had with him, by her servant Roger, she provided him twenty pounds the same day, for the which Mistress Drurie laid certain plate of her own and of Mistress Saunders to gauge.[11] And upon the next day being Thursday morning (having in the meantime had intelligence that Browne was sought for), they sent him six pounds more by the said Roger, and warned him to shift for himself by flight, which he forslowed not[12] to do. Nevertheless, the Lords of the Queen's Majesty's Council caused so speedy and narrow search to be made for him in all places that upon the 28th of the same month he was apprehended in a man's house his own name at Rochester[13] by the Mayor of the town; and being brought back again to the Court, was examined by the Council, unto whom he confessed the deed, as you have heard, and that he had often times before pretended and sought to do the same, by the instigation of the said Widow Drurie, who (as he says) had promised to make a marriage[14] between him and Mistress Saunders, (whom he seemed to love excessively), the desire of which hope hastened him forward to dispatch the fact. Nevertheless, he protested (however untruly) that Mistress Saunders was not privy nor consenting thereunto. Upon this confession, he was arraigned at the King's Bench in Westminster Hall[15] on Friday the 17th of April, where, acknowledging himself guilty, he was condemned as principal of the murder of Master Saunders, according to which sentence he was executed in Smithfield Monday the 20th of the same month, at which time (though untruly, as she herself confessed afterward), he laboured by all means to clear Mistress Saunders of committing evil of her body with him, and afterward was hanged up in chains near unto the place where he had done the fact.

Thus much concerning the very case of the murder itself, and the punishment of the principal doer thereof. As for the acknowledgement of the former wickedness of his life, and the hearty repentance that he pretended for the same, even to his very death, I defer them to the last part of this matter, to which place those things do more peculiarly pertain. In the meantime, Mistress Drurie and her man being examined, and as well by their own confessions as by the falling out of the matter in consequence, and also by Browne's appeachment,[16] thought culpable, were committed to ward.[17] And anon after Mistress Saunders being delivered of child & churched (for at the time o' her husband's death she looked presently to lie down)[18] was, upon Mistress Drurie's man's confession and upon other great likelihood and presumptions, likewise committed to ward, and on Wednesday, the 6th[19] of May, arraigned with Mistress Drurie at the Guildhall, the effect of whose several indictments is this: That they had by a letter written been procurers of the said murder, and so accessories before the fact, and knowing the murder done, had by money and otherwise relieved and been aiding to the murderer, and so accessories also after the fact. Whereunto they both of them pleaded not guilty. And Mistress Saunders, notwithstanding the avouchment[20] of Mistress Drurie's man face to face, and the great probabilities of the evidence given in against her by Master Geoffrey, the Queen's Majesty's Sergeant, stood so stoutly still to the denial of all things (in which stout denial she continued also a certain time after her condemnation) that some were brought in a blind belief that either she was not guilty at all, or else had but brought herself in danger of law through ignorance, and not through pretenced[21] malice. Howbeit forasmuch as bare denial is no sufficient bar to discharge manifest matter and apparent evidence, they were both condemned as accessories to Master Saunders's death, and executed in Smithfield the 13th of May, being the Wednesday in the Whitson week,[22] at which time they both of them, confessed themselves guilty of the fact, for which they were condemned, and with very great repentance and meekness, received the reward of their trespass in the presence of many personages of honour and worship and of so great a number of people as the like hath not been seen there together in any man's remembrance. For almost the whole field and all the way from Newgate was as full of folk as could well stand one by another, and besides that, great companies were placed both in the chambers near about (whose windows & walls were in many places beaten down to look out at) and also upon the gutters, sides, and tops of the houses and upon the battlements and steeple of St. Bartholomew's.

Mistress Drurie's man was arraigned at Newgate on Friday the 7th of May, and being there condemned as accessory, was executed with his mistress, at the time and place aforesaid.

Thus have ye heard the murdering of Master Saunders, with the apprehension, arraignment, condemnation, and execution of the principal and of the accessories to the same; now let us proceed to the incidents that happened from the times of their apprehensions to the time of their deaths, and so to the admonition,[23] which is the conclusion and fruit of this whole matter.

Whereas it was determined that Mistress Saunders & Mistress Drurie should have suffered upon the next Saturday after their condemnation, which was Whitsun even,[24] the matter was stayed till the Wednesday in Whitsun week, upon these occasions ensuing.[25] The book of Master Saunders's accounts and reckonings, whereupon depended the knowledge of his whole estate, was missing. Certain sums of money were said to be in the hands of parties unknown, the intelligence whereof was desired and sought for to the behoof[26] of Master Saunders's children. The parties convicted were to be reformed to Godward, and to be brought to the willing confessing of the things for which they had been justly condemned, and which as yet they obstinately concealed. And besides all this, one Mell, a minister that had heretofore been from her condemnation to Newgate, and conferring with her, as it suspended[27] from his ministry, accompanying Mistress Saunders, had been to give her good counsel and comfort, was so blinded with her solemn asseverations and protestations of innocence, that notwithstanding he had heard her indictment, with the exact and substantial trial of her case: yet notwithstanding, he persuaded himself that she was utterly clear, and thereupon falling in love with her, dealt with Mistress Drurie to take the whole guilt upon herself, undertaking to sue for Mistress Saunders's pardon. And so, what by his terrifying of her with the horror of mischarging and casting away of an innocent, what with his promising of certain money to the marriage of her daughter, and with other persuasions, she was so wholly won that way, that as well before certain personages of honour, as also before the Dean of St. Paul's & others, she utterly cleared Mistress Saunders of the fact, or of consent to the same, taking the whole blame thereof to herself, and protesting to stand therein to the death, contrary to her former confession at the time of her arraignment.

Mistress Saunders also, after the laying of this plate, stood so stoutly to her tackling,[28] that when the Dean of Paul's gave her godly exhortation for the clearing of her conscience, and for the reconciling of herself unto God, as the time and case most needfully required (as other had done before), he could obtain nothing at her hand.[29] By means whereof, he was fain to leave her that time, which was the Friday, not without great grief and indignation of mind to see her stubborn unrepentedness. In the meanwhile, the said Mell, discovering his purpose and whole platform to an honest Gentleman, whom he unskillfully took to have been a well-willer[30] to obtain the pardon [for] Mistress Saunders, was partly by that means, and also by other follies of his own, cut off from his enterprise. For when he came to sue for her pardon, which thing he did with such outrage of doting affection that he not only proffered sums of money, but also offered his own body and life for the safety of the woman, whom he protested, upon his conscience, to be unguilty. The Lords of the Council, knowing her to be rightly condemned by good justice, and being privy to the state of the case beforehand, and also finding him out by his own unwise dealings (whereof among the other one was, that he intended to marry her) not only frustrated his desire, but also adjudged him to stand upon the pillory, with apparent notes and significations of his lewd and foolish demeanor. According to the which appointment, be was set upon a pillory by the place of execution at the time of their suffering, with a paper pinned upon his breast, wherein were written certain words in great letters containing the effect of his fact, to his open shame: *videlicet*,[31] "For practicing to color the detestable fact of George Saunders wife," which was a very good lesson to teach all persons to refrain from any devices or practices to deface or discredit the honourable proceedings of counselors and public and lawful form of trials and judgments according to Justice, or to hinder the beneficial course of so good examples.[32]

By this occasion Mistress Sanders was utterly unprovided to die at that time,[33] and therefore as well in respect of mercy, as for the considerations aforesaid, a further respite was given to them, unwitting, and a reprieve was sent by M[aster] MacWilliams for a time if need were. In the meantime, (that is, to wit, upon the Saturday morning), the constant report goeth, that as certain men came talking through Newgate, one happened to speak aloud of the gallows that was set up and of the greatness and strongness of the same, saying it would hold them both and more, the sound of which words did so pierce into the watchful ears of Mistress Saunders, who lay near hand, that being stricken to the heart with the horror of the present death which she looked for that day, she went immediately to Mistress Drurie, and telling her that she knew certainly by the words which she had heard, that they should by all likelihood be executed that day, asked her if she would stand to her former promise. But Mistress Drurie after better consideration of herself, counseling her to fall to plain and simple dealing, telling her, that for her own part she was fully determined not to dissemble any longer, nor to hazard her own soul eternally for the safety of another body's temporal life. Then Mistress Saunders, who had determined to acknowledge nothing against herself, so long as she might be in any hope of life; howbeit that she always purposed to utter the truth, whensoever she should come to the instant of death, as she herself confessed afterward; being stricken both with fear and remorse, did by the advice of Master Cole, (who laboured very earnestly with her to bring her to repentance, and was come to her very early that morning, because it was thought they should have been executed presently), send for the Dean of Paul's again, and bewailing her former stubbornness, declared unto him and Master Cole, Master Clark, and Master Yong,[34] that she had given her consent and procurement to her husband's death, through unlawful lust and liking that she had to Browne, confessing her sinfulness of life committed with him, and humbly submitting herself to her deserved punishment, besought them of spiritual comfort and counsel, which thing they were glad to perceive, and thereupon employed their travail to do them good, and laboured very painfully to instruct them aright, for (God wot[35]) they found all the three prisoners very raw and ignorant in all things pertaining to God and to their souls' health, yea, and even in the very principles of the Christen religion. Nevertheless, through God's good working with their labour, they recovered them out of Satan's kingdom unto Christ, insomuch that, besides their voluntary acknowledging of their late heinous fact, they also detested the former sinfulness of their life, and willingly yielded to the death which they had shunned, uttering such certain tokens of their unfained[36] repentance, by all kind of modesty and meekness, as no greater could be devised. For Mistress Saunders the same day sent for her husband's brothers and their wives and kinsfolk that were in the town, which came unto her the day before her death, in whose presence she, kneeling mildly on her knees, with abundance of sorrowful tears desired of them forgiveness for bereaving them of their dear brother and friend, whereunto Master Saunders, the Lawyer, in the name of them all, answered that as they were very sorry both for the loss of their friend, and also for her heinous fault, so they heartily forgave her, and, in token thereof, kneeled down altogether, praying to God with her and for her, that he also would remit her sin.

Besides this pitiful submission, she also bewailed her offence toward her own kindred, whom she had stained by her trespass, and toward the whole world, whom she had offended by her crime, but especially her children, whom she had not only bereft both of father and mother, but also left them a coarsie[37] and shame. Wherefore, after exhortation given to such of them as were of any capacity and discretion, that they should fear God and learn by her fall to avoid sin, she gave each of those a book of Master Bradford's meditations, wherein she desired the foresaid three preachers to write some admonition as they thought good.[38] Which done, she subscribed them with these words, "Your sorrowful mother Anne Saunders"; and so blessing them in the name of God and of our Savior Jesus Christ, she sent them away out of her sorrowful sight and gave herself wholly to the settling of her grieved heart, to the quiet receiving of the bitter cup,[39] which she drank of the next day, as hath been told before. Howbeit, without doubt, to her everlasting comfort.

And Mistress Drurie, no less careful of her own state, besides her humble repentance in the prison, and her earnest desiring of the people to pray for herself, and the others with her as they came toward execution, did upon the cart[40] not only confess her guiltiness of the fact, as Mistress Saunders had done, but also with great lowliness and reverence, first kneeling down toward the Earl of Bedford and other noble men that were on horseback on the east side of the stage,[41] took it upon her death that whereas it had been reported of her that she had poisoned her late husband, Master Drurie, and dealt with witchcraft and sorcery, and also appeached divers[e] merchants men's wives of dissolute and unchaste living, she had done none of those things, but was utterly clear both to God and the world of all such manner of dealing. And then with like obeisance, turning herself to the Earl of Derby, who was in a chamber behind her, she protested unto him before God that whereas she had been reported to have been the cause of separation betwixt him and my Lady his wife; she [Drurie] neither procured nor consented to any such thing. But otherwise, whereas in the time of her service in his house, she had offended him, in neglecting or contemning her duty, she acknowledged her fault and besought him for God's sake to forgive her, who very honourably, and even with tears, accepted her submission, and openly protested himself to pray heartily to God for her.

Her servant also, having openly acknowledged his offence, kneeled meekly down, praying severally with a preacher, as each of them had done at their first coming to the place. Which done they were all put in a readiness by the Executioner, and at one instant (by drawing away the cart whereon they stood) were sent together out of this world unto God.

And Browne also, a good while afore, during the time of his imprisonment, coming to a better mind than he had been of in time past, confessed that he had not heretofore frequented sermons, nor received the holy sacrament, nor used any calling upon God private or public, nor given himself to reading of holy Scripture, or any book of godliness, but had altogether followed the appetites and lusts of his sinful flesh, even with greediness and outrageous contempt both of God and man. Nevertheless, God was so good unto him, and schooled him so well in that short time of imprisonment, as he closed up his life with a marvelous appearance of hearty repentance, constant trust in God's mercy through Jesus Christ, and willingness to forsake this miserable world.

Now remaineth to show what is to be gathered of this terrible example, and how we ought to apply the same to our own behoof.[42] First I note with St. Paul that when men regard not to know God or not to honour him when they know him, God giveth them over to their own lusts, so as they run on from sin to sin, and from mischief to mischief, to do such things as are shameful and odious, even in the sight of the world, to their own unavoidable perils. And when the measure of their iniquity is filled up, there is no way for them to escape the justice of God, which they have provoked.[43] Insomuch that if they might eschew all bodily punishment, yet the very hell of their own conscience would prosecute them, and the sting of their mind would be a continual prison, torment, and torture to them, wheresoever they went. Again on the other side we must mark the infinite greatness of God's wisdom and mercy, who perceiving the perverse willfulness of man's forward nature to sinning, suffereth men sometimes to run so long upon the bridle[44] till it seem to themselves that they may safely do what they list, and to the world, that they be past recovery unto goodness; and yet in the end catching them in their chief pride, he raiseth them by their overthrow, amendeth them by their wickedness, and reviveth them by their death, in such wise blotting out the stain of their former filth, that their darkness is turned into light, and their terror to their comfort. Moreover, when God bringeth such matters upon the stage unto ye open face of the world, it is not to the intent that men should gaze and wonder at the persons, as birds do at an owl, not that they should delight themselves & others with the fond and peradventure[45] sinister reporting of them, nor upbraid the whole stock and kindred with the fault of the offenders. No. Surely, God mean-est no such thing. His purpose is that the execution of his judgments should by the terror of the outward sight of the example drive us to the inward consideration of ourselves. Behold, we be all made of the same mold, printed with the same stamp, and endued with the same nature that the offenders are. We be the imps of the old Adam and the venom of sin which he received from the old serpent, is shed into us all, and worketh effectually in us all.[46] Such as the root is, such are the branches, and the twigs of a thorn or bramble can bear no grapes. That we stand it is the benefit of God's grace, and not the goodness of our nature, nor the strength of our own will. That they are fallen, it was of frailty, wherefrom we be no more privileged than they, and that should we oversoon[47] perceive by experience, if we were left to ourselves. He that looketh severely into other men's faults is lightly blind in his own, and he that either upbraideth the repentant that hath received punishment or reproacheth the kindred or offspring with the fault of the ancestor or ally how great so ever the same hath been, showeth himself not to have any remorse of his own sins, nor to remember that he himself also is a man, but (which thing he would little think) he fully matcheth the crime of the mis-doer,[48] if he do not surmount it by his presumptuousness.

When it was told our Savior Christ that Pilate had mingled the blood of certain men with their own sacrifice, what answer made he? Did he [Christ] detest the offenders? Did he declaim against their doings? Did he exaggerate the fault of the one, or the cruelty of the other? No. But framing and applying the example to the reformation of the hearer, "suppose ye" (said he) "that those Galileans were greater sinners than all the other Galileans, because they suffered such punishment? I tell you, 'Nay, but except ye repent ye shall all likewise perish.' Or think ye that those eighteen upon whom the tower in Silo fell, and slew them, were sinners above all yet dwelt in Jerusalem? I tell you, 'Nay, but except ye repent, ye shall perish likewise.'"[49] Let us apply this to our present purpose. Were those whom we saw justly executed in Smithfield greater sinners than all other English people? Were they greater sinners than all Londoners? Were they greater sinners than all that looked upon them? No verily, but except their example lead us to repentance, we shall all of us come to as sore punishment in this world, or else to sorer in the world to come. Their faults came into the open theatre & therefore seemed the greater to our eyes, and surely they were great in deed; neither are ours the less, because they lie hidden in the covert of our heart. God, the searcher of all secrets, seeth them, and if he list,[50] he can also discover them. He hath showed in some what all of us deserve, to provoke us all to repentance, that all of us might have mercy at his hand, and show mercy one to another & with one mouth, and one heart glorify his goodness. It is said by the Prophet Samuel that disobedience is as the sin of witchcraft.[51] Let every of us look into himself (but first let him put on the spectacles of God's law and carry the light of God's word with him) and he shall see such a gulf of disobedience in himself, as he may well think there is none offender but himself. I say not this as a cloaker[52] of offences, that white should not be called white, & black black, or as a patron of mis-doers, that they should not have their deserved hire,[53] but to repress our hasty judgments and uncharitable speeches that we might both detest wickedness with perfect hatred and rue the persons with Christian modesty, knowing that with what measure we mete unto others, with the same shall it be moten to us again.[54]

Finally, let all folks both married and unmarried, learn hereby to possess & keep their vessel in honesty and cleanness. For if the knot between man and wife (which ought to be inseparable) be once broken, it is seldom or never knit again. And though it be, yet is not the wound so thoroughly healed, but there appeareth some scar ever after. But if the sore rankle & fester inwardly (as commonly it doth except the more grace of God be), in the end it bursteth forth to the destruction or hurt of both parties, not lightly without great harm to others also besides themselves, as we see by this example. For when the body which was dedicated to God to be his temple and the tabernacle of his holy spirit is become the sink of sin & cage of uncleanness, the devil ceaseth not to drive the parties still headlong unto naughtiness, till they be fallen either into open shame and danger of temporal law or into damnable destruction both of body and soul, according as Solomon in his Proverbs saith, that the steps of a harlot lead down unto death, and her feet pierce even unto hell.[55] Therefore, good reader, so hear and read this present example as the same may turn to the bettering of thy state, and not to occasion of slander, nor to the hurt of thine own conscience, nor to the offence of thy Christian brethren. Fare well.

Anne Saunders's confession as she spoke it at the place of execution.[56]

Good people, I am come hither to die the death, whereunto I am adjudged as worthily & as deservedly as ever died any. I had a good husband, by whom I had many children, with whom I lived in wealth & might have done still, had not the devil kindled in my heart, first the hellish firebrand of unlawful lust & afterward a murderous intent to procure my said husband to be bereaved of his life, which was also by my wicked means accomplished, as to the world is known. And as I would if he could hear me, if it might be, prostrate upon the ground at my husband's feet, ask mercy with plentiful tears of him, so that which I may & I ought to do, I ask mercy of God, I ask mercy of all men and women, of the world, whom by my deed & example I have offended, and especially I bewail my husband and ask mercy of my children, whom I have bred of so good a father. I ask mercy of his kindred and friends whom I have hurt & of all my friends & kindred of whom I am abashed and ashamed as being of myself unworthy of pity. Yet I beseech them all & you all & all the whole world of the same, even for God's sake, and for our Savior Christ's sake. And I thank God with my whole heart, he hath not suffered me to have the reign and bridle of sinning given me at my will, to the danger of my eternal damnation, but that he hath found out my sin, and brought me to punishment in this world, by his fatherly correction, to amend, to spare, and save me in the world to come; & I beseech him grant me his heavenly grace, that all who do behold or shall hear of my death, may by the example thereof be frayed[57] from like sinning. And I beseech you all to pray for me and with me.

THE PRAYER

which was said by Anne Saunders at the place of execution, the copy whereof, she delivered unto the right honourable the Earl of Bedford.

As I do confess with great sorrow (O dear Father) that I have grievously, and oftentimes sinned against heaven and against thee, & am unworthy to be called thy daughter, so (O dear Father) I acknowledge thy mercy, thy grace & love toward me, most wretched sinner, offered me in my Lord & savior Jesus Christ, in whom thou givest me an heart to repent. And by repentance hast put away my sins and thrown them into the bottom of the Sea. O dear Father, increase and continue this grace until the end, and in the end. I testify this day (O Lord my God) thy love, O Lord, thy saving health is life everlasting, and joy without end; and because thou hast touched my sinful heart with the displeasure of my sin, and with a desire of thy kingdom, O dear Father, for thy Christ's sake, as I hope thou wilt, so I beseech thee to finish that good work in me. Suffer me not, merciful & loving Father, to be troubled with death when it layeth hold on me, nor with the love of life when it shall be taken away. O Lord, now as thou hast, so still lift up my soul as it were with an eagle's wings unto Heaven, there to behold thee. Lord, into thy hands I commit my body, that it be not troubled in death, and my soul that it see not damnation. Come Lord Jesu, come assist me with thy holy Spirit, a weak woman in a strong battle. Come Lord Jesu, come quickly; save thy handmaid that putteth her trust in thee, behold me in Christ, receive me in Christ, in whose name I pray, saying, Our Father &c.

Anne Saunders dying to the world and living to God. After this she also said a godly Prayer out of the Service book which is used to be said at the hour of death.[58]

A NOTE OF A CERTAIN SAYING

which Master Saunders had left written with his own hand in his study.

Christ shall be magnified in my body whither it be through life or else death. For Christ is to me life, death is to me advantage. These words were Mr. Newel's theme, which he preached at the burial of my brother Haddon upon Thursday being the xxv [twenty-fifth] day of January Anno do. [anno domani, or AD] 1570, Anno Reginae Elizabeth 13.[59] Among other things which he preached this saying of his is to be had always in remembrance, that is, that we must all (when we come to pray) first accuse and condemn ourselves for our sins committed against God before the seat of his Justice, and then after cleave unto him by faith in the mercy and merits of our Savior & Redeemer Jesus Christ whereby we are assured of eternal salvation.

John Stow, *The Annales of England Faithfully*
Collected out of the Most Authenticall Authors,
Records, and Other Monuments of Antiquitie
John Stow or Stowe (1524/5–1605), a self-taught historian and lifelong Londoner, was the only nonelite member of the Society of Antiquaries (founded in 1586). He was a member of the

Merchant Taylors' Guild; an intrepid collector of manuscript chronicles, charters, ecclesiastical and municipal records, wills, literary works, and treatises; and a prolific writer. Among his own publications that were often reprinted and continue to be cited are long histories: *Chronicles of England* (1580) and *Annales of England* (1592), which covered Roman times up to Stow's own lifetime under the newly crowned King James I. Stow also published an edition of Chaucer's works (1561), and he edited a multivolume collection of John Skelton's works (1568). The story of the Sanders's murder is one of the entries in *Annales*. Stow's most famous work, *A Survey of London* (1598, 1603), is a topographical survey of London and its suburbs that draws on primary sources such as public and civic records, secondary materials from contemporary, classical, and medieval historical literature, and Stow's own experience and personal knowledge of his city. Stow also contributed to Holinshed's second edition of *Chronicles*. Stow was married to a woman named Elizabeth (last name unknown) and had three daughters. Some unfounded accusations of Catholic sympathies swirled around Stow, but as Barrett L. Beer shows, "Throughout his long life Stow detached himself from religious controversy and had a generally tolerant attitude for the age in which he lived."[60] (From John Stow, *The Annales of England Faithfully Collected out of the Most Authenticall Authors, Records, and Other Monuments of Antiquitie*. Vol. 1. London: Ralfe Newbery, 1592.)

The 25th of March being Wednesday in Easter week, and the Feast of the Annunciation of our Lady, George Browne cruelly murdered two honest men near unto Shooter's Hill in Kent; the one of them was a wealthy merchant of London named George Sanders,[61] the other John Beane of Woolwich, which murder was committed in manner as followeth.

On Tuesday in Easter week (the 24th of March) the said George Browne receiving secret intelligence by letter from Mistress Anne Drurie that Master Sanders should lodge the same night at the house of one Master Barnes in Woolwich, and from thence go on foot to St. Mary Cray the next morning, lay in wait for him by the way, a little from Shooter's Hill, and there slew both him and John Beane, servant to Master Barnes, but John Beane having ten or eleven wounds, and being left for dead, by God's Providence revived again, and creeping away on all fours, was found by an old man and his maiden and conveyed to Woolwich, where he gave evident marks of the murderer.

Immediately upon the deed doing, Browne sent Mistress Drurie word thereof by Roger Clement (among them called Trusty Roger); he himself repaired forthwith to the court at Greenwich, and anon after him came thither the report of the murder also. Then departed he thence unto London, and came to the house of Mistress Drurie, where, though he spoke not personally with her, after conference had with her servant, Trusty Roger, she provided him twenty pounds that same day, for the which she laid certain plate of her own and of Mistress Sanders to gauge. On the next morrow being Thursday (having intelligence, that Browne was sought for) they sent him six pounds more by the same Roger, warning him to shift for himself by flight, which thing he foreslowed not to do: nevertheless, the lords of the Queen's Majesty's Council[62] caused speedy and narrow search to be made for him, that upon the 28th of the same month, he was apprehended in a man's house of his own name at Rochester, and being brought back again to the court, was examined by the Council, to whom he confessed the deed as you have heard, and that he had often times before pretended and sought to do the same, by the instigation of the said Mistress Drurie, who had promised to make a marriage between him and Mistress Sanders (whom he seemed to love excessively). Nevertheless, he protested (though untruly) that Mistress Sanders was not privy nor consenting thereunto. Upon his confession, he was arraigned at the King's Bench in Westminster Hall the 18th of April, where he acknowledged himself guilty, and was condemned as principal of the murder, according to which sentence, he was executed in Smithfield on Monday the 20th of April, at which time also untruly (as she herself confessed afterward), he laboured by all means to clear Mistress Sanders of committing evil of her body with him, and he flung himself besides the ladder; he was after hanged up in chains near unto the place where he had done the fact.

In the meantime, Mistress Drurie and her man being examined, as well by their own confessions, as by falling out of the matter (and also by Browne's appeachment thought culpable) were committed to ward. And after Mistress Sanders being delivered of child, and churched (for at the time of her husband's death she looked presently to lie down) was upon Mistress Drurie's man's confession and other great likelihoods, likewise committed to the Tower [of London], and on Wednesday the sixth of May arraigned with Mistress Drurie at the Guild Hall, the effect of whose indictment was, that they, by a letter written, had been procurers of the said murder, and knowing the murder done, had by money and otherwise relieved the murderer, whereunto they pleaded not guilty; howbeit, they were both condemned as accessories to Master Sanders's death, and executed in Smithfield the thirteenth of May, being Wednesday in Whitsun Week, at which time they both confessed themselves guilty of the fact. Trusty Roger, Mistress Drurie's man, was arraigned on Friday the 8th of May, and being there condemned as accessory, was executed with his mistress at the time and place aforesaid. Not long after, Anthony Browne, brother to the forenamed George Browne, was for notable felonies conveyed from Newgate to York, and there hanged.[63]

A Ballad in the Voice of Anne Sanders

Rollins transcribed the manuscript, breaking it into numbered stanzas. I retain that format. (From "The woeful lamentacon of Mrs. Anne Saunders, which she wrote with her own hand, being prisoner in Newgate, justly condemned to death." Sloane MS 1898, fols. 8–11. Reprinted in *Old English Ballads, 1553–1625, Chiefly from Manuscripts*, edited by Hyder Edward Rollins, 340–48. Cambridge: Cambridge University Press, 1920.)

I lament, I repent, I believe, I rejoice,
I trust in the lord Christ; he will hear my voice.
[I]

O high and mighty God,
which reignst the skies above,
with watered eyes I much commend
thy Providence and love.
With woeful broken heart,
with swollen and blubbered face,
I wail my wanton life long spent,
which had no better grace.
[2]
I make my moan to thee,
with sighs and sobbing tears;
In what distress and heavy case,
my conscience witness bears.
Deprived of worldly joy,
which late I had at ease,
Deprived of wealth and clad with care,
which sought not thee to please.
[3]
Deprived of pleasures great,
bewrapped[64] in grief and pain,
And all through sin, which thus to mourn,
Dear God, doth me constrain.
My babes and children dear,
can heart of mine but sob
To lose them thus—O gripping[65] grief—
can entrails[66] cease to throb!
[4]
Alack, I cannot stay,
mine eyes will not bide dry,[67]
To think what sin hath brought me to—
out on me, wretch—fie, fie![68]
Let tender mothers judge
and gush out tears with me,
Whenas they weigh my inward doubt
and eke[69] my anguish see.

[5]

For naught beside my fact,[70]
I more lament than they;
God send them better grace to live
and not to walk my way.
For wealth did prick me so,
being well and could not see,
O sweetest God, I say thou knowest
this is performed in me.

[6]

And righteous is thy rod,
a plague procuréd long;
And those that warned me of my fault,
I thought they did me wrong.
I linked myself in love
to hateful bitter bale,[71]
Through which my bark is overturned
with quite contrary gale.[72]

[7]

Anne Drurie, woe to thee,
which drew[73] me to decay!
And woe the time I loved thy lure,
woe me and well away!
Woe worth thy false intent,
woe worth thy bloody mind,
And woe thy flattering words which made
my doting heart so blind!

[8]

And, Roger, woe to thee,
in whom it was to stay[74]
Browne's hands from slaughter of my dear
and us from this decay!
Take heed, all honest dames,
what servants ye retain,
For if thou, Roger, hadst feared God,

we had not felt this pain.

[9]

O righteous God, thou knowest
their counsel[75] wrought me ill;
And yet, Anne Saunders, woe to thee
that leanest so much theretill![76]
My husband to betray (a grief to say or think),
And justly weighed as I have brewed
this bitter draft to drink.

[10]

Behold, all honest wives,
and finest London dames,
Bear to your husbands trusty hearts,
procure not to your shames.
Take pattern plain by me,[77]
well view my race and end,
And while you stand, see to your steps,
and let the fault amend.

[11]

For God, though long he bears,
at length will sharply pay,[78]
As may be seen[79] by my first state
and now by me decay.
Trust never trustless tales,
detest that odious love,
Defy such friendship fraught with fraud,
as matrons doth behoove.

[12]

For I bewailing told
of this my fault the cause,
I had no perfect love nor care
to God's word, nor yet his Laws.
My Love was daily hate;
my faith was flattering sure.
Curséd Satan, I lament[80]

thou didst me so allure!
[13]
I yielded too, too much
to thy foul hellish lure.
I gave thee reign to rule
the flesh, which now I rue full sore.[81]
For grudging at my state,[82]
I thought to mend the same,
Though which, instead of life, to death
a foul and hateful shame.
[14]
See what a gain is got—
O God, see what a gain,[83]
of my children, goods, and friends,
and more which doth remain.
A loss far mounting this,
for breach of my dear,
My Soul and Body both quite spilt,
Christ, were it not for thee.[84]
[15]
Christ, for thy precious death,
Thy wounds, and bloody heart,
Which are my pardon, by thy cross,
and my relief from smart.
Thou art all which now remains,
come deignéd wroth dismay,[85]
Thou, Christ, art all my anchor-hold,[86]
which hast my Ransom pay.
[16]
Which cheers my wounded heart,
and makes me glad to die,
A thousand times more cruel death
myself I quite defy.
Out of this carnal world,
Dear God, I long for thee:

O, when shall I be rid of sin
that I thy face may see!
[17]
I am full ready pressed;[87]
my sins I do repent.
O, for my bloody fact,[88]
O God, let not my Soul be shent![89]
No, no, I am full sure
Thy promise is full just;
Christ's blood my bloody fact hath cleansed,
and thereto will I trust.
[18]
And now behold and see
what for me God hath done:
A lost and infected[90] wandering sheep
his merry home hath won.
Whose love so let me fall,
and justice threw me down,
From worldly pomp to foul reproach,
and loss of all renown,
[19]
That he might raise me up
from death to state of bliss,
From Satan's baits, by his rebukes,
to be a child of his.
In flower of constant age,
my days to end with shame,
To my immortal bliss
and joy set free from sin and blame.[91]
[20]
And yet what shame is this
for me, so clad with sin,
To take no more than I shall taste
the lasting throne to win?
And, therefore, now farewell,

all things corrupt and vain,
It is not long till heavenly throng
will take me up again.[92]
[21]
In this my very flesh
to see Christ with mine eyes,
And soul and body dwell
with him above the crystal skies.
For whom my friends prepare,
and so I you commend
To Jesus Christ, who shall ye keep,
and thus I make an end.

Dorothy Leigh's *The Mother's Blessing. Or, The godly counsell of a gentle-woman, not long since deceased, left behinde her for her children. Containing many good exhortations, and good admonitions profitable for all parents to leaue as a legacy to their children.*

Though Dorothy Leigh's *The Mother's Blessing* was published after *A Warning* (in 1616), it is part of a longer tradition of writing by women that offers an important context for understanding Anne Sanders and *A Warning*. Leigh's *The Mother's Blessing*, subtitled, *The Godly Counsaile of a Gentlewoman, not long since deceased, left behind her for her Children*, saw twenty-three editions between 1616 and 1674; it was extremely popular, and influenced subsequent writers in the genre of "mothers' legacies," which were prayers and instructions for children when the mothers themselves were ill, near death, or felt that they were going to die. (In Leigh's case, she did die shortly after drafting the manuscript.)[93] As Iman Sheeha explains, "Surviving mothers' legacies are concerned first and foremost with the religious and moral instruction of the children who are to be left behind motherless."[94] Although nominally addressed to Leigh's own school-aged sons, George, John, and William, whom she advises on practical as well as spiritual topics—from choosing good wives and managing their servants to performing private prayer and religious services—she also speaks forcefully about other subjects, including universal literacy for children (including girls) in order to read the Bible. Leigh is highly critical of people, especially ministers, who attend more to worldly things than spiritual ones, boldly singling out "the unthankfulness of rich men" and ministers, whose "honorable calling . . . [is] stained by worldliness." As a widow (her husband was Ralph Leigh, a gentleman of Cheshire who served under the Earl of Essex at Cadiz, who seems to have died in 1616), she hopes that her boys will become Puritan preachers, which some critics view as her "vicarious pleasure" because women could not serve in this capacity in the Anglican church. Indeed, Leigh's "blessing" does read like a sermon at times.[95] Leigh purposely chose to advance this advice in print, a somewhat daring move for a woman in this period, and she dedicates the work to the influential Protestant Princess Elizabeth, whose father was King James I and husband was the Elector Palatine. As one biographer argues, "Leigh aligns herself with Princess Elizabeth and thereby sets her own writerly effort to propagate true religion among her posterity not merely on a public, but on an international stage."[96] This genre of women's writing shows how private and even personal statements could have a public impact.

To illustrate the flavor of the longer *Blessing*, which runs forty-five short chapters, I have selected the opening poem, which follows the dedications to the author's patron and her "beloved sons," and the table of contents. (From John Budge, London, 1616. Reprinted in *Women's Writing in Stuart England: The Mother's Legacies of Dorothy Leigh, Elizabeth Joscelin, and Elizabeth Richardson*, edited by Sylvia Monica Brown, 15–76. Thrupp, Stroud, Gloucester: Sutton, 1999.)

Counsell to my Children

My sons, the readers of this book,
I do you not entreat
To bear with each misplacéd word,
for why, my pain's as great
To write this little book to you
(the world may think indeed)
As it will be at any time
for you the same to read.

But this I much and oft desire,
that you would do for me,
To gather honey of each flower,
as doth the laborious Bee.
She looks not who did place the plant,
nor how the flower did grow,
Whether so stately up aloft,
or near the ground below.

But where she finds it, there she works,
and gets the wholesome food
And bears it home, and lays it up
to do her country good,
And for to serve herself at need
when winter doth begin;
When storm and tempest is without,
then she doth find within.

A sweet and pleasant wholesome food,
a house to keep her warm,
A place where softly she may rest,
and be kept from all harm.
Except the Bee that idle is,
and seeks too soon for rest,

Before she filléd hath her house,
whereby her state is blest.

And then as she did rest too soon,
too soon she sorrow knows:
When storms and tempests are without,
then she herself beshrews.[97]
She looketh out and seeth death,
ready her to devour.
Then doth she wish that she had got
more of the wholesome flower.

For why, within, her store is spent,
before the winter's past,
And she by no means can endure
the stormy winter's blast.
She looketh out and seeth death,
and finds no less within.
Then too, too late for to repent,
you see she doth begin.

Therefore, see you not idle be,
this I would have you know,
Be sure still that the ground be good,
whereout[98] the plant doth grow.
Then gather well and lose no time;
take heed now you do see,
Lest you be unprovided found,
as was the idle Bee.
—D. L.

The Mothers Blessing. Table of Contents

Notes

Preface

1. Whipday, *Shakespeare's Domestic Tragedies*, 93.
2. Quoted in Smith, "'Goodly Sample,'" 181.
3. Martin, *Women, Murder, and Equity*, 81.
4. Golding, *Briefe discourse*, (appendix 135–50).
5. Munday, *View of Sundry Examples*, B–B4.
6. Martin, *Women, Murder, and Equity*, 83, 81.
7. Simpson, *School of Shakespere*, 210.
8. Berek, "'Follow the Money,'" 175.
9. Gurr, *Shakespeare Company*, 133, 134.
10. Lopez, "Shadow of the Canon," 109.

A Note about the Text

1. This document is available in Word format online: https://www.coursehero
.com/file/30726277/A-Warning-for-Fair-Women-With-Introduction-Edited
-by-Gemma-Leggott-1doc/. Leggott's edition was prepared in connection with
the *Editing a Renaissance Play* module of Sheffield Hallam University's master's
degree in English Studies (https://extra.shu.ac.uk/emls/iemls/resources.html).
2. Richard Simpson (1878), A. F. Hopkinson (1904), J. S. Farmer (1912), and
Charles Dale Cannon (1975).
3. Cannon, *Warning for Fair Women*, 23.
4. Cannon, *Warning for Fair Women*, 16.
5. Quoted in Cannon, *Warning for Fair Women*, 17.
6. Cannon, *Warning for Fair Women*, 16. Cannon describes at length the differences between a play that derived from a printer setting type from a prompt
copy versus an authorial copy and compares typographical and spelling practices of the two printer compositors, who were the print house workers who
set the type for the quarto of *A Warning*. For example, Compositor A used the
"ie" ending for "Tragedie" and "Drurie," while Compositor B preferred the "y"
ending. Cannon, *Warning for Fair Women*, 11. A few other points from Cannon about the text: the printer Valentine Sims and bookseller William Aspley
also worked on Shakespeare plays (10); *A Warning* is similar in length to other
Chamberlain-King's Men plays (15).

Introduction

1. Although another anonymous domestic tragedy, *Arden of Faversham*, that also dramatized an actual case of a wife murdering her husband was published in 1592, *A Warning* was still "a remarkable and noteworthy innovation" for the Chamberlain's Men; neither the Theatre nor the Rose had comparable plays in their repertory. Gurr, *Shakespeare Company*, 131. On the relative dating of the two plays, see Martin, *Women, Murder, and Equity*, 225n29. Besides *Arden*, other plays involving domestic crime from adultery to murder include *Two Lamentable Tragedies* (1601), *A Yorkshire Tragedy* (1608), *and A Woman Killed with Kindness* (published 1607).

2. These titles from 1564 and 1565 appear in the *Stationers' Register*. See also Simpson, *School of Shakespere*, 212. On this note, Cannon suggests that *A Warning*'s dramatist purposefully "align[ed] himself with a popular tradition." Cannon, *Warning for Fair Women*, 45.

3. The following stage direction is a good example of this level of detail: "Enter Frankford as it were brushing the crumbs from his clothes with a napkin, and newly risen from supper" in Heywood, *A Woman Killed with Kindness*, sc. 8, osd 22.

4. Holbrook, *Literature and Degree*, 86–87.

5. Holbrook, *Literature and Degree*, 86–87.

6. I cannot overstate how rarely a tragedy had a London and middle-class setting; the prologue spoken by Tragedy announces not only the play's generic innovation of domestic tragedy, but also the fact that it is "set in London that tells a true story from London's recent history." Gurr, "'Stage Is Hung with Black,'" 68. See also Wiggins, *Shakespeare and the Drama*, 25.

7. Gurr, "'Stage Is Hung with Black,'" 68–69.

8. This combination of realistic and symbolic styles is the focus of Dolan, "Gender, Moral Agency, and Dramatic Form." See also Holbrook, *Literature and Degree*, 93–94.

9. Suzuki, "Gender, Class, and the Social Order," 31.

10. See Orlin, *Private Matters*.

11. See Dolan, "Gender, Moral Agency, and Dramatic Form"; and Martin, *Women, Murder, and Equity*.

12. See Richardson, *Domestic Life*; Richardson, "Tragedy, Family and Household"; and Greenberg, *Metropolitan Tragedy*.

13. See Balizet, *Blood and Home*; and Christensen, *Separation Scenes*.

14. For fascinating new work in these areas, see Sheeha, "'[M]istris Drewry'"; and Birdseye, "Finding Her Conscience," 133–70. Atwood theorizes domestic space in early modern drama in her unpublished dissertation, *Spatial Dra-*

maturgy and Domestic Control in Early Modern Drama. Atwood's paper at the Durham Early Modern Studies conference (July 2019), "Inside Out: Domestic Tragedy and the Dramaturgy of Extrusion," introduced a fascinating approach to stage liminality.

15. Belsey, *Subject of Tragedy*, 9. See also Belsey, "Alice Arden's Crime." Jonathan Dollimore also defined the genre of tragedy in new ways, arguing that Jacobean tragedy was "radical" in that it worked to demystify power relations. See Dollimore, *Radical Tragedy*. See also Drakakis, "Revisiting the Subject of Tragedy."

16. The following studies illustrate feminist scholarship on topics related to my discussion here: Dolan, *Marriage and Violence*; Dowd, *Dynamics of Inheritance*; Longfellow, "Public, Private"; Orlin, *Locating Privacy*; Orlin, *Private Matters*; and Wall, *Staging Domesticity*.

17. A factor affecting the performance run was the theater-closing scandal of *The Isle of Dogs*, a play that allegedly satirized the Queen and other dignitaries, was suppressed, and led to an acting prohibition in the summer of 1597. Wiggins dates the writing of *A Warning* definitely before 1598 and likely in 1595 (personal email correspondence, June 2018).

18. Hopkinson reviews other dating points, including "the business hour on the Exchange" and the mention of a play performed at Lynn (in the conversation about murder-will-out cases at Beane's deathbed). Hopkinson, *Warning for Fair Women*, iv–vi.

19. See https://www.nps.gov/jame/learn/historyculture/tobacco-the-early -history-of-a-new-world-crop.htm.

20. Cannon, *Warning for Fair Women*, 44–45.

21. Gurr, *Shakespeare Company*, 282.

22. Wiggins and Richardson, *British Drama*, 401.

23. The company had four title changes, but "stayed remarkably the same" in its forty-eight-year existence, owning/producing over 168 plays (only that number survive), and doing about two hundred performances per year for a total of approximately ten thousand performances (Gurr, *Shakespeare Company*, xiv, xv). James Marino argues that the company tightly controlled some of Shakespeare's work, but allowed other plays to go forth easily into print. *A Warning* seems to be one of these "unclaimed" texts. Marino, *Owning William Shakespeare*, 30–40. See also Roslyn Knutson's essay, "Repertory System." I thank S. P. Cerasano for her discussions with me about this (personal email correspondence, May 2018). Wiggins has also kindly discussed attribution and other matters with me, also by email correspondence (June 2018).

24. Charry, *Arden Guide*, 155–56.

25. Charry, *Arden Guide*, 157–58.

26. Marlowe's *Tamburlaine the Great* title page is similar—as it was "sundry [or many] times showed upon stages in the City of London" with a good bit of plot summary too. As another example, Jonson's *Bartholomew Fair* begins with the title and genre ("a comedy"), followed by "acted in the year 1614 by the Lady Elizabeth's Servants and then dedicated to King James of most blessed memory by the author, Benjamin Johnson"; next comes a Latin epigraph by Horace, an emblem of the printer's initials (JB for John Beale), and "London, Printed by J.B. for Robert Allot, and are to be sold at the sign of the Beare, in Paul's Churchyard, 1631."

27. See Cannon, *Warning for Fair Women*, 25–43.

28. Cannon, *Warning for Fair Women*, 26–27.

29. Hopkinson, *Warning for Fair Women*, xi. See Hopkinson's survey of authorship issues (pp. viii–xiv.); for Leggott's summary, see pp. 7–13 Research techniques and tools have improved in recent decades, making some of the older arguments easily refutable. Still, one admires the breadth of knowledge in this century-old scholarship.

30. Cannon, *Warning for Fair Women*, 31.

31. Cromwell, *Thomas Heywood*, 139. For more information about Adams, see Shapiro, *Shakespeare in America*.

32. Cannon, *Warning for Fair Women*, 35–43.

33. Leggott, "Warning for Fair Women," 7, 8–18.

34. Each year members of the institute read aloud in chronological order, the complete dramatic canon of a sixteenth- or early seventeenth-century playwright. See Silvia Morris's post at http://theshakespeareblog.com/2016/06/the-thomas-dekker-marathon/. As noted in acknowledgements, the institute did a second reading of *A Warning for Fair Women*, June 29, 2020.

35. Balizet first suggested this breakdown to me (personal email correspondence, June 2018).

36. Shakespeare, *The Rape of Lucrece*, line 117.

37. Balizet, *Blood and Home*, 80.

38. Gurr, "'Stage Is Hung with Black,'" 68–69.

39. Shakespeare, *The Taming of the Shrew*, Ind. 1, 2.

40. Mehl, *Elizabethan Dumb Show*, 90; Dolan, "Gender, Moral Agency, and Dramatic Form," 211.

41. Dessen and Thomson, *Dictionary of Stage Directions*, 19.

42. Purkiss, "Masque of Food," 95.

43. Cannon, *Warning for Fair Women*, 71.

44. Bradbrook, *Themes and Conventions*, 14, 18.

45. Dessen and Thomson, *Dictionary of Stage Directions*, 80.

46. Mehl, *Elizabethan Dumb Show*, 21. Mehl also observes dumb shows' frequent use of a "large number of stage properties," a point he illustrates with the banquet and tree in *A Warning* and *The Battle of Alcazar*. Mehl, *Elizabethan Dumb Show*, 25n1; see also pp. 21, 90–96, 98, 100. Dieter Mehl and Bernard Spivak each provide compendious accounts of dumb shows in Elizabethan plays that Dolan engages in original ways in her essay, "Gender, Moral Agency, and Dramatic Form."

47. Dolan, "Gender, Moral Agency, and Dramatic Form," 211.

48. Mehl, *Elizabethan Dumb Show*, 93.

49. There is a play from 1639 attributed to T.D. called *The Bloody Banquet*. *The Battle of Alcazar* features a bloody banquet, and William Davenant's *Albovine, King of the Lombards* has a stage direction that reads, "a skull, made into a drinking bowl" (quoted in Dessen and Thomson, *Dictionary of Stage Directions*, 202).

50. See Dessen and Thomson, *Dictionary of Stage Directions*, 100, 188.

51. Flowers are associated on stage with the funerals and other ceremonies, and they are strewn or worn in women's hair. I can find no other instance of a flower changing color, though Barbara Sebek reminded me of Oberon's story of the flower "[b]efore, milk-white, now purple with love's wound" in *A Midsummer Night's Dream* (2.1.173) (Sebek, personal email correspondence, June 2018). See also Dessen and Thomson, *Dictionary of Stage Directions*, 94–95.

52. Golding's account mentions the gallows and the children's appearance. See appendix 135–50.

53. See Gillis, *For Better, For Worse*; and Stone, *Family, Sex and Marriage*. For current U.S. data, see https://www.dailydot.com/irl/average-age-marriage-by-state/.

54. Studies that inform my understanding of home and work include Martin and Mohanty, "Feminist Politics"; Kerber, "Separate Spheres, Female Worlds"; Reverby and Helly, "Converging on History"; Haritgan-O'Connor, *Ties That Buy*; Korda, *Shakespeare's Domestic Economies*; Wall, *Staging Domesticity*; and Dowd, *Women's Work*.

55. Muldrew, *Economy of Obligation*, 4.

56. Alice Clark is a notable exception. See Clark, *Working Life of Women*.

57. Harkness, "View from the Streets," 84. Mary Floyd-Wilson explores the many dimensions of "women's occult knowledge." Floyd-Wilson, *Occult Knowledge, Science, and Gender*, 14–15. See also Fissell, "Introduction: Women, Health, and Healing"; and Park, *Secrets of Women*.

58. Christensen, *Separation Scenes*, 9–12.

59. Bartolovich, "Mythos of Labor," 140.

60. See Atwood, "Inside Out."

61. This discussion develops ideas from my book *Separation Scenes* (79–91).

62. Superb studies of housewifery in the early modern period include Boydston, *Home and Work*; Roberts, "'To Bridle the Falsehood'"; Wall, *Staging Domesticity*; Dowd, *Women's Work*; Korda, "'Judicious oeillades'"; Helgerson, *Adulterous Alliances*; and Warnicke, *Women of the English Renaissance*.

63. Warnicke, *Women of the English Renaissance*, 6.

64. Holbrook: "It does not take long to batter down Anne's scruples with images of her in a 'gowne of silk,' riding in a 'coach,' attended by a 'dozen men all in a liverie' (711–13)." Holbrook, *Literature and Degree*, 93. Orlin offers a welcome intervention into this line of criticism of Anne. See Orlin, *Private Matters*, especially 109. Dolan sees Anne as ambitious to expand "the limitations of her role as industrious, dependent, and neglected wife" that Drurie's seduction promises. Dolan, "Gender, Moral Agency, and Dramatic Form," 210. In performance, this could go either way.

65. Jeanne Boydston stresses that what looks like consumption by early modern housewives was really production. Women contributed to their household economies by acquiring goods for family use, whether through foraging, bartering, or shopping. Boydston, *Home and Work*, 14–17.

66. Dolan observes Anne Sanders's relative passivity in the relationship. Dolan, "Gender, Moral Agency, and Dramatic Form," 210.

67. Golding, *Briefe discourse*, 219–20.

68. For example, in narrating Browne's attempt to cover for Anne Sanders, Golding repeats that his protests are "untru[e]" and refers to Anne's sinful life. Golding, *Briefe discourse*, 219, 223.

69. Martin, *Women, Murder, and Equity*, 83.

70. On this point I am indebted to Cheryl Birdseye's paper, "'[I]n danger of lawe through ignorance': Female Testimonial Reliability in *A Warning for Fair Women*" presented at the 2018 Death and Domesticity conference. In fact, for Birdseye, Anne Sanders's final staged confession is itself suspect.

71. Suzuki, "Gender, Class, and the Social Order," 37.

72. For Dolan, the ambiguity stems from married women's problematic legal status in the period in England. Dolan explores the interplay between Anne Sanders's "moral culpability" (in the dumb show) and her "legal accountability" (in the court and execution scenes). Dolan, "Gender, Moral Agency, and Dramatic Form," 213–16.

73. Scholars view this special kind of performative speech either as evidence that the state (through the justice system and the church) controlled the meaning of punishment for the onlookers to reinforce its authority, or, alternatively, as a freer moment of "carnivalesque celebration of . . . inversion" left up to interpretation. Lake and Questier, "Agency, Appropriation and Rhetoric," 64. See also Sharpe, "'Last Dying Speeches.'"

74. Hehmeyer, "'Twill Vex Thy Soul to Hear,'" 172.

75. Golding, *Briefe discourse*, 142, see also 143.

76. Martin, *Women, Murder, and Equity*, 89.

77. Golding, *Briefe discourse*, 145.

78. Other cases of women and crime were retold in news accounts, plays, and other kinds of texts. On criminal women in early modern England, see Dolan *Dangerous Familiars*; Gowing, *Domestic Dangers*; Lake and Questier, "Agency, Appropriation and Rhetoric"; Martin, *Women, Murder, and Equity*; and Salkeld, *Shakespeare among the Courtesans*. For interesting discussions of sources, see also Cannon, *Warning for Fair Women*; Martin, *Women, Murder, and Equity*; and Orlin, *Private Matters*. Annabel M. Patterson addresses issues relating to source study and early modern historiography in *Reading Holinshed's Chronicles*.

79. Aughterson, *Renaissance Woman*, 229.

80. Aughterson, *Renaissance Woman*. See also Stavreva, *Words Like Daggers*, especially chap. 8, "Writing and Speaking."

81. Dolan, "'Gentlemen,'" 163, 168.

82. Golding, quoted in Dolan, "'Gentlemen,'" 168–69n32; see appendix 135–50.

83. For Kristin Poole, the small but enduring genre of published advice books by women called mothers' manuals invites us to "reconsider the perception and reception of women's writing in Jacobean England." Poole, "'Fittest Closet for All Goodness,'" 69.

84. Sheeha, "Devotional Identity," 100.

85. Dolan, "'Gentlemen,'" 159.

86. Lake and Questier, "Agency, Appropriation and Rhetoric," 82–83.

87. Sheeha, "Devotional Identity," 107.

88. Resurgens Theatre Company uses modified original practices that are distinct from the Shakespeare Tavern's home company. For Resurgens, see "About the Company" at http://www.resurgenstheatre.org/About_RTC.html; and for Shakespeare Tavern, see "About Us" at https://www.shakespearetavern.com/index.php?/about_us. For more on their production of *A Warning*, see http://resurgenstheatre.org/Past_Productions.html.

89. In her review, Pearson disagrees, noting that despite the "contagious energy of much of this production," some "structural flaws of the play itself" endure, such as the "lengthy indictment of Mrs. Saunders as the worst woman, wife, and mother of all time. By the time Anne apologizes to her children before she is executed, one feels like *Seinfeld*'s Elaine watching *The English Patient*: 'Just die already! Die!!'"

90. Pearson, Review of *A Warning for Fair Women*, https://bloggingshakespeare.com/reviewing-shakespeare/warning-fair-women-dir-brent-griffin-resurgens-theatre-company-atlanta-ga-usa-nov-2018/.

91. For more on the season, see http://resurgenstheatre.org/Past_Productions .html.

92. Atwood, review, 395.

93. According to Cheryl Birdseye, "There was certainly a ballad pertaining to Anne Sanders in circulation in 1576; however, we cannot confirm that this was *The wofull lamentacon of Anne Saunders* and so the date remains unknown." Birdseye, "Finding Her Conscience."

94. Atwood, review, 395.

95. See Smith, *Musical Response*, 104, quoted in Whipday, *Shakespeare's Domestic Tragedies*, 106n17, 18, 19.

96. Brent Griffin, author interview, March 2019.

97. Notably, women wrote and translated religious and spiritual books more commonly than other kinds of writing. See McQuade, *Catechisms and Women's Writing*.

98. In fact, "cunning men and women were fully ensconced in the community, providing assistance to folk in their daily lives"; these practitioners had "knowledge of nature's secrets" that could be used to keep ordinary people healthy. Floyd-Wilson, *Occult Knowledge, Science, and Gender*, 55. Women surgeons had a small but significant presence, according to Doreen A. Evenden's study (quoted in Floyd-Wilson, *Occult Knowledge, Science, and Gender*, 55).

99. Munday, *View of Sundry Examples*, Bii.

Cast of Characters

1. See figure 1: Melpomene.

2. See figure 2. Based on pronouns and classical and period conceptions, the Furies are female, while Lords, for example, would be gendered male. However, in performance any roles could be played by any gender. The Resurgens Theatre production, for example, doubled Tragedy and the two Furies—all played by women—as the Justice and Lords in the play's closing scene.

3. See "Greenwich and the Tudors."

A Warning for Fair Women

1. The public stage where *A Warning* was performed had an entry point or "door" on each side of the stage, and actors entering or exiting separately could show their disagreement or opposition, as in battle scenes when each of the factions would use a different door. An ensign is a banner or flag that one would carry in battle.

2. See figure 3: Tragedy (Resurgens Theatre production, 2018).

3. Something foolish and unnecessary, referring either to the stage properties (the drum and flag, i.e., "luggage") that the actor carries, or perhaps to History's general demeanor that Tragedy finds inappropriate for "her" stage.

4. The drum.

5. Doughtie or doughty (pronounced to rhyme with "cloudy") meant worthy, brave, or formidable as in this quotation from 1600: "Certaine Tribunes and marshals, valourous and doubtie good men." *OED online*, s.v. "Doughty," accessed November 3, 2019, https://www.oed.com. History uses the term sarcastically here.

6. See figure 4: Comedy and History (Resurgens Theatre production, 2018).

7. Disgraceful, contemptible, and low rather than dirty or lewd. Fiddle strings were literally made of cat's intestines stretched out into thin strands.

8. Tragedy compares the fiddling to unpleasant sounds—the creaking of the wheels of a wooden cart and feet scraping. Think nails on a chalkboard.

9. Short for "get up" and "giddy up," an exclamation of derision, remonstrance, or surprise. Today we might say, "Get lost." Buskin referred to a type of boot worn by actors of Athenian tragedy in ancient Greece, and by extension, in the early modern period, associated with tragedy. Comedy is making fun of Tragedy by calling her "mistress buskins with a whirligig," which might refer to her whip continually whirling.

10. For Melpomene, see cast of characters. "Whose mare [or dog] is dead?" was a saying that meant, "What's all the fuss?"

11. A beadle was an inferior parish officer or constable appointed by the vestry to keep order in church, punish petty offenders, and act as the messenger of the parish generally. Comedy is undermining Tragedy's gravity by using the title of the low-level servant employed by Murder.

12. "What wonder's toward": Comedy thinks it is a "wonder" or rare occurrence that the three of them are "together," suggesting that the three genres are at odds, but actually, as this play itself shows, historical material could be tragic and also have some comic elements. In the next line, History says that she had intended to perform that day, but that Tragedy shooed her off the stage.

13. Unless.

14. Comedy is saying that the audiences will not "attend" or pay to see only tragedies; they need variety.

15. Tragedy implies that her peers rely on stock performances, even shtick to draw from, and that this level of entertainment would appeal only to injudicious ("injudicial" in the next line) or indiscriminate viewers.

16. Whining, complaining, or crying.

17. Rigorous and severe, self-disciplined. On the ability of poetry to "move" readers to virtuous action, see Sidney, *Apologie for Poetry*. The rest of the speech lists the psychological and even physiological effects of powerful drama. This entire discussion points to a dramatist's theorizing his craft.

18. To "rack" meant to stretch, and to "rap" meant to seize; compare to "rapture." What tragedy is professing here sounds rather painful for an audience to endure.

19. This speech pokes fun at popular drama of the period, including Thomas Kyd's revenge play, *The Spanish Tragedy*, as well as Shakespeare's history plays, which were in repertory with *A Warning*.

20. Outer garment.

21. *Vindicta* is a cry of revenge in Latin; compare our word "vindicate." It is probably a reference to the historical play *The Battle of Alcazar* (published in 1594) attributed to George Peele; that play also has a Chorus and a dumb show.

22. An oil distilled of turpentine, possibly used to make fire or an explosion (special effects) on stage.

23. A firecracker.

24. A small pointed dagger, and also an instrument used by tailors for piercing holes in cloth. Comedy uses understatement here to mock the typical tragic performance. Notably, Browne does stab a handkerchief in scene 8.

25. The quality of being finished or in fashion. Again, the tone is sarcastic.

26. Soon. In other words, "If you keep this up, she will soon be even angrier."

27. "Wisp unto a scold"—the phrase may be proverbial, used here to suggest that Comedy's teasing ("jests") just make Tragedy angrier ("mad"). It refers to an apparent practice (how common, I do not know) of taunting a woman accused of being a "scold" or "shrew" with bound strands of straw to shame her for being unruly. In the ca. 1630 ballad, "The Cucking of a Scold," townsfolk try different means to punish a loud, disruptive woman, including violent and humiliating actions and this "label": "a mighty wisp / Was borne before her face. / The perfect tokens of a scold / Well known in any place" (lines 116–19). See also Dyce, *Glossary to the Works of Shakespeare*, 510–11.

28. A shade of red or the quality of being bloody. For "buskins," see note 9.

29. Pointless talk and insults generally, not in our sense of comparisons using "like" or "as."

30. Paper playbills or posters advertising plays were posted near the theaters.

31. Tragedy claims to be sent by the god Apollo, patron of music and the arts.

32. History draws attention to the stage itself, saying in effect, "I just noticed black curtains that signal 'tragedy' to the audience; we better leave." See my introduction and Gurr, "'Stage Is Hung with Black,'" 67–82.

33. Other plays also allude to the apparent practice of draping the stage in black: in John Marston's *The Insatiate Countess* (1613) for example, "The stage of heaven is hung with solemn black / A time best fitting to act tragedies." Quoted in Hopkinson, *Warning for Fair Women*, 97n75. It might seem odd that Tragedy should "be entertained" and the spectators should "give entertainment" to her rather than the other way around, but to entertain here means something like be hospitable to, accommodate.

34. A color unsuitable for comedy or history, since black is traditionally associated with death and sad or tragic events.

35. Notice that the exit lines of Comedy and History appear in rhymed couplets that Tragedy then picks up to close this scene. This is not uncommon for signaling a shift in thought to mark a conclusion; Shakespeare often closes scenes in clinching rhymes like this.

36. Used as a stage direction to indicate that two or more performers leave the stage. Literally, "They exit."

37. The "fair circuit" and "this round" refer to the world or to the rotund theater space itself, but probably not the Globe, based on dating. The Globe was built in 1599, the same year that the play was printed; critics generally agree that performances preceded publication sometimes by years.

38. Fain: feigned or false. "I am telling a true story, unlike the usual fare at the theaters."

39. Although "courteous" retains the meaning of being well-mannered and gracious, it also has the connotation of "courtliness," meaning that one's behavior befits the station of a courtier or courtly gentleman.

40. In the sixteenth century English people occupied and ruled colonies, also called "plantations," in Munster, the southwest part of Ireland, which was also called "the Pale" (see 1.17). Ireland, Scotland, and Wales were frequently represented in English texts and maps as the uncivilized frontiers or "dark corners" of the land, and the native inhabitants were often brutally treated by newcomers. Ireland also remained Catholic after the Protestant Reformation. The play is not specific about what Captain Browne's association with Ireland was (i.e., born of English, Irish, or mixed parentage?). But he defends Ireland as civil, orderly, and law-abiding. See Ohlmeyer, "Literature and the New British and Irish Histories."

41. This language echoes discourses that promoted colonial expansion. Sir Walter Raleigh, for example, speaks of the "large store," variety, and fecundity in "The Discoverie of the Large, Rich and Bewtiful Empyre of Guiana" (279–85).

42. This language of incivility and wildness was used for non-English people and dark-skinned people, such as first-peoples of America; compare the

Welsh rebel, Owen Glendower, known as "irregular and wild" in Shakespeare's *Henry IV, Part 1* (1.1.40).

43. The English Pale was the eastern border of Ireland around Dublin that was officially ruled by Tudor monarchs. Browne, while challenging the common representation of Irish as lawless, also suggests that "the rest [of Ireland]" will "be reduced" or led from error, sin, immorality, etc.; to restore to the truth or the right faith. *OED online*, s.v. "Reduce," accessed November 3, 2019, https://www.oed.com. See Canny, *Elizabethan Conquest of Ireland*.

44. This conversation is entirely invented by the playwright; the sources stipulate that the two men did not know each other. See appendix 137–38.

45. Except.

46. A mild oath; "truly" or "indeed."

47. The term of service from an apprentice; likely Roger came to the Drurie household in his early teens and now may be in his early twenties.

48. Compensate or repay.

49. To come back here. Compare "hither and yon," which means here and there, or yonder.

50. Browne here puns on Roger's geographical path and his own crooked or immoral desire.

51. A kind of oath, also said as "by this good light" or "by God's light."

52. Merry. From this confession, it seems as though he just now fell in love. Browne's claim, "my heart is not my own," is a sentiment common in melancholy love songs, such as "I Left My Heart in San Francisco."

53. The image of the golden wire refers to the Greek and Roman myth that Hephaestus/Vulcan fashioned an unbreakable net to capture his adulterous wife Aphrodite/Venus with her lover, Ares/Mars. (I thank Emma Tan for reminding me of this story.) The metaphor of Love as casting nets, lures, or traps for lovers was common in Elizabethan poetry.

54. Thou art, compressed for meter.

55. Demure, proper in manner and conduct; not forward, impudent, or lewd; a trait desirable for women in particular in this period (and, in some ways, even now).

56. To achieve, obtain.

57. Browne is flattering Drurie's "good nature" and excusing his own bad manners ("nurture") in calling her back. In this conversation, all three parties are cautious and calculating because what they are speaking of is indeed criminal, despite Browne's assurance that his plot is not "treason" or "felony"; adultery and murder, which he seems interested in committing, were, of course, criminal acts.

58. "Handsome features" or attractiveness. This is the first of many remarks on Browne's physical attractiveness, the basis of which seems to be his fine clothes

that Roger has hopes to inherit. To "stead" someone is to take their part as a substitute or proxy, as we say today, "instead of him."

59. Along with its legal meaning of an offense against a monarch or the country, "treason" could refer generally to betrayal or a treacherous action. Killing a superior (as when a wife or servant kills a husband or master, for example) was a crime of petty treason; so, in fact, Browne's eventual plot with Anne Sanders is a form of treason. See Dolan, "Gender, Moral Agency, and Dramatic Form" and *Dangerous Familiars*.

60. Legally, felonies were a certain class of serious crimes, but colloquially, the word indicated wickedness or villainy.

61. This is one of the many references to specific locations in and around London. What is now London was called Londinium by Romans who encircled the area with a wall in the second or third century. For example, the Newgate and Aldersgate areas take their names from the gates into the city at those places. For more on urban topography in the genre, see Greenberg, *Metropolitan Tragedy*. See map of London in figure 5.

62. Mistress Drurie is a surgeon, a rare but not unknown profession for a woman in the period; all the medicines she lists in her next speech were forms of "cordial waters," popular cures for different ailments made from distilled flowers and plants, spice such as ginger and cinnamon, and mixed with a liquor.

63. Medical skill, associated with women's housewifery. Browne is being metaphoric—like saying he needs a "cure" for his sudden attraction, and the "medicine" is Anne Sanders. (Love is often troped as a disease or a drug, from Petrarchan sonnets to modern pop songs.)

64. "Excess," with specific meaning of an illness attributed to excessive eating or drinking. This exchange is a bit funny, with Browne complaining of his lovesickness and Drurie assuming that he has gas! Below, Drurie recounts the story of a woman whom Anne Sanders had helped after the woman "had surfeited / With eating beans" (1.112–13).

65. *Rosa solis* was a liqueur distilled from a carnivorous plant, the sun dew, and proclaimed to cure consumption used in various recipes found in such cookbooks as *A closet for ladies and gentlewomen. Or, The art of preserving, conserving, and candying* (cited in Roberts, "Little Shop of Horrors"). Dr. Stevens's (or Stephens's) Water was a popular cure-all recipe from the sixteenth and seventeenth centuries that appears in print in *The Queen's Closet Opened* and Hugh Platt's *Delights for Ladies* (1602), and Gervase Markham's *English Housewife* (1623). *Pharmacopoeia Londinensis* (1618) lists "Aque Doctoris Stephani" among the approved recipes of the College of Physicians. I thank Edith Snook for sharing this information (personal email June 2018). Although it might seem to us that Drurie speaks of quack cures, these were well known and com-

monly practiced basic recipes with different variations. Interestingly, in another play with a domestic tragedy plot that is also a true story, Thomas Heywood's *Edward IV*, neighbor women use the "rosa-solis" balm to "animate the spirits" of a wounded man (*Part 2*, 18.32–35). Another similarity between *A Warning* and *Edward* is that the wife (Jane Shore) is led astray by another meddling widow (Mistress Blague), who later betrays Jane. See Christensen, "Settled and Unsettling: Home and Mobility in Heywood's King Edward IV (1599)."

66. Excellent or "the perfect thing."

67. Spelled "peate," an endearment used to refer to a young woman.

68. "Quotha" was used after sarcastically repeating the words of another to indicate quotation. This is the equivalent of saying "quote, unquote" or using air quotes to bracket a repetition during a conversation.

69. A person who transported and sold fresh water in London.

70. Flatulent. This little anecdote—about a workingwoman with bad gas—might get a laugh from the audience, but it probably doesn't amuse Browne, anxious to move on his desire for Anne Sanders.

71. Kidney stone or gallstone.

72. One-eighth of a fluid ounce of medicine, a small draught of cordial, stimulant, or spirituous liquor. The next line explains that Anne Sanders's medicine was a fast-acting purgative that helped ("holp") the woman pass the kidney stone or otherwise recover after sweating.

73. "T'faith" is a compression of the oath "in faith"; the "I" is not the personal pronoun. Drurie says, "Ah ha, now I understand what you mean! Are you in love?" In performance Drurie could play dumb, having a joke at his expense, or she may really be confused about "what ails him."

74. Intimate, familiar, and confidential. Browne is asking if Drurie is Anne Sanders's confidant or close friend. "Inward" is a telling expression, given the importance of spatial access in the plot and also Browne's own metaphors for his "secret malady" and "inward grief" (1.88, 92). See Maus, *Inwardness and Theater*.

75. As my Shakespeare students (Spring 2018) pointed out in a discussion board thread, Drurie's statement of this specific amount seems noteworthy since Drurie does indeed wrong her friend for less.

76. A ring or earring. When Drurie says that she'd like its "fellow," she is hinting broadly that she wants that piece of jewelry, not really one just like it, and Browne hands over the item. See also Shylock's "turkey-stone" or turquoise ring in *The Merchant of Venice* (3.1.119–22). In the late sixteenth century, such rings were "the height of masculine fashion." Boswell, "Shylock's Turquoise Ring," 483. On male fashion in the period, see Bailey, *Flaunting*.

77. As above, the characters have started to rhyme, perhaps here to signal the formality of the contract they are making.

78. Under the condition that or provided that you help me to access Anne Sanders.

79. To expose (a person) by divulging their secrets.

80. Wise and shrewd, meant here as a compliment (as in a savvy business-man), but "subtle" also had a negative cast: crafty, cunning, and devious. See "The Argument" to Book IX in Milton's *Paradise Lost*: "The Serpent finds her alone; his subtle approach, first gazing, then speaking, with much flattery extolling Eve above all other creatures" (202).

81. One of the twenty-five wards or districts of London, Billingsgate was the city's original water gate, located on the north bank of the River Thames between London Bridge and Tower Bridge.

82. Roger's claim that Mistress Drurie is "studying the law" is interesting. As a widow she held property of her own, requiring legal knowledge, and though women had no access to formal education in law, other training in informal networks would have served. (Wealthy girls and women had private tutors.) Or Roger might be attempting to make his mistress sound even more skillful to advance Browne's suit. "Strait-laced" could mean both prudish (excessively rigid or scrupulous in matters of conduct; narrow or overprecise in one's rules of practice or moral judgment) as we use it today, but also stingy or grudging in gifts or concessions. *OED online*, s.v. "Strait-laced," accessed November 3, 2019, https://www.oed.com. Here, and throughout the dialogue, Roger stresses compensation (gifts, tips, requiting, and so on).

83. Browne is making a transactional promise with the gift of the ring: "If you help me, then you may command [ask for] my chain [necklace], my hand [loyalty?], and my heart blood [life?]."

84. "Circumspect" here refers to Anne Sanders's modesty or lack of showi-ness; "respective" means attentive, mindful, and considerate of her good name.

85. If you like, or if you wish.

86. This interplay sounds like a con game; Roger is pretending that Drurie needs persuading.

87. To ensure his success. Drurie may mean that she will do all she can, but cannot guarantee success, or that she can't bear the thought of refusing to help this good-looking and well-paying man, this "goodly creature."

88. By "second my onset" (or "onslaught"), she means "follow my lead in the attack." "Break the ice" literally refers to boats and ships breaking up ice floes ahead of them in order to pass through; a "ford" is a shallow point in a river or stream.

89. See figure 6: Drurie and Browne (Resurgens Theatre production, 2018).

90. The Royal Burse or Exchange looms large in the play because it is where George Sanders spends a lot of time, though no scenes are set there. A long

four-story building with arched galleries, it was the first purpose-built meeting place where merchants conducted business in London from the 1570s, when Queen Elizabeth opened the first Royal Exchange building in Cornhill, until it was destroyed in the Great Fire of 1666. Although others discussed the need for such a space (since before then merchants met in the open-air streets), Sir Richard Gresham is credited with the idea and initial design after he saw the bourse (or Burse) at Antwerp; Venice also had a famous bourse that included the Rialto area where much of *Merchant of Venice* is set. It was Richard's son, Thomas Gresham, "King's Merchant" at Antwerp, who saw the plan through in London. See figure 7: The Royal Exchange.

91. "Be strange" here describes aloofness. Drurie is correct; Anne Sanders shows no interest in Browne as demonstrated in the next scene.

92. The phrase sounds proverbial—women prefer men who persist in their courtship—and reflects the enduring myth that women "play hard to get," when in fact, then as now, no means no. "Tried" means tested.

93. To requite (quit) or pay back for your trouble ("pain"). This contract-making scene, like all the encounters among these three characters, centers on different forms of currency—from the ring Browne promises to "recompense" Drurie to the "suit" of clothes that Roger expects as his own payment.

94. This discussion of the two different St. Dunstan's churches, one in the west and one in the east of London, shows the specific sites of London that the audience would know well. See Greenburg, *Metropolitan Tragedy*.

95. To "speed" is to succeed. Browne means, "When I get Anne, you get paid." This is one of the many examples of language associated with tips and bribes on stage. Browne may "pour" some coins into his hand in a dramatic show of largesse, or he may somehow gesture that the tip can be spent pouring drinks at a tavern later.

96. Pledge or bet.

97. Drurie is boasting that any woman would have to work very hard ("much ado") to resist her advocating ("woo"). Roger also attests, "Few women can my mistress's voice withstand," which suggests that Drurie has a history of pandering, also implied in Golding's *A Briefe discourse*. See appendix 144–45.

98. A cast-off or hand-me-down suit of clothes. Roger puns on the idea of lawsuit and suit of clothes; in the next line, Browne promises a second-hand suit and a new one (uncast). Clothing in this period was a form of currency, with masters and mistresses giving servants and others their used clothing and many people from all levels of society pawning their clothing. See Jones and Stallybrass, *Renaissance Clothing*; Hayward, "Clothing," 178; and Hentschell, "Moralizing Apparel."

99. The evening meal; dinner was like our lunch in the United States. This is one of a number of references to meals: later, George Sanders leaves an associate's house on Lombard Street, having just supped; at the same time, the conspirators perform a "bloody banquet" in the dumb show.

100. The Royal Exchange. See figure 8: Anne Sanders and her child (Resurgens Theatre production, 2018).

101. Gladly or willingly. The boy seems to want an afterschool snack, but his mother, like parents today, tells him he must wait for mealtime ("forbear").

102. In preparation for. We would say "for." The boy asks for a set of bow and arrows for a school outing, and his mother agrees, adding a new Easter outfit as long as he does well in school.

103. A chatterbox. To prate meant to prattle or chatter idly—an accusation more often directed at women than children, and rarely at men, though notice that later in the scene Anne Sanders complains that Browne too "prates."

104. "Th'art" elides "thou art." The boy jokingly threatens to "take some [fruit]" as payment for delivering the message to his sister. "Sir sauce" is Anne Sanders's way of calling her son a smart aleck; to be saucy was to talk back to authority. "Wag" was a term of endearment used for mischievous boys, most often a parent's term for children. For example, Falstaff calls his younger friend, Prince Hal, a "sweet wag" and a "mad wag" in Shakespeare's *Henry IV, Part 1* (1.2.17, 24).

105. Dark, out-of-the-way.

106. Appearance, countenance. Hamlet praises the actor's ability to perform grief: with "tears in his eyes, distraction in his aspect" (*Hamlet* 2.2.585).

107. Here Browne relies on conventional rhetoric about Cupid's arrows. Notice generally his highly inflated rhetoric in this soliloquy that Hopkinson likens to Romeo's speech. "It seems she hangs upon the cheek of night, / Like a rich jewel in an Ethiop's ear" (1.5.52–53). Hopkinson, *Warning for Fair Women*, 100n119–22.

108. This inner dialogue states the classic dilemma: passion, not "reason," is leading. In Shakespeare's poem, "The Rape of Lucrece," Tarquin, a prince and army commander, avows similarly: "Desire my pilot is," ignoring his duty and raping one of his subjects (line 330).

109. Browne considers Drurie to be his "tutor" in wooing Anne Sanders.

110. Passersby. He asks if Anne Sanders is outside people-watching, but she insists that the only "passenger" she cares about is her husband, whom she expects any minute.

111. Browne here puns on the "exchange" of vows in marriage and the Exchange as in the trading area where George spends so much time. He uses puns often. See figure 9: Browne courts Mistress Sanders (Resurgens Theatre production, 2018).

112. This dialogue might be played with some flirtation on Anne Sanders's part, but she seems to be rather contentedly waiting for ("attending") her spouse when a virtual stranger, Browne, shows up, malingering on her stoop ostensibly to thank her for her "company" last night. His "salute" or greeting seems more an annoyance than a "courtesy" to her, and she is comfortable in giving him the brush off. But he is slow to take the hint, later even pretending to Drurie that he has made progress.

113. "Herb John" is another name for Saint-John's-wort, a tasteless herb. Anne Sanders's comparison, as she explains in her next line, shows her indifference to Browne's company; we might say, "I can take it or leave it." This is clearly meant as an insult.

114. Browne seems to say that when he met George Sanders at the feast, the two men hit it off and Browne inferred ("conceived") a way to assist the merchant through his own connections to the Queen. Browne is boasting of his ability to curry favor at the English court, offering to be a "go-between" for Sanders, but Mistress Sanders states that her husband has plenty of friends at court. Merchants and other Londoners, including city officials (such as aldermen, sheriffs, and mayors), had sometimes-delicate relationships with the Crown and courtiers. For example, citizens might vie with courtiers for royal favors such as lucrative monopolies and patents, and kings and queens had to be granted (pro forma) "permission" from the lord mayor to "progress" through the city.

115. Free of charge. Browne offers to "effect" or facilitate George Sanders's requests with the Queen as a special favor.

116. Anne Sanders's response shows her confidence in her husband's abilities; George Sanders does not need an intermediary to "speed" or succeed. Again, she rebuffs Browne's come-on.

117. "Do as you wish!"

118. Anne Sanders complains of an enduring problem—pushy men pestering women whom they find attractive. Her term for Browne, "an errand-making gallant," puns on "errant" as wandering (compare knight *errant*) and as "erring" or transgressing. In another way, though, the phrase also points to the fact that it is her own spouse who is almost always "errant" or away from home. Calling Browne a gallant suggests that she, as a middle-class woman, finds courtly men like Browne idle, prideful, and not interesting.

119. Proverbial.

120. Although Anne Sanders referred to her son as a wag earlier, this is a more general use; to "play the wag" meant to be a joker or to be entertaining.

121. That is, Browne enters after the other two and approaches them.

122. Miserly or stingy.

123. Roger and his mistress have not seen Browne in a while and they are joking at his expense. They know that he cannot succeed ("anchor" or settle down with Anne Sanders) unless Drurie pilots the "ship," and nothing will happen on this front until he pays them. The tone of the ensuing dialogue is tricky to follow. Cannon inserts an "aside" here, but I think it makes better sense that Drurie speak to the audience in a false aside; she is "acting innocent," in effect saying, "What are you talking about? There is nothing fishy about this operation; we all know that Browne comes here to court my daughter," wink-wink. At the end of scene 1, Drurie and Roger are quite open about Browne's intent to commit adultery with their help. I take this to be a kind of "performance" between the two of them that shows they enjoy role playing and admire one another's skill in it.

124. Roger praises her clever "cover story" ("cloak for the rain"). "Must needs" works the same way as "necessarily."

125. To like or have affection for.

126. Drurie praises her servant's quick wit and in the next lines contrasts him with a stupid or slow servant. A "drawlatch" was literally a string hanging on the outside of a door used to draw it open or closed, and, figuratively, a lazy person who lags behind; this kind of dull servant would need a month to untangle her web of deceit. The idea that Roger is her "heart's interpreter" suggests the kind of "inwardness" or intimacy that the two women also share.

127. A device, trick, or scheme.

128. A commonly cited myth in the early modern period was that women were more malleable or more easily impressionable than men. The narrator in Shakespeare's poem "The Rape of Lucrece" puts it this way: "Men have marble, women waxen minds" (line 1291). This belief (buttressed by English women's lack of legal status) could protect wives from some legal action since they were "covered" by their husbands through the laws of coverture.

129. The phrase comes from falconry: to trick the hawk using a decoy or "lure" to which the bird comes swooping down. This imagery for training an animal was commonly used to characterize teaching students, servants, and women. For example, Petruchio in Shakespeare's *The Taming of the Shrew* refers to his wife as a falcon: "Thus have I politicly begun my reign, / And 'tis my hope to end successfully. / My falcon now is sharp and passing empty, / And till she stoop she must not be full-gorged, / For then she never looks upon her lure. / Another way I have to man my haggard, / To make her come and know her keeper's call" (4.1.188–94).

130. Roger refers to the role of the brothel-keeper with himself as the lookout. Othello in his late-phase paranoia imagines Emilia to play this role for Desdemona. See *Othello* 4.2.

131. Follow my advice. "Be ruled" also points up the shifting dynamic between the characters relative to the hierarchies of gender and class (and possibly age): Drurie is the mistress and likely older than Roger, yet he advises her, showing her dependency on him. Browne's entrance below introduces a new facet to these relationships—despite *his* rank as a wealthy "proper" gentleman, he depends on a woman and her servant to obtain his goal. This conversation also shows in miniature the play's obsession with requiting debts. Notice again the many references to "recompense" and "quittance" among these three, which also plays out on the Exchange offstage and among the merchants.

132. A female advocate. However, the *OED* dates the first recorded usage not until 1654. *OED online*, s.v. "Spokeswoman," accessed November 3, 2019, https://www.oed.com. Roger recommends—and Drurie has already thought of this—against advocating solely for either Browne or Anne Sanders, but to be flexible and gain the most profit from both about-to-be lovers.

133. "The money I will make between the two of them." In predicting to draw profit from Anne Sanders, they seem to assume that she will fall for the seduction and pay them to keep her cover.

134. My reward, like dessert.

135. Know, as in "you know what." Drurie uses this to avoid directly naming the crime they are about to commit.

136. Leave.

137. A term of address often used for male servants and children, especially when the speaker has (or assumes) a higher status. Not always but often an insult or show of contempt, as when white people in the southern United States called a Black man "boy." Here, however, "sirrah" seems like a neutral way to call for the servant, and also part of their "performance" for Browne's behalf.

138. Contemptuous phrase meaning "nonsense"; it is worth no more than the inedible nub of a fig.

139. Browne's hyperbole—that Mistress Sanders is absolute perfection—sounds like a sonneteer praising his mistress; recall Browne's poetical soliloquy about her beauty just before he strolls up to her porch. As above, "salute" means to greet.

140. In Browne's retelling, it is not Anne Sanders's rebuff that derails his progress, but rather his worry that passers-by and servants might get "jealous" (i.e., suspicious), as he knows neighbors would be, of him hanging around Anne while her husband is away.

141. His conclusion—that Mistress Sanders "may be won"—does not follow logically from the encounter with the woman who rebuffed him in scene 2, but Browne seems to follow Drurie's motto that "women love most, by whom they are most tried" (sc. 1). Interestingly, though Browne hires Drurie to be his "mediator," at this moment in the negotiations, Roger acts like the mediator

between his mistress and Browne, since he in the next lines tries to persuade her on Browne's behalf.

142. If Mistress Drurie has doubts about my ability to pay.

143. An English gold coin, named for the angel on its face and worth about 10 shillings (or half a pound) under Elizabeth I. Browne promises 100 pounds, or about $10,000 in today's U.S. currency, as a marriage portion, a gift to Drurie's daughter.

144. Anne Sanders.

145. Note the highly rhetorical tone in Browne's speech: building from the compare-and-contrast mode, and using alliteration and antithesis, it ends with his proclamation of superior love. That he is pursuing a married woman adds a perverse Petrarchan cast to his language.

146. As earlier, Roger plays the mediator in the negotiation, asking Drurie how she can stand idly by while Browne anguishes for love, and also assuring Browne, man to man, that were it up to him [Roger], the deal would be done. Recall that Tragedy used the same word to describe the effect of her style of play: "I must have passions that move."

147. See reference to "pouring" coins (n95).

148. Brooding, a fit of abstraction. This image of Drurie in rapt contemplation furthers the performativity of this scene. Drurie and Roger are doing a classic con move (or good cop/bad cop) in pretending that one person needs persuading by the other.

149. "Study" means to contemplate; here likely to overthink; "no . . . labor" means it's no big deal.

150. "This is just our friend George Browne. Please help him out."

151. Made certain of; assured or informed.

152. Browne asserts that he will not enjoy anything until he hears from Drurie again.

153. Proverbial, meaning something like "if we don't profit from this situation, no one can." The first recorded use of the phrase is in John Heywood's *A dialogue conteinyng the nomber in effect of all the prouerbes in the Englishe tongue*, 1546: "An yll wynde that blowth no man to good, men say."

154. Promissory notes, like an IOU. From the next line, we learn that George Sanders's debtors have paid up, and so he is now able to pay his own debts, 1,500 pounds to one Master Ashmore. This is about $195,000 in U.S. currency given current exchange rates. *The Big Problem of Small Change* index shows an approximately 100 to 1 ratio of present prices to prices around 1600. Sanders's 1,500-pound deal would be 150,000 GBP today. The 30-pound purchase would be 3,000 GBP today or approximately $4,000, a large but not unreasonable

amount for a wealthy merchant household. Sargent and Velde, *Big Problem of Small Change*. I thank Steve Deng for this reference.

155. Offered in advance.

156. With good credit, financially solvent. Mr. Bishop is "good for it" or can pay back a debt or loan.

157. The Exchange.

158. To free someone from debt.

159. Her debt is about $4,000 (see above).

160. Workaround, alternative.

161. A draper is one who made or sold textiles, such as linen and woolen cloth. Milliners sold higher-end wares, such as accessories, and articles of apparel. These men are apprentices or journeymen, not the master merchant, as becomes clear upon their exit.

162. The original printed text uses "1 and 2" as the merchants' speech tags; I have changed them here.

163. Slap you across the mouth.

164. This conversation illustrates the potential for complexity, if not discord, between a mistress and a male servant, both of whom are hierarchically below the master. The servant is vulnerable to abuse as he navigates competing orders about the money from master and mistress, yet he also clearly enjoys his master's trust, revealed in his intimate knowledge of George Sanders's accounts depicted also earlier in the scene. Meanwhile, the mistress is embarrassed by the awkward situation that the man has put her in—a well-off woman with an apparent lack of access to the household resources. Still, the man is attuned to the delicacy of her position. Drurie further exacerbates the tense mood, and the servant tries his best to calm it down: "Feed not my mistress's anger."

165. Be useful or helpful. Anne Sanders is saying that she does not have the money that she needs.

166. Act of obtaining, usually a payment or repayment.

167. Mary, the mother of Jesus, used as an oath.

168. Wishes or desires.

169. The breaking of her agreement to purchase the goods she had ordered; critics refer to this as the "breach of contract" scene.

170. Both men take great pains to extend credit to this obviously regular and good client, though the extent of their assurances seems extreme ("were it thrice the value").

171. The most common coin in circulation (in both gold and silver), worth 5 shillings, or $135 in today's money.

172. Berated, in trouble. The apprentice or journeyman fears his master's anger if he loses the sale and returns back to the shop with the goods.

173. Don't ask me again.

174. Of little worth or account; here simply, a lowly servant. Drurie is insinuating that George places ("reposes") more trust in his servant than in his wife.

175. By what sign did you know you'd be upset ("chafed"). How did you know?

176. To requite or replace the evil with good fortune. See figure 10: palm reading (Resurgens Theatre production, 2018).

177. The life line in palm reading is one of the three major lines (along with head line and heart line). It starts between thumb and forefinger and extends to the root of the thumb.

178. This is one way that the play obliquely alludes to Golding's *Briefe discourse*. In her confession, Mistress Drurie clarifies that, despite reports, she did not poison her own husband or "deal with witchcraft and sorcerie" (appendix 144–45). In this scene her boast may be more false advertising than a factual assertion that she did practice palmistry. Earlier, Roger says that she makes her living by being a bawd, and he also claims she is "studying the law" (1.162). Many people, especially single women who lived on the margins, cobbled together a living and participated in informal economies that historians call "the economy of make-shift" or "make-do."

179. The logic of Drurie's argument is insidious in a few ways: she uses religion to countenance what will become two grave sins; she suggests that Anne Sanders's husband is better off dead because he will be in heaven with God; and she attests that it is God's plan for Anne Sanders to remarry. Yet Drurie also tries to seduce Anne with earthly temptations (new clothes, a large staff of servants, a coach).

180. A French hood, a head covering worn by women, usually associated with wealth and status. See figure 11: French hood.

181. Marry, like Mary above—an oath.

182. Complain.

183. If compelled, I could tell you his name.

184. Ironic since this is likely Anne Sanders's wedding ring.

185. The adverb "iwis" meant truly or indeed. The *OED* notes a common misreading of iwis: "The writing with capital I, and separation of the two elements, have led later authors to understand and use it erroneously as *I wot, I know*, as if a present of *I wist*." *OED online*, s.v. "Iwis," accessed November 3, 2019, https://www.oed.com. The quarto prints as two words, "I wis," which has led to this misreading.

186. Drurie claims to have the skill to be able to restate ("rehearse") the exact conversation between Anne and Browne that day on the stoop (sc. 6). This claim is disengenuous, yet technically true, since Browne in fact told her about their conversation.

187. Meantime.

188. This is a soliloquy in the tradition of a villain, such as Shakespeare's Richard III, who lets the audience know what he plans to do next, even as he figures this out himself. See *Richard III* 1.1.1ff.

189. In this precise moment or location; compare "in the nick of time."

190. See figure 12: Tragedy with a bowl of blood (Resurgens Theatre production, 2018).

191. Past participle of "sit." We would say "sat."

192. This is another reference to the black ("sable") curtains from the induction. Tragedy's distinction between the power words and deeds ("acts") was a point debated in literature from the period. Her speech also changes the tone from "comic" to "tragic" with words like "hideous" and "dreadful."

193. Ebony. Tapers were long candles usually used for ceremonial purposes.

194. Windows.

195. The "train" refers to the cast of characters who will enact the dumb show—Lust, Chastity, Anne Sanders and Browne, Drurie and Roger. The Furies set out candles and goblets and such and then "usher" in the humans.

196. Drinking cups or goblets. Muriel Bradbrook conjectures that "the tradition of these diabolical suppers" informs *Macbeth*'s cauldron scene, adding, "a great deal of painstaking and elaborate work went into the staging of atrocities." Bradbrook, *Themes and Conventions*, 18.

197. Cannon cites Bradbrook on the soundscape's importance, including the striking of the clock, music, and bells. Cannon, *Warning for Fair Women*, 182n799–800; Bradbrook, *Themes and Conventions*, 119. "Within" meant inside or offstage.

198. The human figures. This section is the printed stage direction for the dumb show's symbolic action; Tragedy repeats some of the information in her speech. In performance, she would speak as the action unfolds.

199. Toasts.

200. This seems to be the only proof of their sexual relationship, since the play does not show the lovers together until after the murder, when they argue. See introduction.

201. Performances at court that included courtiers performing dances and speeches. Professional playwrights, including Ben Jonson, wrote masques for royal performances, which could be outlandishly expensive to produce. Tragedy means that this show presages the "real" action that follows in the human world.

202. Seems to refer to Anne Sanders, given the next line.

203. The tone takes on a new gravity, with references to hell and devils. Here Tragedy informs the audience of the indisputable fact that Roger and Drurie are plotting together. "Drifts" means impulses, tendencies, while "broker" was a

synonym for retailer, but when used contemptuously ("base"), referred to dealers in criminal activities as in pawnbroker as used today.

204. Although it may seem that Murder is personified, it is only capitalized; Murder is not a character in the dumb show.

205. Anne Sanders.

206. Tragedy asserts Anne Sanders's "consent" to or at least knowledge of her spouse's murder, but the degree of Anne Sanders's complicity remains ambiguous throughout the play proper. For example, see scene 6 when she says, "Pray God that Captain Browne hath not been moved / By some ill motion, to endanger him" (lines 98–99).

207. A "magic wand"?

208. Until recently.

209. Cannon changes the line "Murther ('Murder') settes downe her blood" to read "Tragedy," correctly noting that Murder is not a character; one of the Furies who had poured wine earlier might also be carrying the bowl with which to bloody the humans' hands. Cannon explains that murder is a state of mind—the human actors permit "Murder into all their hearts" (*Warning for Fair Women*, 182–83).

210. To use or into practice. Compare "inured," which means used to, as in "he was inured to his discomfort."

211. "Because you make me comfortable at your house, I come often, and would rather you think me rude than too formal." George Sanders repeats the sentiment again soon after when he says he would rather be "unmannerly than ceremonious."

212. The play never specifies what this "occasion" is, but it seems that George Sanders has more business doings on his way home.

213. "Passion of me" was an oath referring to Christ's passion or suffering. Think of the man as striking his forehead because he almost forgot something— perhaps George Sanders's account book, a document, or a package of leftovers to send home with Sanders.

214. In this soliloquy Browne begins logically, talking about why he has chosen this spot to assault George Sanders and which route Sanders is most likely to take because it's so late. He addresses himself ("George"). Then his rhetoric, as in previous speeches, soon escalates to tragic, dark, and even demonic, as he launches into an apostrophe: "O, sable Night," claiming to "hate the light," which sounds like something a fallen angel would say. He asks "Night" or darkness to "cover" his deed. See also "The Rape of Lucrece": "Till sable Night, mother of Dread and Fear, / Upon the world dim darkness doth display" and Lucrece's apostrophe to night (168–69, 808–50). Hopkinson rightly

hears Macbeth's "Come, sealing night" speech (3.2.52–56). Hopkinson, *Warning for Fair Women*, 105n37–38.

215. To let flow out. George Sanders's "life" (the fact that he is alive) hinders or inhibits Browne's love.

216. Browne asks Night personified to be his cloak or "cover."

217. George Sanders is getting close ("fair") to where Browne stands.

218. It's good to see/meet you.

219. Lombard Street is an ancient Roman road in an area that was given to northern Italian goldsmiths (from the Lombardy region) by King Edward I in the thirteenth century, and until fairly recently, Lombard Street was the banking and financial center of London. This detail, like other street names and landmarks (e.g., St. Dunstan's Church) supports Tragedy's initial claim that this is a story "too well known"—that is familiar to London audiences. See also the introduction.

220. With the good food, drink, and company, George Sanders has lost track of the time. "Gone past" or "surpassed."

221. Obliged, grateful. "I owe you one."

222. In this soliloquy, Browne reflects on his failure to stab George Sanders, addressing, in turn, his intended victim ("thou"), personified Night, the torch ("brand"), and Sanders again, and earlier he spoke to himself, "George."

223. The sense of fate operating in the world is strong in the play, as when Drurie convinces Anne Sanders that she is destined by God to remarry (sc. 4). Divine Providence and fate are similar to a belief in the supernatural, which is a motif in the play. *Julius Caesar* is another good example of these beliefs operating side by side, where signs and augurs figure so centrally.

224. Ominous, threatening.

225. Browne is cursing the Night and the servant's torch for thwarting his assassination. A "masque" here means a company or troupe.

226. Browne is addressing the torch ("brand") and sounds a bit like Macbeth talking to the "dagger of the mind" (2.1.50).

227. Come back.

228. An officer of the royal household of England in charge of payments and oversight of the other officers. A coffer was a strong box and metonymically the treasury; the cofferer was like a treasurer.

229. We never learn the nature of this "matter at Saint Mary Cray," but presumably it is some real estate or other business. The name refers to the ancient parish church in a village that developed into a market town in the Middle Ages.

230. The "holy-day" of Easter Week. "Spittle" or "Spital" is short for a charitable hospital, which housed the poor and the sick. Sermons were preached on Easter Monday and Tuesday from a special pulpit at St. Mary Spital outside

of Bishopsgate. Originally part of a Catholic priory, this hospital survived the dissolution of the monasteries under Henry VIII.

231. The road from Woolwich to East London's Blackwell was dangerous, according to Beane, a rustic who may have in mind the "sailor town" area of East London, notoriously rough and chaotic. Recent histories of these working-class neighborhoods challenge such stereotypes.

232. Insult referring to a head void of sense; Barnes is both punning on Beane's desire for the choice meat of "calf's head" and calling him stupid. The master here totally discounts the servant's actually good advice as well as his ultimately justified sense of foreboding about travel.

233. The Thursday before Easter, also called "Holy Thursday." In the historical accounts and the play, George Sanders dies on the Tuesday after Easter.

234. Flat or even ground.

235. Beane seems to think his stumbling just as he sets off on his journey is a bad omen, and it was proverbial. See *Henry VI, Part 3*, when Richard of Gloucester finds his army locked out of a town: "The gates made fast? Brother, I like not this. / For many men that stumble at the threshold / Are well foretold that danger lurks within" (4.7.10).

236. Catches refers to the water taken with the oar at the beginning of a stroke, and hoyes are small boats usually used to carry passengers or goods over short distances. Beane is trying to calm his anxiety by talking to himself about the trip.

237. He says he can stop a thief ("false knave") with his hedge trimmers ("hedging bill"). Old John's eagerness to fight would probably be played for laughs, especially if he is cast or played as truly aged.

238. With the introduction of these rural working characters comes a shift to prose, something that playwrights did often to contrast the elevated speech of the upper classes. At the same time, Old John's and Joan's speech is vivid and even lyrical.

239. The most umber, or numerous. It could mean that the flowers in Joan's dream were umber-colored—deep red or dark brown (dead?). The *OED* cites this line as their sole entry for "umberst," defining it as "most numerous" because "umber" as a noun or verb sometimes meant number. *OED online*, s.v. "Umberst," accessed November 3, 2019, https://www.oed.com.

240. Carnations. A ruff was a starched and ruffled collar around the edge of a garment. A yeoman servant like John would wear a plain collar, not a fancy ruff like one sees in portraits of gentry and nobility from the period. See figure 13: a man's ruff collar.

241. Joan's dream contains imagery of death and burial (Beane's white shirt, blood, lying in a meadow). A bloody handkerchief does appear later in the

play (sc. 8). Reports of dreams advance the play's themes of the supernatural and superstition.

242. See also Mistress Quickly's report of Falstaff's death: he "babbled of green fields" (*Henry V*, 2.3.17).

243. Barking is a part of East London—too far off to actually be heard in Woolwich.

244. Past of "trow"; to suppose or imagine.

245. Old John's dream seems to attest to Anne Sanders's beauty; his reference to her visit to the Barnes household "last summer" corroborates information from the other merchant that the wives (or at least Anne) occasionally traveled with their husbands. For more information on women in mercantile domestic contexts, see Schleck, "Marital Problems"; Fury, *Tides in the Affairs of Men*; and Andrea, *Lives of Girls and Women*.

246. A close was an enclosed yard or field; here, a field where John has his cattle graze. Shooters or Shooter's Hill was the highest natural point in an area southeast of the city (now incorporated in London). Originally named for its association with archery practice in the Middle Ages, the area was an isolated and hence dangerous place to walk because of highwaymen ("shooters" of another sort). Shooter's Hill was also where certain convicted criminals were hanged, and where Browne's body eventually does hang. If George Sanders met Barnes at St. Mary Cray, which is south of Woolwich, and they spent the night at Woolwich, as Roger contends, then he and Beane are walking south again to Shooter's Hill and will then head west to London. Recall that earlier, Beane said the route just east of London was "the worst" part of the trip.

247. Joan refers to a dress or shift whose loose sleeves needed to be tied up. Used as an adjective, carnation meant some shade of pink or red. A groat was a coin valued at about four pennies. See Costard's question to Barone in Shakespeare's *Love's Labour's Lost*: "How much carnation ribbon / may a man buy?" (3.1.153–54).

248. The men call each other "father" and "son" to express their intimacy rather than any blood relationship. The old man wishes he had given Beane a bottle to be refilled with a strong distilled alcohol (such as brandy) at the Black Bull Tavern in an area in central London called Battle Bridge or Battlebridge, an ancient crossing of the River Fleet.

249. Quarrelers, troublemakers. Joan is saying, "Stay out of trouble!"

250. Don't give it another thought. "But let that pass" is a phrase that Margery Eyre uses often in Thomas Dekker's London comedy, *The Shoemaker's Holiday*.

251. Thought of as or considered.

252. Proverbial sounding, the phrase is clearly racist, meant to express an insurmountable disparity: "A coward who fails to follow through with the

murder does not deserve Anne Sanders in the same way that a [B]lack man (of any rank) has no right to 'embrace' (touch, have a relationship with) a (presumably white) queen." Embedded in such language is a fear of miscegenation and a sense of white superiority, though Englishmen traveled to, were captives in, or voluntarily relocated to areas throughout the Mediterranean where some married local women of color. A similar saying appears in Ben Jonson's *Masque of Blackness* (1605), performed by female courtiers in blackface, which proved scandalous for the white women. An Ethiopian goddess promises a sun: "Whose beams shine day and night, and are of force / To blanch an Æthiop, and revive a corse. / His light sciential is, and, past mere nature, / Can salve the rude defects of every creature" (lines 240–44). The idea conveyed is one of impossibility, like "when pigs fly," but ideas like this were rooted in the presumed unchangeable nature of black skin, parallel to a belief that one's basic nature was immutable. Shakespeare and many white European authors use terms such as "Egyptian," "Moor," or "Ethiope" to stand for Black, often as a negative comparison to "fair" (as white and even good); see for example, *The Two Gentlemen of Verona* (1594): "And Silvia—witness Heaven, that made her fair!—/ Shows Julia but a swarthy Ethiope" (2.6.25–26) and Romeo's praise of Juliet, who "hangs upon the cheek of night / Like a rich jewel in an Ethiope's ear" (1.5.42–43). "To wash the Ethiop white" was another long-lived phrase that originated in Aesop's fable about a Black slave trying to whiten himself to please his master. Another phrase meaning "that will never happen" was anti-Semitic, illustrated in Andrew Marvell's poem "To His Coy Mistress," where the male lover jokes that a woman will refuse to comply with his desires indefinitely, or "until the conversion of the Jews" (line 10). Gurr suggests that the negro/queen saying in *A Warning* may be an allusion to Aaron, the Black Moor and his lover, Tamara, the Queen of Goths, both taken captive to Rome in Shakespeare's first tragedy, *Titus Andronicus*. Gurr, *Shakespeare Company*, 134. Also notable is that Aaron appropriates the anti-Black racism to claim his own racial pride: "Coal-black is better than another hue, / In that it scorns to bear another hue; / For all the water in the ocean / Can never turn the swan's black legs to white, / Although she lave them hourly in the flood" (4.2.103–7). When readers encounter this kind of imagery, they should consider what it is doing in the context of the speech, work, and period, but they should not ignore racism because it appears in a historical document. Consulting contemporary sources (such as the *OED* and Open Source Shakespeare) can lead to some interesting discoveries. Among the excellent critical work on race in general and Blackness in particular in the early modern period are Chapman, *Anti-Black Racism*; Charry, *Arden Guide to Renaissance Drama*; Erickson and Hall, "Special Issue on Race"; Hall, *Things of Darkness*; Little, *Shakespeare Jungle Fever*; Loomba and Burton, *Race in Early Modern England*; Newman, "'And Wash the Ethiop White'"; and Thompson, *Colorblind Shakespeare*.

253. Lose heart or despair of obtaining Anne Sanders. Next follows Drurie's pep talk.

254. Follow, track, like a hunting dog.

255. Coarsely abusive name, like "bastard," here meant playfully.

256. Browne seems to imply that the information Roger brings will make up for the time lost while Roger was out tracking George Sanders.

257. This speech could be played for laughs in the way that Juliet's nurse enters panting with news of Romeo that Juliet is impatient to hear (*Romeo and Juliet*, 2.5).

258. Cornhill, part of London where Leadenhall Market and the Royal Exchange were located. "Cornwell" appears on the first map of London from 1559, though the actual name of the street was Cornhill, from Old English *corn* and *hyll*, a hill where corn was grown or sold. Cornhill is also the name of the ward of the city where the Royal Exchange stood, so it was natural for merchants to be there. Mills, *Dictionary of London Place-Names*.

259. The chief meal of the day, eaten at midday; the equivalent of our modern-day lunch.

260. Some kind of royal officer, based in Greenwich.

261. Roger says that he himself ferried ("in a pair of oars") in order to keep up his close pursuit. Note the play's many references to the Thames, its ferry boats, quays/keys, and watermen. Greenwich Palace, built along the river, was one of the royal palaces where the Tudors held court. The riverside was an appealing site because water travel was easier, faster, and safer than unpaved roads. Greenwich was both close to the city and also a kind of country estate, where the royal family and their guests could escape the increasingly crowded city with its perceived smells, noise, and disease. Elizabeth I was born there and, as queen, used Greenwich, especially in the summer. See "Greenwich and the Tudors" on the Royal Museums Greenwich website. Recall that earlier Barnes sent Beane to the palace with a message for the cofferer. Later, Browne goes to Greenwich to form his alibi.

262. Lion's Quay or Key was a ferry stop along the Thames just east of London Bridge. From there, the Sanderses could walk home. See figure 5: Map of *A Warning*'s London.

263. A mildly offensive expression that people said in anger; here the phrase means something like, "I'll be darned." Drurie is giving Browne a broad hint to tip the messenger for his "pains."

264. Presumptuous.

265. You can hide out at my house.

266. The best place to lie in wait.

267. In my opinion.

268. Closed-off, well-concealed.

269. Another ferry landing just to the east of Lion's Key.

270. Be quiet to avoid being discovered.

271. Suspect.

272. A key or quay was a stone or metal platform lying alongside or projecting into water, where ships and ferries land to load and unload cargo and passengers.

273. Voice.

274. Silver coin worth two shillings and sixpence; about forty dollars in today's money; a huge tip.

275. "I had no choice or say in the matter." Later in this scene Sanders accepts another professional obligation—Barnes's insistence on a "Tuesday" meeting without consulting his wife.

276. Know, think.

277. Probably a meal or drink that Anne Sanders provided at her house.

278. Browne seems to speak this as if Roger is not there, and his words increasingly admit religious significance to the failed murder, assuming that George Sanders is "guard[ed]" or protected by divine power or prayer.

279. Compare the saying, "The third time's the charm."

280. In a financial context "to pay home" meant to pay back the full amount borrowed or for a purchase, but it was also used metaphorically to mean to punish someone as much as they deserve, to take revenge on; in this context, to the point of killing him. *OED online*, s.v. "To pay home," accessed November 3, 2019, https://www.oed.com. Interestingly in *Arden of Faversham*, the killers use this phrase for the cuckolded husband whom they track from Kent to London and finally kill at "home" (1.515). In modern revenge movie language: "It's payback time!"

281. Compare "blind fury."

282. This scene represents and also recaps the consummation of the love affair via the "embrace" (dumb show 2.25, 31, 42), action that does not take place in the play proper; the dumb show also, especially as explained by Tragedy, predicts the murder that has not yet happened.

283. Private or secretive; the viewer is never told what the "secret business" is regarding St. Mary (or Marie) Cray, which was an area known for a church and a market. See Martin, *Women, Murder, and Equity*, 81.

284. The quarto text reads "shere the labouring vitall threed of life." To shear is to cut, and the three Destinies (called Moirae and Fates) were sister goddesses who were thought to control people's destinies by cutting their life threads. We still say, for example, that someone's life is "hanging by a thread."

285. Presumably this pronoun refers to Anne Sanders, though it is not totally clear.

286. Gladly.

287. A reference to the first dumb show, when, as Tragedy explains, Drurie, Browne, and Roger "thus with blood their hands shall be imbrued," while dipping only Anne Sanders's finger in the bowl (76, 90).

288. An ambiguous pronoun referent; is Lust or Browne "the only actor"?

289. Browne is clearly jumpy here, first panicked at the thought that George Sanders is not alone, and then proclaiming that he could handle "ten thousand lives" and massacre ten men (8.7, 27–30).

290. A youth or adolescent male; here used dismissively. Browne is still angry that Beane disrupted the previous murder attempt by showing up with Mistress Sanders at Lion's Key.

291. Greenwich Park; the grounds around Greenwich Palace. Blackheath is the green space south of Greenwich.

292. There are two of them.

293. Fight.

294. Care; compare "reckless."

295. Joan will later note that the day is "dismal" (8.138–39). Both instances give a sense of foreboding and further the idea of signs or omens operating.

296. Sanders means there is another traveler (whom they do not recognize as Browne) on the road ahead who might keep them "company."

297. Keep going.

298. John Beane is thinking of Joan's dream of him in a meadow with carnations (gilliflowers), and she herself will mention yet another dream about Beane when she next appears. Some characters put more weight on dreams than others. George Sanders scoffs at "visions," as does Old John. (Recall Old John's similar assertion that "dreams are but fancies" [6.79–80] or fantasies.) On the popularity or dream interpretation and other folk practices, see Thomas, *Religion and the Decline of Magic*.

299. Ruined or destroyed.

300. Lowly servant. Interesting use of class markers in this scene; in the next line Sanders plays on Browne's gentle status as a reason not to kill him.

301. Meant as plural, "sins."

302. Untimely; Anne Sanders later calls Browne the "author" of her woe (11.68).

303. The holes made in the cloth bring to mind Julius Caesar's cloak that Mark Antony uses as a prop in his funeral oration (*Julius Caesar* 3.1). Hieronimo in Kyd's *The Spanish Tragedy* also dips his handkerchief in blood. For a brilliant analysis of bloody "napkins" on the stage, see Balizet, *Blood and Home*. See figure 14: Browne with the handkerchief (Resurgens Theatre production, 2018).

304. Unholy, profane.

305. Browne's soliloquy shows his instantaneous regret.

306. Browne's regret is so strong that he would not kill again for all the wealth of "a kingdom." This moment ushers the rhymed couplets that close the verse portion of the scene, after which Old John and Joan enter speaking prose.

307. Browne confesses that he is now afraid of his own shadow.

308. "Creeping" is a term from Golding's account. This is the type of stage direction that Cannon considers more descriptive than theatrical.

309. The phrase was apparently newly coined in the sixteenth century, according to the *OED*. *OED online*, s.v. "The coast is clear," accessed November 3, 2019, https://www.oed.com.

310. Expression used to communicate grief, regret, or surprise. Juliet's nurse and mother each cry "Alack the day" when they think that Juliet is dead (*Romeo and Juliet* 4.5).

311. Unwilling; my life does not want to leave my limbs; I don't want to die.

312. Nearby.

313. This phrase seems nonsense to Cannon, but I think "harlotries" refers to the cattle themselves, as worthless or bad because they have run off. In fact, the *OED* provides an illustration from 1598 that uses the term to describe undesirable cattle: "harletry runts." *OED online*, s.v. "Harlotry," accessed November 3, 2019, https://www.oed.com. "Bespoken" means ordered or commissioned, and here, by extension bewitched, possessed.

314. Wandering. Old John's herd has dispersed and he thinks they are "bewitched"; this unusual or unnatural behavior he takes as evidence, like the "dismal" weather, of some evil. See also *Macbeth*: on the night of Duncan's murder, horses "Turned wild in nature, broke their stalls, flung out, / Contending 'gainst obedience, as they would / Make war with mankind," and there are rumors that the horses did "eat each other" (2.4.20–24).

315. Early modern almanacs were books of tables and calendars outlining astronomical data, church holidays and other anniversaries, and astrological and meteorological forecasts, including *dies male* (or evil or unlucky days, from which the word "dismal" derives). See also Cannon, *Warning for Fair Women*, 185n1436.

316. Short for "belong," owed to or attributable to. Joan runs through possible explanations for the strange occurrences—from the bereft cow's madness to the "dismal day," from her bloody nose to her dream that Beane was married and the cow killed.

317. Tawny, brown.

318. Joan's nosebleed and her belief in its portent echo Anne Sanders's yellow spots—both are somatic manifestations of something amiss. See also Balizet, *Blood and Home*.

319. Marie, or Mary, was Jesus's mother; said as an oath.

320. Make the sign of the cross; bless yourself. See figure 15: Old John and Joan discover Beane (Resurgens Theatre production, 2018).

321. Ginger is still used as a remedy for nausea and for reviving someone from fainting and delirium. There are countless references in English medieval and early modern texts to this spice/root that was imported from South Asia.

322. "Sweb" and "swound" each mean to faint or swoon; by "cut my lace" Joan means that her dress is holding her ribcage too tightly and she may pass out. Cleopatra asks for her lace to be cut when she fakes a fainting spell (*Antony and Cleopatra* 1.3.85).

323. "God forbid."

324. Old John asks whether Beane has attempted suicide.

325. Handkerchief.

326. Joan curses the murderer: "Let him have no joy and be rewarded with execution." Mead meant reward.

327. Or wer-a-day. Exclamation of sorrow or lamentation. See the nurse in Shakespeare's *Romeo and Juliet* when she tells Juliet that Tybalt is dead (3.2.42).

328. "Desperate Dick" seems to have been a colloquial phrase for a criminal and the subject of ballads in the period; the name "Dick" was more common for a lower-class man. Interestingly, of course, the killer is not some lowborn criminal, but a fine captain. Anthony Munday includes this name among his list of other bad men, like "Sim Swashbuckler" (Biir). "Desperate Dick" is an entry in John Taylor, the Water Poet's *EPIGRAMMES* (London, 1630): "Dick is a desperate fellow, but at what? / He hath no mercy on his meat, or Wench. / He drank a Dutch man drunk as any Ratt, / He's stouter at a Trencher, then a Trench" (#65, reprinted in Spenser Society's *Works of John Taylor, the Water-Poet*). In Shakespeare's play, *Love's Labours Lost*, Berowne assumes that someone betrayed him: "Some mumble-news, some trencher-knight, some Dick, / That smiles his cheek in years and knows the trick / To make my lady laugh when she's disposed, / Told our intents before" (Folger 5.2.509–12).

329. "Are you finished binding the wounds?"

330. Gently.

331. Slipping away.

332. Master was a title; today we say "mister." James seems to be a kind of legal functionary who is later appointed to manage this case against Browne.

333. See cast of characters.

334. Ale is an alcoholic drink made from fermented grain and bittered with herbs, and beer is bittered with hops. In this period both were important sources of nutrition. "Small beer," also known as table beer or mild beer, which was highly nutritious, contained just enough alcohol to act as a preservative

and provided hydration without intoxicating effects. These drinks were made domestically and sold by women (alewives), a profession later taken over by male guilds (Brewers) and later still moved into industrial settings. See Bennett, *Ale, Beer, and Brewsters*.

335. This is a nod to Queen Elizabeth's largesse. Notice how the staff comment on Browne's status of "gentleman"; the citizens of London and Rochester will also later express regret that a man of this high stature could be capable of such a crime.

336. A jack was a vessel for liquor (either for holding liquor or for drinking from) and a court dish was a little tray of snacks, like a sampler platter, as suggested in the *OED* example from G. Goodman's *The Court of King James I* (ca. 1656): "The King caused his carver to cut him out a court-dish, that is, something of every dish, which he sent him, as part of his reversion." *OED online*, s.v. "Court-dish," accessed November 3, 2019, https://www.oed.com.

337. Thirsty.

338. Refill. The steward is offering to top off Browne's cup.

339. He looks as though he has traveled far.

340. Eltham was a town due south of Shooter's Hill and about eight miles from London. It was home to English kings in the Middle Ages; for example, Edward III was born at Eltham House in 1315 and held Parliament there during his reign.

341. Startle or scare animals. A "brace" is two, a pair.

342. Browne's quick thinking explains away his bloody hose: he chanced upon some rabbits, killed one, and as he gutted the animal ("garbage" meant entrails or guts), the blood "befell" or happened to stain his socks, but the men agree that "it will [come] out again."

343. Portion of the day before noon.

344. Chamber of Presence, where a distinguished person receives visitors; in this case, Queen Elizabeth.

345. Sign, token, emblem. Recall in the induction, History carried an ensign, like a flag in battle.

346. A list or record of any kind, not necessarily the days of the week as we think of today. Significantly, "calendar" also referred to a docket of prisoners' names, and this "red lettered text" ("bloody letters") points to church holy or feast days that almanacs marked in red ink, and, by extension, to Anne Sanders's "future 'red-letter days' in the court, jail, and gallows." Balizet, *Blood and Home*, 79.

347. Outraged, frantic. Like Browne after he kills George Sanders in scene 8, Anne Sanders immediately regrets the action.

348. Reveal or betray.

349. The closeness of neighbors is mentioned a number of times in the play, a reference to the increasing density of London's buildings. See Orlin, *Locating Privacy*; Capp, *When Gossips Meet*; and Greenberg, *Metropolitan Tragedy*.

350. A covert plan.

351. Unnatural, out of order.

352. Exclamation of disgust.

353. In this context "pampered" has the likely meaning of "excessively indulging" in an emotion or thought rather than living luxuriously.

354. Enticing; Anne Sanders blames her beauty for being alluring. Browne will do the same (11.70–71).

355. Anne Sanders is playing on the words "do," "done," and "misdone." Her idea is that in the "misdeed" of killing her husband, she may as well do violence on herself since in marriage the husband and wife become one. The phrase "the better part" is an allusion to the biblical book of Genesis and the Anglican marriage service, where a couple becomes "one flesh." Even today, some people refer to their partner as their "better half." "Therefore shall a man leave his father and his mother, and shall cleave unto his wife: and they shall be one flesh" (Gen. 2:24 [King James Version (KJV)]).

356. Private room or inner chamber, not the place to store clothes as it is for us.

357. Drurie hopes that Browne might ease Anne Sanders's fit of suffering. "Haply" means "perhaps," not happily, but the pun is also operating.

358. Careful, cautious.

359. A game of betting on "heads or tails," originally called in French *croix ou pile* based on the images on a coin.

360. Tokens or coins.

361. I'll put down a stake or lay a bet like a *proper* gambler ("gamester"). Young Sanders wants to play a full game, when Harry suggests a kind of winner-take-all in the line above.

362. George Sanders was in fact en route from his meeting with Barnes, who lives in Woolwich, when he was slain. It is worth noting that the Sanders family members seem to know where the father is, and he is rarely at home (as in scene 2). See Christensen, *Separation Scenes*, 69–102.

363. Harry is offering his coin; "good" in this context meant not counterfeit. *OED online*, s.v. "Good," accessed November 3, 2019, https://www.oed.com.

364. Upset, hysterical.

365. The uptick in Browne's tone shows his own jumbled emotions and guilty thoughts, as he realizes that this murder did not bring him together with Anne Sanders at all, but rather divided them ("at variance").

366. Full of shock or fear.

367. Nearest.

368. Something that brings about bad luck or misfortune.

369. Later, in fact, the wounds of Beane, his other victim, will bleed freshly (sc. 15).

370. Roger may be referring to the boy's schoolmaster or his father, but in any case—an unfounded threat meant to scare the boys away.

371. Whipped, slapped, punished.

372. A conflation of "godfather," this title of address was used when speaking to an older man.

373. A piece of ribbon or cord used to lace a garment or fasten a shoe; Sanders Jr. and Harry try to pay off Roger not to reveal their petty crime.

374. A mythical reptile said to kill the person who looked at it. This begins a list of impossibilities that Anne Sanders compares to finding comfort from her husband's killer. The tenor of Anne's speech throughout the scene is heightened and poetic, reflecting her emotional state.

375. To excessively consume food or drink; recall Drurie's story about the water bearer's wife who had "surfeited" on beans.

376. Soothed or consoled.

377. Origin or cause.

378. Figure out, plan.

379. Heal.

380. The Cimmerian people were thought to be the earliest known inhabitants of Crimea in Asia Minor; their first mention in Western literature may be Homer's *Odyssey* (book 11.14), a people who lived in perpetual mist and darkness near Hades, the land of the dead. The proverbial expression was used to signify any kind of dense darkness or gloom.

381. Device, strategy, or trick.

382. This image alludes to the story of Jesus's entrance to Jerusalem at the end of his life, when everyone is celebrating. But "some of the Pharisees from among the multitude said unto him, Master, rebuke thy disciples. And he answered and said unto them, I tell you that, if these should hold their peace, the stones would immediately cry out" (Luke 19:39–40).

383. These could be small boxes with papers and supplies or some kind of wooden structure; a jury box or witness box, though the *OED* records this usage only in 1822. *OED online*, s.v. "Boxes," accessed November 3, 2019, https://www.oed.com.

384. This lord is shocked that the murder took place so close to the Queen's residence, as if the killer were deliberately flouting the law. "Durst" means "dares."

385. They are amazed that one so gravely injured as Beane is able to positively identify the murderer, or "tell [his] marks."

386. Like a police APB (all-points bulletin), "hue and cry" was a call from street to street or town to town to pursue a felon.

387. Spoken of or rumored.

388. The speech tag reads "Lo." (for Lord) without specifying which one.

389. A place where liquor and/or provisions are stored.

390. Officers of a town or borough with various legal and civic duties, including keeping prisoners.

391. Identify Browne by these markers—clothes, bloody stockings, and so forth.

392. Otherwise.

393. A collective noun for gold or silver vessels and utensils. Roger has been asked to pawn some of the women's household items to raise money for Browne's flight; Anne Sanders in her later arraignment denies this and accuses Roger of being a thief (sc. 17). The trade in second-hand clothing and other goods was a staple of the London economy and the theater business in particular and was very often conducted by women. See Korda, *Labors Lost*.

394. "Taken," elided into one syllable in order to maintain the pentameter line.

395. Figure something out. Recall that in scene 4 George Sanders tells his man that his wife must "shift it" or make do with waiting for her money.

396. A position or juncture where one can do no more, a hopeless extremity.

397. Contrive, manage to obtain.

398. Lying under a curse; doomed to perdition or misery. Each of the conspirators blames the other: Drurie and Browne in this dialogue accuse each other of prompting the crime, and Browne also earlier suggested that Anne Sanders's incomparable beauty made him kill her husband; Anne calls him the "author" of her misery.

399. He is afraid to seek out his family members ("mine own") for aid.

400. Pawned.

401. Roger enters as if on cue, suggesting perhaps that he (or he and Drurie) are scamming Browne. Roger reports that Anne Sanders can "make," or come up with, only six pounds. "Take it in worth" means take whatever you can get for the plate.

402. Proverbial: "Poverty parts friends."

403. Nan was another name for Anne. It does seem odd that both the women are named Anne and both the husband and lover (and the milliner) are named George.

404. Drurie is clearly shaken up and refuses to go out of her house to Anne's; to "keep close" was to be enclosed or private.

405. Browne addresses his victim in an apostrophe, the gist of which is, "Sanders, if you were alive, I would not have engineered your death (which was done from my love and impatience) for all the money in London." He prays

for other men not to do such crimes. "Tall" here refers not to height but means proper, honorable, or good.

406. The meaning of this couplet is not clear, but the gist of it seems to be that Browne blames his lust ("heat of love") for leading to his ambition ("climbing") to win Mistress Sanders, though perhaps he refers to climbing up to the gallows. See also Hopkinson, *Warning for Fair Women*, 114n45.

407. Providing the opportunity for the murder to occur. Personified Sin has lured the parties to desire, had them agree to act on that desire, and provided the opportunity for them to commit the sin.

408. Savagery, brutality.

409. Hidden or kept from sight. Tragedy accurately explains how, after the murder, everyone involved expresses anger at the others and are unhappy with the outcome. The lines that follow are full of ironic antitheses—that the "rest" or relief they sought became "unrest" and anxiety, "delight" or happiness at being together in fact grew "danger[ous]" and fearful, while "confidence" or hope in their accomplishment turned to "despair."

410. Dismissed.

411. The act of murder ("lawless actions and prodigious crimes") damages not only the victims but also the perpetrators ("their ministers").

412. To lay oneself facedown on the ground.

413. Sprinkled.

414. Gentle and softening. Mercy tries to calm Chastity, who is crying and acting wildly; "humility" below means that Mercy is trying to get Chastity to act more decorously, to be less demanding and so forth.

415. Presented as proof or an example of something. Along with the main actors, some "officers" carry in Sanders's body.

416. Immediate questioning, straightaway.

417. "Judge not, that ye be not judged. / For with what judgment ye judge, ye shall be judged: and with what measure ye mete, it shall be measured to you again" (Matt. 7:1–2 [KJV]) and "Whoso sheddeth man's blood, by man shall be shed" (Gen. 9:6 [KJV]). See also Balizet, *Blood and Home*, 80; and Siegel, "*Measure for Measure*."

418. Odd, strange.

419. Captain Browne explains in a lie that the inn where he usually stays ("wont to host") is occupied by "Frenchmen"—a curious detail, likely referring to French Protestants, or Huguenots, who were religious refugees living in England. Elizabethan audiences would know Rochester's history of martyrdom on both Catholic and Protestant sides and its reputation as a refuge for poor wayfarers. In the first half of the sixteenth century, John Fisher was bishop of Rochester, later becoming a cardinal. Henry VIII executed Fisher

because he refused to sanction the King's divorce from Catherine of Aragon. (Fisher became a Roman Catholic saint in 1935.) The next bishop of Rochester, Anglican Nicholas Ridley, became a Reformation martyr, executed by Queen Mary (1550). In addition, in 1579 (after the events of the play, but before it was performed and published), one Richard Watts left money in his will to expand the Rochester Almshouse in order to accommodate "six poor travellers." It seems the playwright had this history of hospitality in mind as much as the prose accounts of Browne's flight when he wrote this episode. In any case, Captain Browne seems to be thinking on his feet, as he did at Greenwich with his "brace of hares" alibi to explain his bloodied stockings.

420. Plain, simple.

421. Captain Browne delivers a backhanded compliment here: "Despite my rank of gentleman, I willingly acknowledge familial ties to the lowest Browne around—even lower than a Rochester butcher!"

422. Misfortune, calamity.

423. Browne's invented creditor has had him declared to be outside the protection of the law. Outlawry status was a common problem for those unable to pay debts.

424. Browne explains that he is hiding out from London until the invented debt problem is resolved.

425. A junior heraldic officer attending a nobleman; here like a guard.

426. James, as the representative of the Queen's Privy Council, works in concert with the civic magistrates of Rochester, a provincial town, and London, the capital, to do official state business. Notably, the Mayor of Rochester is portrayed as competent in this play, when country magistrates were elsewhere depicted as either bumpkins or corrupt like Justice Shallow in *2 Henry IV* (3.2).

427. This claim equivocates: Browne wrongly believes that Beane died at the scene, and he trusts his coconspirators to lie for him.

428. The Privy Council was like the Queen's cabinet of advisors, who as a body managed national affairs including defense and royal patronage and other economic, legal, and religious matters. The council oversaw the management of this case, including the appointment of the magistrate and assize judge, the legal and spiritual examination of suspects, the conduct of the trial, and, according to Randall Martin, even the "abject speeches of repentance from the scaffold to justify their handling of the case." Martin, *Women, Murder, and Equity*, 83. Martin explains further that this level of direct intervention in this case by the council was unusual, stemming from "George Saunders' personal connections to government officials" including the Office of Exchequer and the Queen's Guard. Martin, *Women, Murder, and Equity*, 83, 223n7. See also Brooks, "Pam-

phlet by Arthur Golding,"183. These Sanders family connections make Browne's offer to Anne Sanders to use his own contacts at court even more absurd (sc. 2).

429. Misfortune.

430. Barnes is of course speaking of his fellow merchant, Sanders, not his man, Beane.

431. Serious and sober. Barnes may be trying to curry favor with James, a newly appointed member of the Privy Council. In any case, both James and Barnes have been thrust into a kind of celebrity status through their connection to the crime, and they exchange formal compliments and expressions of humility. See also below when Barnes commends the Mayor of Rochester for his contributions to the case (15.56–58).

432. Investigate.

433. One who is experiencing distress, sorrow, or misfortune; compare wretched.

434. As Old John and Joan were his rescuers and his friends, Beane thinks of them. In performance, this rural pair might be at Beane's side, although they have no lines.

435. Thirsty.

436. Barnes means that since the attack, Beane has not remembered things well.

437. With such strength.

438. Recently.

439. Required or appropriate.

440. The Mayor of Rochester explains how he learned of the case, apprehended Browne, and decided to stop at Woolwich en route to court because he knew the bodies had been taken there.

441. Painstaking or careful; one who takes pains, not one who is in pain. We would say "careful."

442. An oath, an elision of "by God's wounds," referring to Christ's pierced hands, feet, and side on the day of his crucifixion.

443. Beane's spontaneous bleeding or cruentation, as Balizet points out, is a "dramatic invention" that depicts "blood as a spectacular and irrepressible force." Balizet, *Blood and Home*, 87. How this bleeding would appear on stage is not clear. A number of contemporary texts report victims' (and even corpses') blood gushing out when their attackers appear. See *Daemonologie* by King James I: "as in a secret murther, if the deade carcase be at any time thereafter handled by the murtherer, it wil gush out of bloud, as if the blud wer crying to the heauen for reuenge of the murtherer" (63). See also Scot, *Discoverie of Witchcraft*, 247; and *Arden of Faversham*, where Alice, who has murdered her husband, cries, "The more I sound his name, the more he bleeds; / This blood condemns me, and in gushing forth, / Speaks as it falls and asks me why I did it" (21.4–6).

444. On tongues in wounds and wounds as voices, see Kahn, *Roman Shakespeare*.

445. To bend or curve something; here, it seems to mean help him sit up.

446. Master James is concurring with Barnes that this strange situation is "the . . . work of God" (the Lord).

447. Requite; in this case, to match.

448. King's Lynn (earlier known as Bishop's Lynn) is a seaport and market town in Norfolk about one hundred miles north of London. This story of how "murder . . . did come to light" via theatrical enactment may be familiar to readers from *Hamlet*, where "The Mousetrap," a "play within a play" stokes the guilty party's response (though not his confession). Another playwright, Thomas Heywood (in *An Apology for Actors*) records a story like this occurring in Amsterdam, and critics are not sure whether Heywood borrowed the contours from *A Warning* or the other way around, or whether the story originated in a Dutch morality play. See Cannon, *Warning for Fair Women*, 188–89n2026; and Ringler, "Hamlet's Defense," 206. Hopkinson reprints a number of such stories. Hopkinson, *Warning for Fair Women*, 116–17n100.

449. This is a kind of advertisement for tragedy: "written by a feeling pen / And acted by a good Tragedian" and recalls the induction, when the character of Tragedy speaks of drama moving even "the strictest eyes" to tears.

450. Whatever the case with these other stories, this one (Beane's revelation) is the work of God.

451. Give my regards.

452. In a lively manner, not "cheerfully."

453. Acknowledged, vouched for.

454. To die, stop breathing, when one's spirit leaves the body. The Bible has a number of examples of this phrase: Gen. 25:8–9, 35:29, 49:33, 50:13; Acts 5:5–6, 5:10; Mark 15:37; Luke 23:46; and Matt. 27:50, 59 (all KJV).

455. Hurry or make "haste" to London and tell the Justices that he wills or commands them to draw up the papers.

456. The mayor does not actually enter yet. See below.

457. This is a command: "Tell the Justices to draw up an indictment."

458. A nonspeaking role. Hopkinson thinks that "Humphries" refers to an actor (Master Humphrey Jeffs), not a character. Hopkinson, *Warning for Fair Women*, 119n. However, that actor seems to have played with Pembroke's Men, not the Chamberlain's Men.

459. Luck, circumstance.

460. Love, have affection for.

461. To do away with, to dispose of, to kill.

462. United, allied.

463. That Anne Sanders knew about the murder.

464. Interestingly, the officials begin to call Anne Drurie "Drurie's wife" now that the legal proceedings have begun—perhaps because women's legal status was tied a male relative. See Gowing, *Domestic Dangers*.

465. Browne makes it sound as though Drurie approached him to "affect the marriage" or make it happen. An "apple-squire" is a pander, an insulting term for the male companion of a bawd. Recall that in scene 3 Roger admits to Drurie that he knows that her sexual go-between work "is your trade, your living . . . . / Drive you the bargain, I will keep the door" (3.38).

466. Spirit, in this case, evil.

467. Acts or duties; neither the play nor the prose accounts provide much backstory for "services" that Browne performed in London, but everyone seems to have liked him.

468. The King's Court used in criminal cases and held at Westminster Hall. Browne's trial occurred here on April 17, 1573; Mistresses Drurie and Sanders were tried and sentenced on May 6 at the Guildhall, which was the sort of town hall where a number of famous trials took place. Readers may be familiar with the much later Zong case, tried at Guildhall in the 1780s, following the massacre of Black slaves, who had been thrown overboard from a ship. The outcome of the case impacted Britain's abolishment of the transatlantic slave trade and was the topic of the 2013 film, *Belle*.

469. Release or clear your conscience; i.e., admit Anne Sanders's guilt.

470. Several.

471. The characters use the word "lusty" in two senses, one meaning "lively" or strong and the other in our sense of "full of lust or sexual desire." Since Browne is presumably shackled, he is now "tame."

472. This dialogue injects a bit of comedy into the scene, as the officer makes jokes at Browne's expense. Like the pastoral characters Old John and Joan and the London carpenters Crow and Peart (sc. 20), working-class characters in early modern drama often contribute a wry commentary on the main action involving their "betters."

473. The railing in a courtroom separating spectators from court officials. The speech is meant to sound like a mouthful of legalese and might get a chuckle from the audience, especially when the price of the sword is mentioned.

474. Browne is using his status as "dead in law," or legally condemned to die, to attest to his truthfulness, as if to say, "why would I lie right before death?" Cannon sees this move as "an implied comparison to a deathbed utterance" and also notes that Browne is lying and his attempt to persuade the Lords of Mistress Sanders's innocence fails anyway. Cannon, *Warning for Fair Women*, 191n2210.

475. Show leniency or mildness toward Mistress Sanders. Presumably the Justice and Lord promise "no wrong" so that Browne will reveal her guilt.

476. Newgate was a London prison used in part as a holding tank where the accused would await their trials.

477. Executed criminals (or their heads) were often displayed as a deterrent to crime and as further punishment. Browne is protective of his image and legacy; he wants no more shame brought upon him by being made a post-mortem public spectacle.

478. The idea of making a good death was common in the period—that one ought to get right with God at the time of death, even if one's life was not exemplary. Compare the report on a traitor: "Nothing in his life became him like the leaving it" (*Macbeth* 1.4.8–9).

479. Together and individually.

480. Abbreviation for Latin *videlicet* or *videre licit*, literally "it is permitted to see," used to introduce something: "namely," "as follows."

481. A person who spun thread, working in the cloth industry; the epithet was appended to names of women, originally in order to denote their occupation. Beginning in this period it became the proper legal designation for an unmarried woman. In this case, the Annes are both widows.

482. 1573; Elizabeth I ascended the throne in 1558.

483. Our Lady's Day or Lady Day was formally known as "The Annunciation of the (Blessed) Virgin Mary," according to *The Book of Common Prayer*. It commemorated the day that an angel announced to Mary that she would bear the son of God. The holy day fell on March 25 in 1573.

484. Clearly revealed or obvious.

485. See figure 16: Anne Sanders in the courtroom wearing a white rose (Resurgens Theatre production, 2018).

486. Tinged or saturated. Recall that Browne stabbed into the cloth and dipped it in George Sanders's blood. The business of the handkerchief is the playwright's invention. See Balizet, *Blood and Home*, 87.

487. Lies, libels.

488. A room (most likely a bedroom) where a woman gave birth and spent time during and after her pregnancy; customarily only other women—a midwife, family members, and friends—would be allowed inside. All the prose accounts of the story specifically mention Anne Sanders's pregnancy during the trial and suggest that the delay of her sentencing was due to her delivering a baby, but here, this information seems to be Anne's last-ditch effort at an alibi. See appendix 139, 153; Martin, *Women, Murder, and Equity*, 83; and Balizet, *Blood and Home*, 87. Cannon concludes, "From the play it is not possible to learn that she had a child, presumably by Browne." Cannon, *Warning for Fair Women*, 185n1274.

489. It is not proper for a man to enter this woman-only space.

490. As other editors have also observed, the Justice is pursuing a line of investigation that the play has not developed in as much detail as the sources do, since the play only represents unchaste behavior via Anne and Browne's dumb show "embrace." In contrast, for example, Golding asserts at Anne Sanders's lustfulness.

491. Heartfelt.

492. The murder of a superior by a subordinate was considered particularly "unnatural" because it upset hierarchy; for this reason, as noted in the introduction, such a crime was petty treason.

493. Probably the actor playing Anne Sanders would have turned around and switched out the flower, as Dessen and Thomson have suggested (personal email correspondence, June 2018). This is how the Resurgens production handled the moment. Cannon adds this stage direction, noting that it turns "probably to scarlet or black"—for sin/lust and death. Cannon, *Warning for Fair Women*, 191n2312.

494. Browne asks why his execution is delayed ("stay[ed]").

495. I emended the punctuation, though the sense is still hard to follow. He seems to say that the children watching him walk to execution are crying for the Sanders children, whom he left fatherless.

496. This rhymed dialogue may sound tinny to our ears, as the Brownes reunite and ask each other about where and when they killed their victims and where they are to be executed. In performance, however, the actors would have to work to keep the tone somehow somber. The Resurgens production cut the brother, and the Shakespeare Institute readers, notably Alexander Thom who read Browne, managed to invoke some real feeling.

497. Convicted criminals were sometimes executed in the place where they allegedly committed their crimes. Recall that Browne begged not to be hanged in chains at Shooter's Hill but buried immediately.

498. An agreement, a promise not to betray Anne Sanders to the authorities.

499. Browne is debating a serious matter for a Christian who is about to die: the salvation of his eternal soul depends on a full confession, but he made a promise ("covenant") to protect Anne Sanders; additionally, he is concerned for his own reputation ("Shall it be said . . . ?"), which is also the reason why he wants his body to be buried and not displayed.

500. An attitude of regret or penitence. To be contrite is to be very sorry.

501. This public "confession" falls within a tradition of stage scaffold speeches as noted in the introduction. Because it seems both hyperbolic and out of the blue, Browne's rap sheet is perplexing; these sins do not seem to match the Browne that the Lords and others so admire in the play. But a version of this confession/speech is part of the public record (see appendix 145). Furthermore,

as Martin shows, criminals needed to be seen as "reprobates" who achieve a kind of spiritual transformation brought on by prison chaplains, who counseled, and, in some cases, exacted confessions or coauthored them. Martin, *Women, Murder, and Equity*, 88–97. Golding stresses that the other three prisoners were "raw and ignorant" about God (appendix 143).

502. Beastly, brutish, barbarous.

503. Brothels.

504. Wasteful gambling.

505. Betrayals or lies.

506. Wearing foreign outlandish clothes. This "sin" seems to flout in a very particular way the Protestant bourgeois values of industry, thrift, and modesty that that play associates with the Sanderses. See Bailey, *Flaunting*.

507. Browne's final couplet delivers a state-sanctioned moral: don't follow my bad example. Anne Sanders likewise provides a cautionary tale to her audience.

508. The Privy Council clearly refuses to comply with Browne's particular status-based request to be buried, *not* hung up in chains.

509. As noted in the introduction, Golding's *Brief discourse* records the case of Mell, the minister who had sued for Anne Sanders's freedom in order to marry her and was put in the stocks. See appendix 141–42.

510. Purely, wholly innocent.

511. The minister claims to have considered the possibilities and probabilities of Anne's guilt and determined her innocence, based on his "evidence," which is essentially Anne Sanders's denial and Drurie's admission of guilt.

512. Requite, to pay, clear from debt. This sounds like a bribe.

513. Arrogant, presumptuous, or prideful.

514. A contrivance; a sneaky plot or stratagem.

515. James's rhetorical question suggests that the minister's plot is obvious to everyone.

516. A wooden framework with holes for the head and hands, otherwise known as the stocks. See figure 17: pillory or stocks.

517. James states that such a large "fault" or indiscretion is an abuse of power that deserves a worse punishment or repayment. "Mean" means small, not cruel.

518. I follow Hopkinson, who changes the "two carpenters" to Tom Peart and Will Crow.

519. I add this detail in the stage direction because in the next scene Anne Sanders explains that she "heard men talk"—overhearing information that struck "her to the heart with horror" and leads her to return to Drurie for assurance. This eavesdropping moment appears in Golding's account, rendered so much more vividly on stage.

520. Something of considerable effect, in other words, "a whopper." The *OED* uses this line to illustrate that definition. Clearly it is primarily a pun on the "swinging" motion of the about-to-be-hanged bodies. *OED online*, s.v. "Swinger," accessed November 3, 2019, https://www.oed.com.

521. A glass or tankard of beer.

522. Smithfield was a popular gathering place in London, home to a livestock market and, later, a cloth fair outside St. Bartholomew's Church; it was also the main execution place in this period, notorious for Queen Mary's execution of condemned Protestants, called the Marian Martyrs, in the early 1550s. The preacher Anne Askew and William Wallace ("Braveheart") were both killed there, as was the preacher John Bradford whose *Works* Anne gives to her children. See "Open City: London."

523. Liberty; the keeper will let the women talk freely.

524. See figure 18: Anne Sanders and Drurie by the prison cell grate (Resurgens Theatre production, 2018).

525. Anne Sanders is using monetary terms to discuss the value of Drurie's love: "current" refers to money that is in circulation and in use (compare "currency") and "counterfeit" refers to false coins. "Unto the touch" meant to test for trueness of the coin.

526. Renounce, take back.

527. Turn over a new leaf.

528. Disguising.

529. Lawbreakers, sinners who refuse to confess and repent. Cannon points out how well both of the women "show a considerable facility with the language of piety," following Golding's *Brief discourse*. Cannon, *Warning for Fair Women*, 195n2634ff. As noted in the introduction, it is also significant that Drurie's ministrations rather than the Doctor's counsel lead Anne Sanders to her change of heart. See also Sheeha, "'[M]istris Drewry.'"

530. One who has been rejected by God. More generally, a wicked or unruly person.

531. Drurie's speech reveals that she has progressed beyond Browne in terms of weighing the pros and cons of salvation; for Drurie, the price of covering up is too high, and she will tell the truth rather than protect Anne Sanders.

532. "Perfect timing because here comes the Doctor now." (He is a doctor of divinity or theology, a minister.)

533. Based on the root "propitiate," which means to appease or reconcile (often with a deity), the gist is that Mistress Sanders's soul and God may regain their good relationship. This word is not in the *OED*.

534. In Golding's published account, Mistress Sanders delivers her penitence in prison before the Sanders family, "kneeling mildly on her knees, with abun-

dance of sorrowful tears" (appendix 141–42). Martin shows that all of these events in prison and on the gallows were orchestrated by the clergymen to "reconstitute Anne's public identity as redeemed sinner" and also provide an example to her audience. Martin, *Women, Murder, and Equity*, 84. Indeed, the speech illustrates necessary stages of salvation: she confesses to being "a grievous sinner," she "repent[s]" and accepts the justice of her punishment, and she is "resolved to go to death." Although she speaks of "the world" and the families, the stage directions and the cast list do not call for any other onstage audience members beyond the Doctor and Drurie. Later, her children enter.

535. The punishment I deserve.

536. A biblical image for the peaceful afterlife and the idea of loving, parental comfort; a place where the soul goes after death, not quite heaven but not hell or Hades either. This is a Jewish concept that Christians picked up. Readers may be familiar with the lovely African American spiritual of the same name.

537. See Psalm 115 for similar language.

538. Jesus, who died on the "Holy Cross." All the imagery is biblical—banquets, blood, fire, sword, and torment (eternal suffering in hell).

539. Sources of support; here, both parents.

540. Represented or written. She means, "If you could see into my heart."

541. See introduction on the "mothers' blessing," an "advice" genre. See also Sheeha, "Devotional Identity."

542. A corrosive, a cause of trouble and grief that eats away at one like rust. This is a term right out of Golding's pamphlet.

543. This mention of kindred appears in Golding's account: Sanders's brother and other relatives visit his widow in prison (appendix 143–44). Notice how she addresses an ever-widening audience including "all men and women in the world."

544. Suffering. Anne Sanders is grateful to be punished for her sins in this world in order to be spared in the afterlife ("in the world to come"). This is presumably where the title comes from.

545. This is an example of a scaffold speech and a mother's blessing combined.

546. Lures, temptations.

547. Bile, proverbially bitter, produced in the gall bladder.

548. I am not sure why the verb tense changes here: she seems to be wishing them a future when they *will live* in some wealth and be well matched, that is, marry appropriate spouses.

549. Sanders wishes her children success (wealthy and suitably mated), but also advises them not to get too prideful about their success.

550. "Are you done counseling the criminals?" The Sheriff asks the clergyman if the accused have confessed and accepted their fates, that is, "made an end"

in preparation for death. The blocking for this scene begins in Anne Sanders's prison cell and continues, with the Sheriff's entrance, with the actors walking out into a public space meant to be Smithfield where the gallows are visible.

551. Bradford; see introduction.

552. This kind of repetition of a single word is unusual, and likely each child (of five) gets one kiss and one "farewell."

553. Literally, a long wooden shaft and an iron or steel head, held by a horseman in charging at full speed. To sluice is to flush or wash out.

554. Like Comedy in the induction, who parodied the cry, *vindicta* in revenge tragedy, Tragedy herself refers to that strain of her genre.

555. See Tragedy's prologue: "My scene is London, native and your own" (line 7).

556. Genre or shape.

557. Perhaps.

Appendix

1. John Considine, "Arthur Golding" in *Oxford Dictionary of National Biography*.

2. This extremely long sentence is built around the following premise: since this event has garnered a lot of rumors, theories, and conclusions, Golding feels it is useful for him to set the story right, which is the purpose of the pamphlet.

3. Attached to. Golding is warning to the reader not to expect every detail to be recounted here so as not to fuel people's further curiosity and judgment.

4. This is the notion that one should "love the sinner, but hate the sin."

5. Golding insists—against "whatsoever report"—that Browne and Sanders were not acquainted with each other. The play opens with the two men talking. I explore significant contrasts between Golding and the play in "What a Lord Chamberlain's Men Playwright."

6. The vividly drawn Old John and Joan of *A Warning* are mere passersby in this account, rather than good friends of Beane's.

7. Cattle.

8. Identified the murderer by his clothing and other "marks."

9. Soon.

10. Although, however.

11. To "lay . . . to gauge" something means to use it as a pledge, or to pawn it.

12. Browne hurried to leave London.

13. The playwright, as in creating backstories for "the old man and the maiden," gives a personality to this man named Browne. This is one of a number of departures that demonstrates the playwright's purposeful and, I argue, sophisticated handling of source material.

14. Or "arrange"?

15. The play does not specifically cite Westminster for the locale. In my stage direction, I place it the scene in Greenwich because we have already seen that locale.

16. Compare impeachment, accusation, or criminal charge.

17. Sent to jail.

18. Mistress Sanders looks as though she is ready to give birth. The time surrounding childbirth was called "lying in." Golding does not conjecture about the baby's paternity.

19. I have regularized numbers in dates, departing from the original, where they are sometimes spelled out and sometimes represented numerically.

20. Testimony. He "vouches" for the story.

21. Intended or purposeful. This part of the report suggests that Anne Sanders had support in the community, though for Golding, this support was rooted in a "blind belief" of her innocence. See also below on the crowds gathered to see the executions.

22. Whitsun week began with Whitsunday, the seventh Sunday after Easter.

23. With this term that meant "warning," Golding repeats his purpose—to caution his readers.

24. Whitsun Eve, i.e., the evening before Whitsunday or Whitsun, is the celebration in England of the Christian feast of Pentecost, observed seven weeks after Easter.

25. Following, as in "the following explains why the trial was delayed."

26. Benefit.

27. Part of the minister's duty was to counsel the imprisoned; this duty followed or "was suspended from" that role. *A Warning* contains the Mell figure (called Minister, whom James condemns to the pillory) within scene 19; the opening stage direction reads: *Enter Master James with the Minister.*

28. Arms, weapons, instruments; figuratively, to "stand to one's guns," to hold one's ground, to maintain one's position or attitude. *OED online*, s.v. "Tackling," accessed November 3, 2019, https://www.oed.com.

29. That is, Anne Sanders thwarts her examiner's attempt to extract a confession; she sticks to her story.

30. Or well-wisher; someone he could trust.

31. Latin for "it is permissible," or namely, as follows. The sign is meant to shame him as it points to him as one who lied about or covered ("color[ed]") the facts.

32. Today we would call this obstruction of justice.

33. Not prepared for death, not in good spiritual condition.

34. These were the prison chaplains who instructed the convicts in prison. Clark is variously spelled Chark and Clearke. In the play Drurie plays a com-

paratively larger role than the clergy in counseling Anne Sanders, as I show in "What a Lord Chamberlain's Men".

35. God knows.

36. Sincere. To fain meant to fake or dissemble.

37. The playwright uses this language almost exactly; I take "coarsie" to mean "corrosive" or annoyance; this word appears in Sanders's final speech in *A Warning* as well.

38. The playwright omits this authorization of the books and folds Golding's various churchmen into one "Doctor," moves which I argue reduce the impact of clerical intervention, and thus leave Anne Sanders's gift to her children unmediated; she goes on to instruct them herself about "keeping the book handy" (Christensen, "What a Lord Chamberlain's Men Playwright").

39. That is, accepting her death sentence and going to the scaffold. On the "bitter cup," see Matt. 26:37–46, Luke 22:42, Mark 10:22, and John 18:11 (KJV).

40. Scaffold.

41. Interesting word choice: as noted in the introduction, "scaffold" came to mean stage in this period, while still retaining its meaning as a place of execution.

42. Here is where Golding shifts clearly to his message—from a record of events to the lessons we are to take away from the story above.

43. See Romans 1:21–26 (KJV).

44. A familiar period metaphor of a horse's bridle or restraining headgear (including a bit in the mouth), with God as the guide of the horse/sinner.

45. Possibly.

46. Reference to the "fall" of Adam and Eve in Gen. 1–19. An imp was literally a shoot or slip of a young tree; and figuratively, the term still means a child, with a specific meaning in the period of a devilish person as in the *OED* example from 1583, Phillip Stubbes's *Anatomy of Abuses*: "An impe of Sathan" (sig. iviv).

47. Quickly.

48. Evildoer.

49. These biblical references to the Galileans and the collapse of the Tower of Siloam are meant to show that those who are punished or suffer might not be worse than anyone else, as Jesus taught (Luke 13:1–5).

50. Wishes.

51. "For rebellion *is as* the sin of witchcraft, and stubbornness *is as* iniquity and idolatry" (1 Sam. 15:23).

52. That is, as one who covers up sins like a cloak covers the head.

53. Payment, in this case, punishment or "just reward."

54. This is the idea of a measure for a measure, or what we judge (measure, and allot or mete out punishment) might come back to us again. "Moten" is a form of the verb "mete," to dispense or allot.

55. Prov. 5:5. This language also echoes "An Homilie against Disobedience and Willful Rebellion."

56. This speech purports to be a record of Anne Saunders's actual words. Compare this form to the verse lamentation in "The woeful lamentacon of Mrs. Anne Saunders" below (appendix 153–59).

57. To affect with fear, make afraid, frighten.

58. Golding refers to "A prayer to be said at the houre of death," one of the "Certain Godly Prayers to be Used for Sundry Purposes" that were often bound with printings of the official Anglican prayer book, *The Book of Common Prayer*. This prayer appears in the 1552 and 1567 versions.

59. In the thirteenth year of the reign of Elizabeth, who was crowned in 1558. The "saying" appears to be a snippet that records something memorable that Saunders heard in a sermon. Literate Protestants were encouraged to do this kind of recording and reflection.

60. Barrett L. Beer, "Stow [Stowe], John" in *Oxford Dictionary of National Biography*.

61. Stow is not consistent with Saunders/Sanders; I regularize to Sanders.

62. The Privy Council.

63. Stow and Holinshed mirror Golding's account almost exactly, but add the detail of the brother Browne, also a criminal to be executed, and also the fact that Browne flung himself from the scaffold, thereby taking his own life.

64. Wrapped up in.

65. As printed, the word is "gryping," which could mean griping or complaining, but being gripped by grief makes more sense to me.

66. Guts or innards; the body, wracked with grief, is shaking.

67. Perhaps she means that her eyes cannot bear (or abide) being dry through excessive crying.

68. She curses herself, as if to say, "Out upon me." Fie is a kind of mild curse.

69. Also.

70. Deed, presumably the murder of her husband.

71. Evil, or the suffering, torment, and misery caused by evil; compare "baleful."

72. A bark is a boat; the metaphor is common that lust sinks the lover/ship. Here the speaker seems to say that the winds have shifted: "contrary gale."

73. This seems to be a pun on Drurie's name. In the line above, we would say "who" not "which."

74. To restrain or hold back. She blames Roger for not stopping the murder since it was he alone who accompanied Browne.

75. Advice.

76. "Theretill" fits the rhyme, but we might say thereto. She assumes the blame for inclining (leaning) toward her tempters.

77. This is the clearest statement of exemplarity; the speaker puts herself forward with "Behold," and tells other women to use her as a "pattern" or example for what not to do. See Smith, "'A Goodly Sample.'"

78. This conveys a sense that God patiently endures ("bears") our sins, but eventually sins will need to be requited ("pay").

79. The line reads "as may be Sine," but elsewhere in the text, "sin" is spelled "Sin" or "synne." The phonetic "seen" makes better sense since the speaker uses her story as a negative example. "By my first state" refers to the belief in "original sin," furthered by the speaker's admission that her own actions also caused her to fall ("decay").

80. She directly addresses Satan in this part of the ballad.

81. She deeply regrets yielding her self-sovereignty to Satan.

82. Here "state" seems to mean her condition, including her financial position as George Sanders's wife. In the play's scene 4 ("the breech of credit" scene), as I have argued, Anne Sanders is persuaded less by worldly status than by Drurie's claim of divine Providence, though other critics disagree.

83. This is meant in a sarcastic tone, as she goes on to say, she has "losses" not gains.

84. The condemned woman is here suggesting that Christ has saved her—an idea continued in the next five stanzas; Rollins points out that the "theological views expressed in the ballad" are "dubious." In his view, according to Protestant teaching, sinners (i.e., all of us) should neither be comforted by or confident in salvation. Rollins, *Old English Ballads*, 341.

85. Printed thus: "com dayned wrothe dismay"; the meaning is unclear to me. Rollins suggests a parenthetical exclamation, "Condemned wrath dismay!"

86. "Anchor-hold" picks up on the nautical imagery from above. It is literally the grip (or hold) of the anchor and where it lodges, and figuratively, the ground to trust, believe in, or hold on to.

87. Either impressed or enlisted in God's service, or to be pressured, pushed, or driven.

88. Deed or act.

89. To be ruined or destroyed.

90. Diseased or impure. Christ is often imaged as a shepherd in the second testament of the Bible.

91. The speaker here envisions God (Christ) rebuking (or chastising) the devil (Satan) and saving the speaker's soul. She sees herself going to heaven ("immortal bliss").

92. Saints or angels will carry her up to the "throne" of God in heaven.

93. See Jocelyn Catty, "Dorothy Leigh" in *Oxford Dictionary of National Biography*.

94. Sheeha, "Devotional," 3.

95. Brown, *Women's Writing*, 5

96. Brown, *Women's Writing*, 6.

97. Castigates or berates herself for being careless. This sounds like a version of the Aesop's fable of the Ant and the Grasshopper.

98. Out of which, the opposite of "within."

99. Before the usual or expected time; early.

100. A "let" is a stay or obstacle, something that gets in the way.

101. In both the table of contents and the text, chapter 17 is listed twice, and there is no chapter 19.

102. Diverse or different (kinds of) people have different troubles.

Bibliography

Andrea, Bernadette. *The Lives of Girls and Women from the Islamic World in Early Modern British Literature and Culture.* Toronto: University of Toronto Press, 2017.

"An Homilie against Disobedience and Willful Rebellion." In *The Norton Anthology of English Literature: The Sixteenth Century and the Early Seventeenth Century,* Vol. 1B, edited by M. H. Abrams, Barbara K. Lewalski, Stephen Greenblatt, and George M. Logan, 556–58. 7th ed. New York: W. W. Norton, 2000.

Arden of Faversham. Edited by Martin White. New York: W. W. Norton, 1982.

Atwood, Emma Katherine. "Inside Out: Domestic Tragedy and the Dramaturgy of Extrusion." Paper presented at the Durham Early Modern Conference, Durham UK, July 2019.

———. "Spatial Dramaturgy and Domestic Control in Early Modern Drama." PhD diss., Boston College, 2015.

———. "*A Warning for Fair Women* Dir. by Brent Griffin (Review)." *Theatre Journal* 71, no. 3 (September 2019): 394–96. doi:10.1353/tj.2019.0066.

Aughterson, Kate. *Renaissance Woman: A Sourcebook; Constructions of Femininity in England.* London: Routledge, 1995.

Bailey, Amanda. *Flaunting: Style and the Subversive Male Body in Renaissance England.* Toronto: University of Toronto Press, 2007.

Balizet, Ariane M. *Blood and Home in Early Modern Drama: Domestic Identity on the Renaissance Stage.* London: Routledge, 2014.

Bartolovich, Crystal. "Mythos of Labor: *The Shoemaker's Holiday* and the Origin of Citizen History." In *Working Subjects in Early Modern English Drama,* edited by Michelle M. Dowd and Natasha Korda, 17–36. London: Ashgate, 2011.

Belsey, Catherine. "Alice Arden's Crime." In *New Historicism and Renaissance Drama,* edited by Richard Wilson and Richard Dutton, 131–44. London: Longman, 1992.

———. *The Subject of Tragedy: Identity and Difference in Renaissance Drama.* London: Routledge, 1985.

Bennett, Judith M. *Ale, Beer, and Brewsters in England: Women's Work in a Changing World, 1300–1600.* New York: Oxford University Press, 1996.

Berek, Peter. "'Follow the Money': Sex, Murder, Print, and Domestic Tragedy." In *Medieval and Renaissance Drama in England: An Annual Gathering of*

Research, Criticism and Reviews, edited by S. P. Cerasano and Heather Anne Hirschfeld, 21:170–88. Madison NJ: Farleigh Dickinson University Press, 2008.

Birdseye, Cheryl. "Finding Her Conscience: Auditing Female Confession in *A Warning for Fair Women*." Unpublished manuscript.

———. "The Rise of Female Testimony on the Early Modern Stage." PhD diss., Oxford Brookes University, 2018.

Boswell, Jackson Campbell. "Shylock's Turquoise Ring." *Shakespeare Quarterly* 14, no. 4 (1963): 481–83.

Boydston, Jeanne. *Home and Work: Housework, Wages, and the Ideology of Labor in the Early Republic*. New York: Oxford University Press, 1990.

Bradbrook, M. C. *Themes and Conventions of Elizabethan Tragedy*. Cambridge: Cambridge University Press, 1935.

Brooks, E. St. John. "A Pamphlet by Arthur Golding: The Murder of George Saunders." *Notes and Queries* 174 (1938): 182–84.

Brown, Sylvia Monica, ed. *Women's Writing in Stuart England: The Mother's Legacies of Dorothy Leigh, Elizabeth Joscelin, and Elizabeth Richardson*. Thrupp, Stroud, Gloucester: Sutton, 1999.

Burnett, Mark Thornton. *Masters and Servants in English Renaissance Drama and Culture: Authority and Obedience*. New York: St. Martin's Press, 1997.

Cannon, Charles Dale, ed. *A Warning for Fair Women: A Critical Edition*. The Hague: Mouton, 1975.

Canny, Nicholas P. *The Elizabethan Conquest of Ireland: A Pattern Established, 1565–76*. New York: Barnes & Noble Books, 1976.

Capp, Bernard. *When Gossips Meet: Women, Family, and Neighbourhood in Early Modern England*. Oxford: Oxford University Press, 2003.

Chapman, Matthieu. *Anti-Black Racism in Early Modern English Drama: The Other "Other."* London: Routledge, 2018.

Charry, Brinda. *The Arden Guide to Renaissance Drama: An Introduction with Primary Sources*. London: Bloomsbury Arden Shakespeare, 2017.

Christensen, Ann C. *Separation Scenes: Domestic Drama in Early Modern England*. Lincoln: University of Nebraska Press, 2017.

———. "Settled and Unsettling: Home and Mobility in Heywood's *King Edward IV* (1599)." In "Door-Bolts, Thresholds, and Peep-Holes: Liminality and Domestic Spaces in Early Modern England," edited by Robert W. Daniel and Iman Sheeha. *Early Modern Literary Studies* Special issue 29 (2020): 1–27. https://extra.shu.ac.uk/emls/journal/index.php/emls/article/view/522/375.

———"What a Lord Chamberlain's Men Playwright Did with Sources: *A Warning for Fair Women* (1599)." Paper presented at the Shakespeare Association of America Seminar, "The King's/Lord Chamberlain's Men and Their Playwrights," Washington DC, April 2019.

Clark, Alice. *Working Life of Women in the Seventeenth Century.* London: Routledge, 1919.

Cromwell, Otelia. *Thomas Heywood: A Study in the Elizabethan Drama of Everyday Life.* New Haven CT: Yale University Press, 1928.

"The Cucking of a Scold (to the Tune of the Merchant of Emden), ca. 1630." In *The Broadview Anthology of British Literature.* Vol. 2, *The Renaissance and the Early Seventeenth Century,* edited by Joseph Black, Leonard Conolly, Kate Flint, Isobel Grundy, Don LePan, Roy Liuzza, Jerome J. McGann, Anne Lake Prescott, Barry V. Qualls, and Claire Waters, 644–46. 2nd ed. Ontario: Broadview Press, 2010.

Deng, Stephen. *Coinage and State Formation in Early Modern English Literature.* New York: Palgrave Macmillan, 2011.

Dessen, Alan C., and Leslie Thomson. *A Dictionary of Stage Directions in English Drama, 1580–1642.* Cambridge: Cambridge University Press, 1999.

Dolan, Frances E. *Dangerous Familiars: Representations of Domestic Crime in England, 1550–1700.* Ithaca NY: Cornell University Press, 1994.

———. "Gender, Moral Agency, and Dramatic Form in *A Warning for Fair Women.*" *SEL: Studies in English Literature, 1500–1900* 29, no. 2 (1989): 201–18.

———. "'Gentlemen, I Have One Thing More to Say': Women on Scaffolds in England, 1563–1680." *Modern Philology* 92, no. 2 (November 1994): 157–78.

———. *Marriage and Violence: The Early Modern Legacy.* Philadelphia: University of Pennsylvania Press, 2008.

Dollimore, Jonathan. *Radical Tragedy: Religion, Ideology and Power in the Drama of Shakespeare and His Contemporaries.* 3rd ed. New York: Palgrave Macmillan, 2004.

Dowd, Michelle M. *The Dynamics of Inheritance on the Shakespearean Stage.* Cambridge: Cambridge University Press, 2015.

———. *Women's Work in Early Modern English Literature and Culture.* New York: Palgrave Macmillan, 2009.

Dowd, Michelle M., and Natasha Korda, eds. *Working Subjects in Early Modern English Drama.* London: Ashgate, 2011.

Drakakis, John. "Revisiting the Subject of Tragedy." *Textual Practice* 24, no. 6 (2010): 987–1002. DOI: 10.1080/0950236X.2010.521667.

Dyce, Alexander. *A Glossary to the Works of William Shakespeare: The References Made Applicable to Any Edition of Shakespeare, the Explanations Rev. and New Notes Added.* 1893. New York: Johnson Reprint, 1970.

Erickson, Peter, and Kim F. Hall, eds. "Special Issue on Race." *Shakespeare Quarterly* 67, no. 1 (2016): 1–135.

Farmer, J. S., ed. *A Warning for Fair Women* (1599). Tudor Facsimile Texts, 1912. archive.org/details/warningforfairwo00unknuoft/page/n9.

Fischer, Sandra K. *Econoligua: A Glossary of Coins and Economic Language in Renaissance Drama*. Newark: University of Delaware Press, 1985.

Fissell, Mary E. "Introduction: Women, Health, and Healing in Early Modern Europe." *Bulletin of the History of Medicine* 82, no. 1 (2008): 1–17.

Floyd-Wilson, Mary. *Occult Knowledge, Science, and Gender on the Shakespearean Stage*. Cambridge: Cambridge University Press, 2013.

Fumerton, Patricia. *Unsettled: The Culture of Mobility and the Working Poor in Early Modern England*. Chicago: University of Chicago Press, 2006.

Fury, Cheryl A. *Tides in the Affairs of Men: The Social History of Elizabethan Seamen, 1580–1603*. Westport CT: Greenwood Press, 2002.

Giese, Loreen L. *Courtships, Marriage Customs, and Shakespeare's Comedies*. New York: Palgrave Macmillan, 2006.

Gillen, Katherine. *Chaste Value: Economic Crisis, Female Chastity and the Production of Social Difference on Shakespeare's Stage*. Edinburgh: Edinburgh University Press, 2017.

Gillis, John R. *For Better, For Worse: British Marriages, 1600 to the Present*. New York: Oxford University Press, 1985.

Golding, Arthur. *A Briefe Discourse of the Late Murther of Master George Sanders, a Worshipful Citizen of London and of the Apprehension, Arreignement, and Execution of the Principall and Accessaries of the Same. Seene and Allowed*. London: Henrie Bynnyman, 1577.

Gowing, Laura. *Domestic Dangers: Women, Words, and Sex in Early Modern London*. Oxford: Clarendon Press, 1996.

Greenberg, Marissa. *Metropolitan Tragedy: Genre, Justice, and the City in Early Modern England*. Toronto: University of Toronto Press, 2015.

"Greenwich and the Tudors." Royal Museums Greenwich. rmg.co.uk/discover /explore/greenwich-and-tudors#rFRHDhbfzWQlprqi.99.

Gurr, Andrew. *The Shakespeare Company, 1594–1642*. Cambridge: Cambridge University Press, 2004.

———. "'The Stage Is Hung with Black': Genre and the Trappings of Stagecraft in Shakespearean Tragedy." In *Shakespeare and Genre: From Early Modern Inheritances to Postmodern Legacies*, edited by Anthony R. Generate, 67–82. New York: Palgrave Macmillan, 2012.

Hall, Kim F. *Things of Darkness: Economies of Race and Gender in Early Modern England*. Ithaca NY: Cornell University Press, 1995.

Harkness, Deborah E. "A View from the Streets: Women and Medical Work in Elizabethan London." *Bulletin of the History of Medicine* 82, no. 1 (2008): 52–85.

Harris, Jonathan Gil, and Natasha Korda. *Staged Properties in Modern English Drama*. New York: Cambridge University Press, 2006.

Hartigan-O'Connor, Ellen. *The Ties That Buy: Women and Commerce in Revolutionary America*. Philadelphia: University of Pennsylvania Press, 2009.

Hayward, Maria. "Clothing." In *The Routledge Handbook of Material Culture in Early Modern Europe*, edited by Catherine Richardson, Tara Hamling, and David Gaimster, 172–84. London: Routledge, 2017.

Hehmeyer, Paxton. "'Twill Vex Thy Soul to Hear What I Shall Speak': Aaron and the Aesthetics of Discomfort." In *Titus Out of Joint: Reading the Fragmented Titus Andronicus*, edited by Liberty Stanavage and Paxton Hehmeyer, 165–76. Newcastle upon Tyne: Cambridge Scholars, 2012.

Helgerson, Richard. *Adulterous Alliances: Home, State, and History in Early Modern European Drama and Painting*. Chicago: University of Chicago Press, 2000.

———. *Forms of Nationhood: The Elizabethan Writing of England*. Chicago: University of Chicago Press, 1992.

Hentschell, Roze. "Moralizing Apparel in Early Modern London: Popular Literature, Sermons, and Sartorial Display." *Journal of Medieval and Early Modern Studies* 39, no. 3 (Fall 2009): 571–95.

Heywood, Thomas. *A Woman Killed with Kindness*. Edited by Brian Scobie. New York: W. W. Norton, 1985.

Holbrook, Peter. *Literature and Degree in Renaissance England: Nashe, Bourgeois Tragedy, Shakespeare*. Newark: University of Delaware Press, 1994.

Homer, *The Odyssey of Homer*. Translated by Richmond Lattimore. New York: Harper & Row, 1967.

Hopkinson, A. F. (Arthur Frederick), ed. *A Warning for Fair Women*. London: M. E. Sims, 1904. archive.org/details/cu31924013127331/.

Ingram, Martin. *Church Courts, Sex and Marriage in England, 1570–1640*. Cambridge: Cambridge University Press, 1987.

James I, King of England. *Daemonologie: In Forme of a Dialogue*. Edinburgh: Robert Walde-graue, 1597. gutenberg.org/files/25929/25929-pdf.pdf.

Jones, Ann Rosalind, and Peter Stallybrass. *Renaissance Clothing and the Materials of Memory*. Cambridge: Cambridge University Press, 2000.

Jonson, Ben. "Masque of Blackness" (1605). In *Masques of Difference: Four Court Masques*, edited by Kristin McDermott, 91–105. Manchester UK: Manchester University Press, 2007.

Kahn, Coppélia. *Roman Shakespeare: Warriors, Wounds, and Women*. London: Routledge, 1997.

Karim-Cooper, Farah. *Cosmetics in Shakespearean and Renaissance Drama*. Edinburgh: Edinburgh University Press, 2006.

Kerber, Linda K. "Separate Spheres, Female Worlds, Woman's Place: The Rhetoric of Women's History." *Journal of American History* 75, no. 1 (June 1988): 9–39.

King James Bible Online (website). kingjamesbibleonline.org/.

Knutson, Roslyn L. "Repertory System." In *The Oxford Handbook of Shakespeare*, edited by Arthur F. Kinney, 404–19. Oxford: Oxford University Press, 2014.

Korda, Natasha. "'Judicious oeillades': Supervising Marital Property in *The Merry Wives of Windsor*." In *Marxist Shakespeares*, edited by Jean E. Howard and Scott Cutler Shershow, 82–103. London: Routledge, 2001.

———. *Labors Lost: Women's Work and the Early Modern English Stage*. Philadelphia: University of Pennsylvania Press, 2011.

———. *Shakespeare's Domestic Economies: Gender and Property in Early Modern England*. Philadelphia: University of Pennsylvania Press, 2002.

Lake, Peter, and Michael Questier. "Agency, Appropriation and Rhetoric under the Gallows: Puritans, Romanists and the State in Early Modern England." *Past & Present* 153 (November 1996): 64–107.

Leggott, Gemma, ed. "A Warning for Fair Women." Master's thesis, University of Hartford, 2011. coursehero.com/file/30726277/A-Warning-for-Fair -Women-With-Introduction-Edited-by-Gemma-Leggott-1doc/.

Leigh, Dorothy. "The Mother's Blessing." In *Women's Writing in Stuart England: The Mother's Legacies of Dorothy Leigh, Elizabeth Joscelin, and Elizabeth Richardson*, edited by Sylvia Monica Brown, 15–76. Thrupp, Stroud, Gloucester: Sutton, 1999.

Little, Arthur L. *Shakespeare Jungle Fever: National-Imperial Re-Visions of Race, Rape, and Sacrifice*. Palo Alto CA: Stanford University Press, 2000.

Longfellow, Erica. "Public, Private, and the Household in Early Seventeenth-Century England." *Journal of British Studies* 45, no. 2 (2006): 313–34.

Loomba, Ania, and Jonathan Burton, eds. *Race in Early Modern England: A Documentary Companion*. New York: Palgrave Macmillan, 2007.

Lopez, Jeremy. "The Shadow of the Canon." *Shakespeare Quarterly* 65, no. 2 (2014): 109–19.

MacGregor, Neil. "City Life, Urban Strife: The Life of London's Apprentices and Shakespeare's Groundlings Told through a Rare Woollen Cap," April 26, 2018. In *Shakespeare's Restless World*, produced by Paul Kobrak. Podcast, MP3 audio, 13:57. https://www.bbc.co.uk/programmes/b01gg8h6.

Marino, James J. *Owning William Shakespeare: The King's Men and Their Intellectual Property*. Philadelphia: University of Pennsylvania Press, 2011.

Martin, Biddy, and Chandra Talpade Mohanty. "Feminist Politics: What's Home Got to Do with It?" In *Feminist Studies / Critical Studies*, edited by Teresa de Lauretis, 191–212. Bloomington: Indiana University Press, 1986.

Martin, Randall. *Women, Murder, and Equity in Early Modern England*. London: Routledge, 2008.

Maus, Catharine Eisaman. *Inwardness and Theater in the English Renaissance*. Chicago: University of Chicago Press, 1995.

McQuade, Paula. *Catechisms and Women's Writing in Seventeenth-Century England.* Cambridge: Cambridge University Press, 2017.

Mehl, Dieter. *The Elizabethan Dumb Show: The History of a Dramatic Convention.* Cambridge MA: Harvard University Press, 1966.

Middling Culture: The Cultural Lives of the Middling Sort, Writing and Material Culture 1550–1650 (website). https://middlingculture.com/.

Mills, Anthony David. *A Dictionary of London Place-Names.* Oxford: Oxford University Press, 2010.

Milton, John. *Paradise Lost.* Edited by Merritt Y. Hughes. New York: Odyssey Press, 1962.

Morris, Silvia. "The Thomas Dekker Marathon." *Shakespeare Blog,* June 12, 2016. http://theshakespeareblog.com/2016/06/the-thomas-dekker-marathon/.

Mukherji, Subha. *Law and Representation in Early Modern Drama.* Cambridge: Cambridge University Press, 2006.

Muldrew, Craig. *The Economy of Obligation: The Culture of Credit and Social Relations in Early Modern England.* New York: St. Martin's Press, 1998.

Munday, Anthony. *A View of Sundry Examples Reporting Many Straunge Murthers.* London: William Wright, 1580.

Newman, Karen. "'And Wash the Ethiop White': Femininity and the Monstrous in Othello." In *Critical Essays on Shakespeare's Othello,* edited by Anthony Gerard Barthelemy, 124–43. New York: G. K. Hall, 1994.

Nichols, John Gough. *Narratives of the Days of the Reformation.* London: Camden Society, 1858.

Nye, Eric W. *Pounds Sterling to Dollars: Historical Conversion of Currency.* Accessed November 3, 2018. uwyo.edu/numimage/currency.htm.

Ohlmeyer, Jane. "Literature and the New British and Irish Histories." *British Identities and English Renaissance Literature,* edited by David J. Baker and Willy Maley, 245–55. Cambridge University Press, 2002.

"Open City: London, 1500–1700 Exhibition Material." Folgerpedia. Last modified July 13, 2015. folgerpedia.folger.edu/Open_City:_London,_1500%E2%80%931700_exhibition_material.

Orlin, Lena Cowen. *Locating Privacy in Tudor London.* Oxford: Oxford University Press, 2007.

———, ed. *Material London, ca. 1600.* Philadelphia: University of Pennsylvania Press, 2000.

———. *Private Matters and Public Culture in Post-Reformation England.* Ithaca NY: Cornell University Press, 1994.

Park, Katharine. *Secrets of Women: Gender, Generation, and the Origins of Human Dissection.* New York: Zone Books, 2006.

Patterson, Annabel M. *Reading Holinshed's Chronicles*. University of Chicago Press, 1994.

Pearson, Meg. "Review of *A Warning for Fair Women*, Directed by Brent Griffin, Resurgens Theatre Company, Atlanta, GA, USA, November 20, 2018." Reviewing Shakespeare. https://bloggingshakespeare.com/reviewing-shakespeare /warning-fair-women-dir-brent-griffin-resurgens-theatre-company-atlanta -ga-usa-nov-2018/.

Poole, Kristen. "'The Fittest Closet for All Goodness': Authorial Strategies of Jacobean Mothers' Manuals." *SEL: Studies in English Literature, 1500–1900* 35, no. 1 (1995): 69–88.

Purkiss, Diane. "The Masque of Food: Staging and Banqueting in Shakespeare's England." *Shakespeare Studies* 42 (2014): 91–105.

Raleigh, Sir Walter. "The Discoverie of the Large, Rich and Bewtiful Empyre of Guiana." In *Amazons, Savages, and Machiavels: Travel and Colonial Writing in English, 1550–1630: An Anthology*, edited by Andrew Hadfield, 279–85. Oxford: Oxford University Press, 2001.

The Recipes Project (website). https://recipes.hypotheses.org/.

Reverby, Sandra M., and Dorothy O. Helly. "Introduction: Converging on History." *Gendered Domains: Rethinking Public and Private in Women's History: Essays from the Seventh Berkshire Conference on the History of Women*, edited by Dorothy O. Helly and Susan M. Reverby, 1–24. Ithaca NY: Cornell University Press, 1992.

Richardson, Catherine. *Domestic Life and Domestic Tragedy in Early Modern England: The Material Life of the Household*. Manchester UK: Manchester University Press, 2006.

———. "Tragedy, Family and Household." In *The Cambridge Companion to English Renaissance Tragedy*, edited by Emma Smith and Garrett A. Sullivan Jr., 17–29. Cambridge: Cambridge University Press, 2010.

Ringler, William. "Hamlet's Defense of the Players." In *Essays on Shakespeare and Elizabethan Drama in Honor of Hardin Craig*, edited by Richard Hosley, 201–13. Columbia: University of Missouri Press, 1962.

Roberts, Edgar V. *Writing about Literature*. 11th ed. Boston: Pearson/Prentice Hall, 2006.

Roberts, Jennifer Sherman. "Little Shop of Horrors, Early Modern Style." *Recipes Project*. Posted January 30, 2014. recipes.hypotheses.org/tag/rosa-solis.

Roberts, Michael. "'To Bridle the Falsehood of Unconscionable Workmen, and for Her Own Satisfaction': What the Jacobean Housewife Needed to Know about Men's Work, and Why." *Labour History Review* 63, no. 1 (1998): 4–30.

Rollins, Hyder Edward. *Old English Ballads, 1553–1625, Chiefly from Manuscripts*. Cambridge: University Press, 1920.

Salkeld, Duncan. *Shakespeare among the Courtesans: Prostitution, Literature, and Drama, 1500–1650*. London: Ashgate, 2012.

Schleck, Julia. "The Marital Problems of the East India Company." *Journal for Early Modern Cultural Studies* 17, no. 3 (Summer 2018): 83–104.

Scot, Reginald. *Discoverie of Witchcraft*. 1584. Edited by Brinsley Nicholson. London: Elliot Stock, 1886.

Shapiro, James, ed. *Shakespeare in America: An Anthology from the Revolution to Now*. New York: Library of America, 2014.

Sharpe, J. A. "'Last Dying Speeches': Religion, Ideology and Public Execution in Seventeenth-Century England." *Past & Present* 107, no. 1 (May 1985): 144–67. https://doi.org/10.1093/past/107.1.144.

Sheeha, Iman. "Devotional Identity and the Mother's Legacy in *A Warning for Fair Women* (1599)." In *People and Piety: Devotional Writing in Print and Manuscript in Early Modern England*, edited by Robert W. Daniel and Elizabeth Clarke, 96–113. Manchester UK: Manchester University Press, 2019.

———. "'[M]istris Drewry, / You Do Not Well': The Gossip as an Ill-Doer in *A Warning for Fair Women* (1599)." *Early Theatre* 22, no. 2 (2019): 89–118. https://doi.org/10.12745/et.22.2.3662.

Sidney, Sir Philip. *An Apologie for Poetry*. London: James Roberts, 1595.

Siegel, Paul N. "*Measure for Measure*: The Significance of the Title." *Shakespeare Quarterly* 4, no. 3 (1953): 317–20.

Simpson, Richard. *The School of Shakspere*. London: Chatto and Windus, 1878.

Smith, Rosalind. "'A Goodly Sample:' Exemplarity, Female Complaint and Early Modern Women's Poetry." In *Early Modern Women and the Poem*, edited by Susan Wiseman, 181–200. Manchester UK: Manchester University Press, 2013.

Smith, Simon. *Musical Response in the Early Modern Playhouse, 1603–1625*. Cambridge: Cambridge University Press, 2018.

Snook, Edith. *Women, Beauty and Power in Early Modern England: A Feminist Literary History*. New York: Palgrave Macmillan, 2011.

Stavreva, Kirilka. *Words Like Daggers: Violent Female Speech in Early Modern England*. Lincoln: University of Nebraska Press, 2015.

Stone, Lawrence. *The Family, Sex and Marriage in England, 1500–1800*. New York: Harper & Row, 1977.

Stow, John. *The Annales of England Faithfully Collected out of the Most Autenticall Authors, Records, and Other Monuments of Antiquitie*. Vol. 1. London: Ralfe Newbery, 1592.

Suzuki, Mihoko. "Gender, Class, and the Social Order in Late Elizabethan Drama." *Theatre Journal* 44, no. 1 (1992): 31–45.

Teague, Frances N. *Shakespeare's Speaking Properties*. Lewisburg PA: Bucknell University Press, 1991.

Thomas, Keith. *Religion and the Decline of Magic*. New York: Scribner, 1971.

Thompson, Ayanna. *Colorblind Shakespeare: New Perspectives on Race and Performance*. London: Routledge, 2006.

Velde, François R., and Thomas J. Sargent. *The Big Problem of Small Change*. Princeton NJ: Princeton University Press, 2014.

Wall, Wendy. *Staging Domesticity: Household Work and English Identity in Early Modern Drama*. Cambridge: Cambridge University Press, 2002.

Warnicke, Retha M. *Women of the English Renaissance and Reformation*. Westport CT: Greenwood Press, 1983.

Whipday, Emma. *Shakespeare's Domestic Tragedies: Violence in the Early Modern Home*. Cambridge: Cambridge University Press, 2019.

Wiggins, Martin. *Shakespeare and the Drama of His Time*. New York: Oxford University Press, 2000.

Wiggins, Martin, and Catherine Richardson, eds. *British Drama, 1533–1642: A Catalogue*. Vol. 3. Oxford: Oxford University Press, 2012.

Index

Page numbers with F indicate illustrations

Anne Sanders (*cont.*)

Clerk of London (character), lxii,
107–9, 111–12
close (enclosed field), 192n246
A closet for ladies and gentlemen,
177n65
clothing, 192n247, 198n322, 201n373,
210n506; exchange of, 9, 176–
77n58, 180n93, 180n98, 202n393
cofferers, 190n228
coin, as exchange medium, lviii,
180n95, 200n363, 211n525
coins, English, 185n143, 186n171,
192n247, 195n274
coin-toss game, 77–78, 200n359
comedies, xx–xxi, xxxvi
Comedy (character), F4; in future,
134; on History, 173n12; in play
structure, xxvi; in recent performance, xlvii–xlviii; rhyming by,
175n35; role description of, lix;
staging for, xxix; Tragedy and,
xx, 3–6, 173n9, 173nn11–12, 173n14,
174n27
"Commentaries" (Caesar), 135
compensation, 179n82, 180n93,
180n95, 184n131
Considine, John, 135
consumption and production,
xxxvii–xxxix, 170n65
Cornhill (London), 180n90, 194n258
corsage, xxxii, xli, 107. *See also* flowers; rose
credit, xxxiv–xxxv, xxxvii, liii–liv,
186n170
Cromwell, Otelia, *Thomas Heywood*,
xxvi
"The Cucking of a Scold," 174n26
Cupid, 181n107
Curtain Theatre, xxiv

Daemonologie (King James I),
205n443
Dangerous Familiars (Dolan), liv
Daughter of George and Anne
Sanders (character), lx
Davenant, William, *Albovine, King
of the Lombards*, 169n49
death, good, 208n478
Death and Domesticity conference
(2018), xlvi, 170n70
De beneficiis (Seneca), 135
Dekker, Thomas, xxiv, xxvi; *The Shoe-
maker's Holiday*, 192n250
Deng, Stephen, liv
Desdemona (character), 183n130
Dessen, Alan, 209n493; *Dictionary of
Stage Directions*, xxx
Destinies (characters), 58, 195n284.
See also Furies (characters)
devil(s), 148, 188n203, 217n91. *See also*
Satan
*A dialogue conteinyng the nomber in
effect* (Heywood), 185n153
Dick (name), 198n328
Dictionary of Stage Directions (Des-
sen and Thomson), xxx
Diligence (character), lix, 89–90
"Discourse upon the" (Golding), 135
Doctor (character), xli, xliii, lxii,
127, 129–30, 132, 211n529, 211n532,
212–13n550
Dolan, Frances, xxi, xxix, xxxi, xliv,
xlv, 169n46, 170n64, 170n66,
170n72; *Dangerous Familiars*, liv;
Marriage and Violence, liv
Dollimore, Jonathan, 167n15
domesticity, xxi–xxii, xxxii–xxxix
Dowd, Michelle, liv; *Working Subjects*, lvi
dowries, 23, 185n143

Floyd-Wilson, Mary, lv, 169n57

food, 199n336

Forms of Nationhood (Helgerson), lvii

"Fortune my Foe," 1

Fumerton, Patricia, lvii

Furies (characters), F2, F3, xxxi, xlvii–xlviii, lix, 35–37, 172n2 (cast), 188n195, 189n209

Galileans, 215n49

gallows, xxxi, xli–xlii, 125–26, 128, 212n534. *See also* scaffolds

gambling, 200n361

Genesis, 200n355

Gentlemen (characters), lxi, 42–44

George Browne (character), F6, F9, F14; alibi of, 69–71, 199n342, 203–4n419, 204nn423–24; on Anne Sanders, 184n139; Anne Sanders on, xl, 27, 33–34, 181n103, 182n118, 196n302; Anne Sanders's motives and, xxxi; appearance of, liv, lviii, 9, 176–77n58; arrest of, 93, 95; blame and, 85–86, 202n398, 207n465; body of, xlv–xlvi; compared to Romeo, 181n107; confession of, xli–xliii, 103–5, 209n499; death of, xxxi, 115, 117–18, 192n246; deception by, 184n140; Diligence and, 89–90; evidence against, 202n391; expressing love, 176n52, 177nn63–64, 185n145; on failed murder attempt, 51, 190n222, 190n225, 195n278; fleeing, 64, 85–87, 93–94; guilty feeling of, xxxiii, 77–79; handkerchief and, 208n486; insult by, 204n421; on Ireland, 175n40, 176n43; John Beane and, 97, 99–101, 204n427; Lust guiding, 37, 57–59; meeting Anne Sanders, 17–20, 77, 79–80,

180n91, 181nn109–11, 182nn112–16, 205n428; meeting brother, 115–17; meeting George Sanders, 9–10; mental state of, 196nn289–90, 200n365; message of, 210n507; mocked, 108, 207nn471–72; murder contract and, 21–26, 183n123, 184nn131–33, 184–85n141, 185n143, 185n146; murdering George Sanders, 61, 64; Nan Drurie and, 27, 33–34, 181n109, 211n531; overview of, xxvii–xxviii; planning murder, 52–54, 61–63; pleading guilty, 107–9; proposal of, 9, 11–16, 176n57, 177n59, 178n70, 178n74, 178n76, 179n83; protecting Anne Sanders, 105–6, 109, 111, 117–18, 207n474, 209n499; in recent performance, xlvii, xlviii–xlix, li–lii; referred to, 75; regrets of, 197nn305–6, 202–3nn405–6, 209n495; reputation of, 199n335, 207n467, 209n499; requests of, 110–11, 119, 208n477, 209n497, 210n508; Roger and, lvi, 180n95, 180n98, 194n256, 194n263, 202n401; role description of, lx; stalking George Sanders, 41, 43–44, 51, 55–56, 63, 189n214; as suspect, 82–83; Tragedy on, 38–39; tree chopping by, xl, 57, 58–59

George Sanders (character): body of, 89–91, 203n415; economic situation of, xxxvii, liii–liv, 27–28, 185–86n154; in everyday life, ix–x, xxxiii–xxxiv, 9–10, 41–44, 63, 181n99, 189n211, 189n214, 190n220, 192n246, 200n362; George Browne on death of, 80, 87, 100, 116, 202n405; as husband, xxxiii, xxx–viii, 17, 20, 31–32, 34, 74–75, 195n275;

Lust (character), xxvii, xxx, xxxi, xlviii, lix, 35, 37–38, 57–59
Luther, Martin, lv
Lyly, John, xxv

Macbeth (character), lv, 61, 189–90n214, 190n226
Macbeth (Shakespeare), xvii, xxx, 188n196, 197n314
Man (character), lx, 27–29
Margery Eyre (character), 192n250
Marian Martyrs, 211n522
Marino, James, 167n23
Markham, George, *English House-wife*, 177n65
Marlowe, Christopher: *Edward II*, xx, 135; *Tamburlaine the Great*, xx, 135, 168n26; *The Troublesome Reign*, xxi
marriage, xxii, xxxii, 200n355
Marriage and Violence (Dolan), liv
Mars, 176n53
Marston, John, *The Insatiate Count-ess*, 175n33
Martin, Randall, ix, xxi, xliii, liv, 204n428, 210n501, 212n534
Marvell, Andrew, "To His Coy Mis-tress," 193n252
Mary, Queen, 204n419, 211n522
Masque of Blackness (Jonson), 193n252
masques (performances in court), 188n201
masques (troupes), 190n225
master and servant relationships, lvi–lvii, 184n131, 186n164, 191n232
Master Ashmore (character), 28, 185n154
Master Barnes (character): anec-dotes of, lv, 101–2; in everyday life,

192n246, 194n261, 195n275; in mur-der investigation, 97–101, 205n431, 206n446; in recent performance, xlix, li; referred to, 56, 62, 95; role description of, lx; treatment of servant by, 45–47, 191n232, 205n430
Master Humphries (character), lxii, 105, 206n458
Master James (character): anecdotes of, 101–2; connections of, 205n431; George Browne and, 69–71, 81–83, 93, 95, 99–101; John Beane and, 97–101; Minister and, 121–23, 210n515, 210n517; role description of, lxi; work of, 104–5, 198n332, 204n426
Masters and Servants (Burnett), lvii
Material London (Orlin), liii
Maundy Thursday, 191n233
Mayor of Rochester (character), lxii, 93, 95, 97, 99–104, 204n426, 205n440
meals, 181n99, 194n259
medical arts, xxiii, xxxv–xxxvi, lvi, 169n57, 172n98, 177nn62–64, 177–78n65, 178n72
Mehl, Dieter, xxix, xxxi, 169n46
Mell (minister), lxiii, 141–42, 210n509, 214n27. See also Minister (character)
Melpomene, F1, xx, lix, 4. See also Tragedy (character)
men, xxii, xxxii, xxxvi, xxxvii, 172n98, 183n128, 184n131, 208n489
Menzel, Adolph von, *Study of a Man with a Ruff Collar*, F13
The Merchant of Venice (Shakespeare), 178n76, 180n90
merchants, xxxii, xxxiii–xxxiv, xxxvi, 180n90, 182n114

tips, monetary, 180n95, 194n263, 195n274

title pages, xiii, xxiv, xl, 168n26

Titus Andronicus (Shakespeare), xx, xlii, 193n252

tobacco use, xxiii

"To His Coy Mistress" (Marvell), 193n252

Tom Peart (character), xxxi, lxi, 125–26

torches, 190n222, 190nn225–26

Tower of Siloam, 215n49

tragedies: comic, xx–xxi; domestic, xix–xxiii, xxxvi, xlvi, lvii, 166n1, 166n6, 178n65; Elizabethan, xx; Jacobean, 167n15; settings of, 166n6; staging of, 175n33; symbols of, 173n9; viewing encouraged, 206n449

Tragedy (character), F1, F3, F12; Comedy and, xx, 3–6, 134, 173n9, 173nn11–12, 173n15; History and, xx, 3–6, 134, 173n3, 173n12, 173n15, 174n32; on London, 7–8, 166n6; on murder, xl, 35–39, 57–59, 90–91, 188–89n203, 189n206, 195n282, 203n409; in play structure, xxvi–xxvii, xxviii; in recent performance, xlvii–xlviii, 172n2 (cast); rhyming, 175n35; role description of, lix; on self, 133–34, 213n554; staging for, xxix–xxx. *See also* Melpomene

tragicomedies, xx–xxi

Trautwein, Matthew, F4, xlvii, li

treason, xxi, 176n57, 177n59, 209n492

tree chopping, xxvii, xxxi, xl–xli, lii, 57, 58–59

trials, 204n428, 207n468

The Troublesome Reign (Marlowe), xxi

Tudor monarchs, lxi, 176n43, 194n261

Two Gentlemen of Verona (Shakespeare), 193n252

Two Lamentable Tragedies (Yarington), xxv, 166n1

umber (word), 191n239

University of Houston, xi–xii, lii–liii; UH Improv Club, lii–liii; UH Shakespeare Club, lii–liii

Velde, François, *The Big Problem of Small Change*, 185–86n154

Venus, 176n53

videlicet, 142, 174n21, 214n31

virtue, lviii

Volpone (Jonson), li–lii

Vulcan, 176n53

Wales, 175n40

Wallace, William, 211n522

A Warning for Fair Women: authorship of, xxiv–xxvi, 166n2, 168n29; beauty in, lviii; church and state in, liv; crime in, xxxix–xli; criticism of, x–xi; dating of, xxiii–xxiv, 167nn17–18; as domestic tragedy, xix–xxiii, 166n1; economic themes in, xxxii–xxxvi, liii–liv; editions of, xiii–xv, 165n1, 165n6; modifications to, xlvi–xlvii, 171n88, 172n2 (Cast); occult in, lv; ordinary life in, ix–x, xix–xxiii; private sphere in, lvii; public sphere in, lvii; recent performance of, xlvi, xlvii–lii, 171n89; scene study of, xxxvi–xxxix; servants in, lvi–lvii; setting of, liii; significance of, xi–xii; sources for, vii–ix, lvii–lviii; speeches in, xli–xlvi; staging of, xxviii–xxxii;

CPSIA information can be obtained
at www.ICGtesting.com
Printed in the USA
LVHW032238270421
685732LV00006B/388

9 781496 225528